The Story of the

RESERVE
BANK OF
INDIA

The Story of the

RESERVE BANK OF INDIA

RAHUL BAJORIA

RUPA

Published by
Rupa Publications India Pvt. Ltd 2018
7/16, Ansari Road, Daryaganj
New Delhi 110002

Sales centres:
Allahabad Bengaluru Chennai
Hyderabad Jaipur Kathmandu
Kolkata Mumbai

ISBN: 978-93-5304-644-6

First impression 2018

10 9 8 7 6 5 4 3 2 1

The moral right of the author has been asserted.

Printed at Gopsons Papers Ltd., Noida

To my parents

Contents

Introduction

More than a printing press

The government of India has very few islands of excellence. While India's institutions have proved to be much more durable than those of its immediate neighbours, they nonetheless face similar issues of corruption, red tape and a general lack of competence. Despite India's crippling governance issues, its financial sector and financial markets are open, deep and generally well regulated. This is somewhat of an anomaly, given India's current level of development.

Since 2016, the role of the Reserve Bank of India—the RBI—has come under immense scrutiny, as it was a critical but perhaps unwilling participant in the government's November 2016 demonetization exercise. Political attacks on the institution, coupled with accusations of collusion, were made, but the staff of the Reserve Bank continued to do their job in a professional manner.

This was not the first demonetization that India had seen. It was also not the first time a large sum of the currency notes withdrawn from circulation returned to the banking system. Previously, in 1946 and then again in 1978, the Reserve Bank undertook similar exercises, but on a slightly smaller scale. The results were largely the same, with little money being extinguished from the system.

In the seventy years of India's independent history, the Reserve Bank of India, an institution older than independent India itself, has played an important role in the nation's economic development. The government has, to a large extent, left the RBI to emerge as an area of relative excellence, and technocrats have been allowed to design policies. The Reserve Bank has been an active participant in most areas, but the policies have often yielded mixed results.

Institutional autonomy vs individual independence

The role and the importance of the RBI increased substantially after 1991, as India's economy opened up and its capital markets grew, perhaps much faster than what was warranted. As a regulator, RBI has had to not only intervene in areas that may be beyond its jurisdiction, but it has also been a key driver of introducing best practices in India's financial markets, especially around bank regulation, minority investor protection and bond market regulation.

With the increase in its importance, the personalities running the bank have come into greater focus, which has sometimes led to clashes between the Reserve Bank and the government of India. The Ministry of Finance, which in a way is the parent institution to the Reserve Bank, has always treated the bank as somewhat of a 'problem child', with disagreements occurring on multiple occasions over a myriad of issues pertaining to India's economic management. This was well summarized by former governor Raghuram Rajan, when he said, 'We (RBI) are the gatekeepers, and sometimes have to say no'. This disavowal, however, was conspicuously absent during the recent demonetization exercise, which the Reserve Bank was widely criticized for, including by former governors.

Indeed, these personality clashes have often resulted in governors leaving their jobs before their terms expire. Most recently, the perceived clash between Raghuram Rajan and the government resulted in the popular governor not seeking another term, highlighting the fundamental difference in the policy objectives of the government on the one hand and the bank on the other.

Such clashes are not new, and they are a common feature of the modern financial system, where central banks occupy a unique position in every government around the world. Indeed, the very first governor of the RBI, Sir Osbourne Arkell Smith, an Australian, resigned due to his differences with the government on policy and personality issues. Similar issues cropped up between Governor Rama Rau and Finance Minister T.T. Krishnamachari, which resulted in a public altercation between the two in the corridors of the Secretariat building's North Block in Delhi, culminating in the former's resignation in 1957.

As Governor H.V.R. Iyengar noted in the 1960s, the Reserve Bank was grappling with four key areas of conflict with the government, namely, interest rate policy, deficit financing, cooperative credit policies and management of sub-standard banks. These issues continue to manifest today, albeit in a slightly different form and spirit.

There are other instances that show at best a frosty relationship between the finance minister and the governor of the RBI. As Governor Y.V. Reddy once quipped, 'The Reserve Bank is independent within the boundaries set by the government.'* The clashes have become slightly more prominent with increasing media scrutiny, but also with the arrival of 'outsiders' to the Reserve Bank itself. Indeed, Governor Rajan was already a reputed economist before his arrival in Indian policy circles, and Governor Urjit Patel has been a private sector economist for most of his career. Before them, the governors usually came from within the government, having served as career bureaucrats dealing with politicians and their agendas at close quarters.

The Ministry of Finance and its mandarins and the Reserve Bank have had different objectives over different periods of time, and it has not always been possible to reconcile them. In the corridors of power in Delhi, the Reserve Bank of India is often described as 'too conservative', a term often used by former employees of the central bank itself. This conservatism has generally served the country well, but has often led to allegations of the bank being 'behind the times' and too 'tight-fisted'.

Nonetheless, most governments have praised the Reserve Bank's critical role in promoting financial inclusion and increasing savings, and have not tinkered around too much with its organizational set-up, thus creating conditions for the autonomous institution to flourish and fulfil its critical role in the government.

Gatekeeper of foreign capital, not policy manager

The word 'rupee' comes from the Sanskrit word 'roopya', meaning shape or form. Used to denominate silver coins, rupee is used as a moniker for

---

*Y.V. Reddy. 'Autonomy of the Central Bank: Changing Contours in India.' Speech, Reserve Bank of India, 3 October 2001. https://rbi.org.in/Scripts/BS_SpeechesView. aspx?Id=88, accessed on 29 October 2017

currency across South Asia and in Indonesia. Currency management, both operational and preserving its value, is a major task of any central bank. The RBI has also had the privilege of being the central banker to many countries, including Pakistan and Burma for short periods of time, along with managing currency systems in several Middle Eastern countries in its early years.

Modern currency management boils down to two primary objectives: ensuring that there is enough currency in circulation, and managing foreign reserves. With regard to foreign exchange, the Reserve Bank is responsible for managing it, not necessarily deciding on its direction. Unlike monetary policy, the sovereign largely controls foreign exchange policy, and hence the RBI does not necessarily control the direction of the currency. It uses tools such as direct currency intervention, its stock of foreign exchange reserves, and even the introduction of special windows and policies to manage the exchange rate.

The RBI is the gatekeeper of capital account transactions in India, such as foreign direct investment (FDI) or investments by institutional investors in India's equity or debt markets. These limits are operated by the RBI, on the instruction of the government of India, and the RBI does not necessarily have the discretion to change the limits on its own. However, in practice, the RBI has a significant amount of clout in deciding these limits, so as to enable its currency operations.

The RBI is also the primary agency interacting with international institutions such as the International Monetary Fund (IMF) and the World Bank on India's behalf, along with the Ministry of Finance. In the past, whenever India has needed funds or support from these multilateral institutions, RBI has usually taken the lead on the negotiations.

Donning multiple hats

Since its establishment in 1935, the Reserve Bank has performed multiple roles. While the financial press focuses more on the RBI's monetary policy, exchange rate management and banking system operations, the central bank also manages government debt, prints currency notes and coins, manages banking system regulation and performs supervision, along with promoting rural credit and financial inclusion.

At times, these multiple objectives have come into conflict, as one function impedes the objectives of another. For instance, during the early days of the implementation of the Pradhan Mantri Jan-Dhan Yojana, while the RBI welcomed the renewed push for financial inclusion, Governor Rajan did point out the risks associated with opening bank accounts without incentivizing their usage, thus putting an extra burden on the public sector banks.

Similarly, when the Reserve Bank forced banks to undertake a rigorous asset quality review in 2015, many in the government blamed the bank for sleeping on the job of banking regulation, and further admonished the governor for keeping policy conditions tight when banks were not in a position to increase lending. The fact is that while lapses were probably made in the early part of the decade when bank lending was expanding aggressively, a sharp redressal mechanism would have had significant negative implications for India's financial system, and in turn the Indian economy.

The RBI has also been able to successfully navigate political headwinds, ensuring critical reforms are passed through different administrations. For instance, when it came to stopping the decade-long practice of deficit financing (RBI would print money to buy bonds from the government directly to finance the budget deficit), the Reserve Bank worked across two different governors, C. Rangarajan and Bimal Jalan, to successfully implement a critical reform that was initiated under P.V. Narasimha Rao and was carried out by the United Front government under I.K. Gujral and then carried forward by Atal Bihari Vajpayee's National Democratic Alliance (NDA) government. It was a classic case of consensus-driven reform and showcased the bank's ability to negotiate across the political spectrum, thanks to its leadership.

The Reserve Bank is also known to protect its turf. For instance, there has been some discussion to set up a debt management office in New Delhi under the Ministry of Finance, but the RBI has not been keen on the proposal, given its conservative nature, but also to protect its turf. The central bank does have a legal mandate to ensure the central government is able to finance its borrowings. The bank also provides banking services to state governments and has greater discretion in managing state finances, with the ability to cut states off from primary bond issuance if it feels the states will exceed their fiscal responsibility and budget management act requirements to contain the borrowings within a certain limit.

However, as the complexities of financial regulation have grown, the government has taken steps to increase the number of institutions managing India's financial markets. Some have been set up with the Reserve Bank's blessings such as the National Bank for Agriculture and Rural Development (NABARD) and the Bank Boards Bureau (BBB). Others, such as the Securities and Exchange Board of India (SEBI) and the Insurance Regulatory and Development Authority (IRDA) have carved out certain functions from the Reserve Bank itself, often contradicting some of the policy objectives. This was apparent in RBI's reluctance to support committees such as those headed by Percy Mistry or the Financial Sector Legislative Reforms Committee (FSLRC) headed by Justice B.N. Srikrishna. Indeed, even the Financial Stability and Development Council set up by Finance Minister Pranab Mukherjee to arbitrate regulatory conflicts between different regulators was cold shouldered by the Reserve Bank, till it got what it wanted, a 'higher' seat at the table.

In recent years, the Reserve Bank has also taken on the role of promoting the use of technology to achieve the overarching objective of financial inclusion. Setting up and encouraging modern payment systems, digital banking and ensuring last mile connectivity through the use of small and payments banks are some of the initiatives the central bank has undertaken. The push to encourage technology has seen the RBI promoting a unified payments interface, or United Payments Interface (UPI) which has provided India with one of the simplest yet most efficient payment systems globally.

In a nutshell, the Reserve Bank occupies the primal position in India's financial labyrinth, and even though other agencies such as SEBI and IRDA have filled important positions as far as the regulatory space is concerned, RBI will continue to remain fundamentally dominant and indispensable to India's body politic for decades to come.

Chapter 1

Origins of the Reserve Bank of India

India's monetary system has gone through multiple transformations in the last few hundred years. From an era of using bullion to the modern-day fractional banking, currency, and more importantly, trade and commerce, have been at the centre of India's development. For India to evolve beyond the use of precious metals to a robust banking system has taken time and effort, at the heart of which the Reserve Bank of India has sat for the last eighty years.

While India's monetary system is ancient, the need for a central bank arose fairly recently. The RBI has been in existence for just over eighty years, but it evolved from a series of dialogues and deliberations, which date back to the eighteenth century. India has always had a relatively sophisticated network of informal banking, which dates back to the Subarnabanik bankers of Bengal around the sixteenth century. Later, the Jagat Seths of Marwar during the nineteenth century helped create an extensive banking network, where transactions were conducted primarily through 'hundis'[1], or bills of exchange, which was a centuries-old Bania innovation, allowing merchants across India to receive or provide payments in hundis instead of cash, thus lowering the risk of theft and introducing an honour system in transactions.

But with regard to modern central banking, it was Warren Hastings, the first de facto Governor General of India under the British East India Company, who mooted the idea of forming a General Bank of Bengal and Bahar[2] in 1773 so the East India Company could conduct its monetary transactions with relative ease.[3] This proposal was quickly shot down, and shortly afterwards, Warren Hastings was impeached on charges of corruption.

1

Nonetheless, the East India Company's business grew fast enough for the government to justify opening the Bank of Bengal in June 1806, with permission to issue currency in Bengal and Bihar. The Bank of Bengal enjoyed a virtual monopoly over issuing currency on a large scale. This monopoly was challenged on two occasions, once in 1807 and then again in 1836, when a trader by the name of Robert Rickards, and later a British merchant body in England, proposed setting up a general bank. Both proposals were shot down by the Bank of Bengal.

However, with the Maratha kingdom in retreat in the early nineteenth century and the Mughals losing their dominance simultaneously, the powers of the East India Company expanded at a rapid pace, and via a network of patronage and business ties, two more general banks, Bank of Bombay (1840) and Bank of Madras (1843) were set up.[4] Together, the three banks, set up in Bengal, Bombay (now Mumbai) and Madras (now Chennai), came to be known as the 'Presidency Banks'. Each had the power to manage and conduct monetary transactions on behalf of their respective states.

The Paper Currency Act and James Wilson

India's first War of Independence came in 1857. After a brief but intense battle, the East India Company reigned supreme, and it handed over control of the dominion of India to the British crown. India's existing monetary system thus came under the control of the crown, and the India Office was set up in London in 1858[5] to manage India's financial matters.

While the India Office was essentially set up to increase the crown's stranglehold on India's borders, it did set up a position for financial matters. James Wilson, a Scottish businessman and founder of *The Economist Weekly* and the Chartered Bank of India, Australia and China, which went on to become the Standard Chartered Bank, was selected to fill the position. Mr Wilson was a free market advocate and made his name in British politics opposing the restrictive corn laws. He took office in 1859 and visited India to redesign its financial system. He proposed the setting up of a national banking establishment, which he envisaged would help extend banking services to unserved areas. However, the bank would not necessarily issue notes, a function he wanted reserved for the government itself.

The government took control of paper currency in 1861, through the Paper Currency Act, which gave the government monopoly control over currency issuance across British India. This was done through the Presidency Banks, which distributed the currency, while the government, through the finance office in Delhi, controlled the money supply. Unfortunately, Mr Wilson's stay in India was short, and he died in 1860 after contracting dysentery in Calcutta (now Kolkata). He was buried in an unmarked grave in Mullick Bazaar, which was only recently discovered and restored.[6]

The troubled years between 1860 and 1900

Between 1860 and 1900, the demand for a central banking establishment was muted. Barring a brief crisis in 1867, the Bank of Bengal remained the dominant financial institution in the country. In 1867, the Bank of Bombay ran into financial troubles, and was of the view that a merger of the three Presidency Banks would help it tide over the crisis. The proposal envisaged amalgamating the three banks into a 'Central Bank for all India',[7] but this was promptly shot down by Bank of Bengal, which wanted to maintain its dominance and autonomy.

Discussion on a central bank was raised again in 1898 by the Indian currency committee under Viscount Fowler, a British parliamentarian. The committee looked into the currency situation in India, which until 1892 had been based on silver; however, the value of silver had declined significantly against that of gold between 1850–1890. During the committee's deliberations, several members raised the need for a central banking establishment in India along the lines of the Bank of England, despite the issue not being within the remit of the committee's discussions. Nonetheless, one of the members, Mr Everard Hambro, a banker and one of the co-founders of a commercial bank called the Central Bank of India, gave a strong pitch for setting up a central banking establishment, and his ideas were dispatched to the government of India in 1899, which actively backed his proposal.[8]

Given the supremacy of the three Presidency Banks, there was a trade-off between amalgamation and setting up a new institution. This was widely debated within the government and financial circles, with varied opinions. Bankers and business interests staunchly opposed the merger of the Presidency Banks, since the move could undermine the two smaller banks. However, the principle behind the merger was to create a large financial institution that could cater to the burgeoning business interests of the British Empire in India, was still of interest, but it did not materialize until 1913, when a certain John Maynard Keynes started analysing India's banking system and its future needs.

Keynes joins the Chamberlain Commission

Keynes had two stints with the India Office in London, where he spent most of his time studying issues related to Indian currency and finance. He first joined the India Office in October 1906, but left in 1908 to pursue a career as a lecturer at Cambridge. However, he never stopped working on his analysis of the Indian economy, and rejoined the India Office in 1913, after having published his first book, *Indian Currency and Finance.* In his second innings, Keynes had joined the India Office as a member of the Royal Commission on Indian Finance and Currency, also known as the Chamberlain[9] Commission. The commission was set up to investigate matters of currency stability and government finance, but it eventually ended up examining the need for a national banking establishment as well.

The issues around the Indian rupee placed before the Chamberlain Commission had been under debate for decades. The East India Company had adopted silver as its base currency standard in 1835. However, gold was easily accepted as legal tender, along with currency notes in some areas, which started being issued after the Presidency Banks were established. However, with gold prices coming under pressure following the gold rush in the nineteenth century in the United States, the convertibility was abruptly withdrawn. Post the handover of the control of the dominion of India to the crown, James Wilson and his successor Samuel Laing shepherded the Paper Currency Act of 1861, which introduced paper notes and some government securities across the country with a silver reserve backing it.

This arrangement continued for several years, until the price of silver started dropping significantly between the 1870s and 1890s, and the rupee fell along with it. Several steps to prevent a budgetary crisis were contemplated, including artificial exchange rate overvaluation. However, these steps did not succeed, and India moved on to a partial gold exchange standard, which continued until J.M. Keynes joined the Chamberlain Commission.

The Chamberlain Commission was set up before the outbreak of the First World War. In his seminal work, *Indian Currency and Finance*, Keynes outlined how the Indian rupee and its various derivatives had become an inconvertible legal tender, given the stoppage of free minting of silver into legal tender in 1893 as a result of depreciation pressures.[10] Also, the Indian rupee, while being issued by British India's currency department, was being increasingly used across different provinces or circles, despite the restrictions on its convertibility. Even with no legal backing to be converted into bullion (whether gold or silver), the rupee was becoming the 'local currency' across the Indian subcontinent, with a relatively stable exchange rate. This development of the Indian rupee as a uniform exchange was not by design but more by evolution. Keynes saw the benefit of having such a system, and along with the other members of the Chamberlain Commission, recommended that the system should continue, with some modifications.

Given that India was still reeling from the aftershocks of a banking and currency crisis in 1907–08, which started in the United States, the government passed a universal Paper Currency Act in 1910, which made rupee notes in the denominations of five, ten and hundred legal tender across British India, breaking down the imaginary barriers that had existed before. The Chamberlain Commission submitted its report in 1914, and concluded that the Indian system of currency and finance was largely functional, despite being experimental in nature. Apart from recommending the continuation of the proportional reserve gold standard system, Keynes in his report to the commission also recommended an amalgamation of the three Presidency Banks, with a possible capital infusion needed to secure 'public' control over its operations. This central banking establishment was envisaged as the issuer of currency and manager of public debt, as well as the manager of financial transactions between the Indian government and the British crown.[11]

The Imperial Bank of India

With the end of the First World War in 1919, the process of setting up a central bank in India was restarted. The Indian government began working on the merger of the Presidency Banks, having seen the benefits of working closely with them during the war. A bill was tabled in India's legislative council in March 1920, and the Imperial Bank of India came into existence in January 1921.

However, its powers were limited. In addition to being the banker of the government and having the responsibility of managing public debt exclusively, it was expected to carry on its normal transactions of business and finance, which gave it a quasi-national character, but it could not issue currency and manage foreign exchange. This was a critical omission, as without these functions, while the Imperial Bank was the largest bank in the Indian subcontinent, but it was not the central banking institution similar to other institutions such as Bank of England. This peculiar characteristic set the stage for years of conflict between the Imperial Bank and the RBI, even in its later avatar as State Bank of India, as the Imperial Bank would later go on to be nationalized in 1955, after a prolonged fight with the bank management over control and command of a planned economy.

The Hilton Young Commission, and the problem of the rupee

The Indian rupee fluctuated significantly during the war years. With several countries restricting the export of gold during the war, the Indian government suspended gold sales in 1914, which led to a spike in the value of silver, as silver was still being exchanged for rupees within the Indian context. As silver rose in value, the currency system broke down in 1917, and the rupee appreciated in value, given its favourable trade surplus (emptied by war reparations). However, once the war ended, the value of the Indian rupee plummeted, and it eventually reached levels similar to those before the war.

This volatility through the 1910s had a debilitating effect on businesses across India, and in 1924, Sir Purshottamdas Thakurdas, a veteran banker and a leading proponent of rupee stability, moved a bill to fix the rupee's value against sterling. This proposal was shot down, but the then finance member agreed to set up a committee to look into the matter. This laid the foundation for the constitution of the Hilton Young Commission under the chairmanship of Edward Hilton Young. This commission would prove to be a critical precursor to the establishment of the Reserve Bank.[12]

The Hilton Young Commission was appointed in 1925, and its primary mandate was to look into matters of currency and exchange and suggest modifications in the interest of India. This was a seminal moment for India's banking history, for the Royal Commission on Indian Currency and Finance was appointed in August 1925, with both British and Indian members invited to sit on it. Despite his differences with the government on the exchange rate of the rupee, Sir Thakurdas was invited to join the panel.

The commission invited comments and testimonies from several leaders in both India and Britain, including the then governor of the Bank of England, Montagu Norman, a widely celebrated and respected banker who presided over the Bank of England from 1920 to 1944. Testimonies from the Indian commentators included the famous testimony by Dr Bhim Rao 'Babasaheb' Ambedkar.

Before appearing in front of the Hilton Young Commission, Ambedkar had written his thoughts on the Indian rupee and its exchange system in his book, *The Problem of the Rupee: Its origin and its solution*. A large part of his book was devoted to the issue of finding a stable and reasonable internal value for the rupee, which would require control over money supply, and also taking away the power of issuing currency from the government, as Ambedkar feared that currency issuance was being done in an inconsistent manner relative to India's internal trade.

Similar thoughts were expressed by several other members, and as setting up central banks was in vogue, the committee, in its final report submitted in July 1926, recommended that a new institution, called the 'Reserve Bank of India', should be set up, which would have the power to issue currency, manage the exchange rate and become the banker to the government.

There was fierce argument over the conversion of the Imperial Bank of India into a central bank. While several members including Sir Purshottamdas Thakurdas were in favour[13] of this move, a few factors went against the Imperial Bank. At the time when the committee met, the Imperial Bank was the biggest financial institution in British India, and had been consistently expanding its regional presence by opening new branches.

Further, the Imperial Bank was in effect a private sector bank, which would mean that the government would be handing over the responsibility of currency issuance to a private body, which could become counterproductive. In his remarks to the commission, Montagu Norman also noted that forcing the Imperial Bank to 'abandon' its commercial banking activities would be 'most undesirable'.[14]

In fact, when asked what the Reserve Bank's role should be vis-à-vis the Bank of England, Lord Norman observed that the RBI should treat the relationship as a 'Hindoo marriage', wherein the RBI would play the passive role of the wife, who would advise, but obey the instructions of the Bank of England.[15] This subservience was also desired by the British government, which eventually led to clashes between the early leadership and the finance secretary.

A private or a public central bank?

The British Indian government promptly accepted the recommendations of the Hilton Young Commission in 1926 and in 1927 tabled the first Reserve Bank bill in the Parliament to set up a central bank with issuing powers and provisions for private capital, and included restrictions on political appointees in order to preserve the institution's independence. The bill immediately ran into trouble and was sent to a joint parliamentary committee for changes. The joint committee itself faced heated debates, but recommended that the Reserve Bank be set up with its share capital wholly subscribed by the government, and also recommended the removal of restrictions on existing members of legislature joining the board of the new institution.

However, the recommendations were not palatable to several members of the committee, and while there was a consensus on what the institution should do, there was little agreement over who should own the RBI and how they should run it. The government then introduced an amended version of the bill in January 1928, which had restrictive individual ownership of RBI's shares and direct appointments of the senior management of the bank. However, with two versions of the bill circulating, the government found it difficult to find support within the legislature for using private capital for a public institution, and the finance member shelved the idea of chaperoning the bill in the house in February 1928.[16]

Although there were no further attempts to pass the Reserve Bank bill for some time after 1928, the debate continued. With independence in sight, several Indian members of the legislature were in favour of an institution that was owned by the government, and several notable figures such as Madan Mohan Malviya, Jamnadas Mehta and Lala Lajpat Rai had previously raised their opposition to the idea of private shareholding in the RBI.

As the Non-Cooperation Movement called for by Mahatma Gandhi in 1920 was peaking, the first Round Table Conference was called in 1930–1931 by the British government, inviting Indian politicians to discuss constitutional reforms in London. Within that, a subcommittee on federal structure revisited the issue of setting up the Reserve Bank of India, and recommended that if constitutional reforms were to be undertaken, then setting up the RBI would be an ideal accompaniment. An internal finance committee in the India Office in London backed an institution based broadly on the recommendations of the Hilton Young Commission, and the government introduced the Reserve Bank of India bill in 1933. The bill was drafted on the basis of recommendations from the internal finance Committee set up by the India office, and recommended a private capital infusion in order to limit political interference. Despite going to a joint committee in the Indian legislature, the bill was approved on 22 December 1933, and was signed into law by the then Governor General, Freeman Freeman-Thomas, on 6 March 1934.

The Reserve Bank of India comes into being

The Reserve Bank of India came into existence on 1 April 1935. Sir Osborne Arkell Smith, an Australian by birth, was appointed the first governor of the new central bank. The bank was initially headquartered in Calcutta, but was shifted permanently to Bombay in December 1937, due to operational challenges. In its early years, the RBI also commissioned the construction of several offices across its major centres in Bombay, Rangoon and Lahore.

Sir Osborne Smith was serving as the managing governor of the Imperial Bank of India when he was asked to head the newly founded institution. Having worked his way up through the Commonwealth Bank of Australia, which had performed a similar fiduciary role of managing currency operations for the crown in Australia, Smith was handpicked by Sir Montagu Norman, governor of the Bank of England, to head the new Reserve Bank, as he believed that Smith's loyalties would be with the Bank of England more than the government of India.

He was well complemented by Sir James Taylor, who had played a key role in the drafting and passage of RBI's legislation, and had spent years working within the Indian bureaucracy, including serving as a Deputy Comptroller of Currency, a function that the Reserve Bank was taking over. To honour the promise of appointing an Indian to the senior leadership, Sir Sikandar Hyat-Khan was the preferred choice, given his strong political connections across party lines, and was appointed as the deputy governor.

Along with the senior leadership, the board for the central bank comprised several eminent personalities from the world of business and finance, including Sir Purshottamdas Thakurdas, who became a director in the institution for the Bombay Register. Rai Bahadur Sir Badridas Goenka, a prominent Marwari businessman from Calcutta, was also on the inaugural board. Goenka was also the first chairman of the Imperial Bank of India, having served in that position for over twenty years.

The senior management selected the bank's official seal. It was designed keeping in mind the East India Company's seal, which comprised a lion and a palm tree, but the lion was replaced by a tiger, to add an 'Indian' feel to it. It was also a reminder of the supremacy of the government over the institution, and the tiger at the entrance of Belvedere Estate in Calcutta (modern-day National Library in New Alipore) was picked as a model for the image that eventually became the symbol. Post-Independence, it remains a reminder of the colonial past of India and the RBI.

To begin with, RBI instituted two key separate departments to perform the two essential functions required of it, the issuance of currency and banking for the government. The Issue department was divided on a geographic basis, based on various currency circles, and had two basic functions, issuing new currency and facilitating exchange across various circles. The Banking department managed various functions required of the central bank, barring issuance. These were public accounts, deposit accounts, public debt, securities and share transfer.

The Imperial Bank of India was appointed as the agent for the Reserve Bank to conduct business for government transactions. In the early years, the Imperial Bank had an overwhelming presence in the Indian banking system and acted as a banker to other banks on matters of liquidity. This agreement was part of the bargain struck with the Imperial Bank to compensate for the loss of some of the functions it had been performing for the state, and was initially approved for twenty years.

The Osborne Smith affair

Even as the RBI was trying to find its place within the evolving Indian economy, there were emerging conflicts within the institution itself. Sir Osborne Smith, who had spent considerable time working within the Indian banking system after he became one of the two managing governors of the Imperial Bank of India, had a general dislike for government interference in his work. He thought the exchange rate was too strong and was in favour of a weaker exchange rate to avoid deflationary pressures. This was at direct odds with the thinking within the government, which favoured a strong but stable exchange rate, and balanced budgets, deflation notwithstanding.

His attitude was evident during his short term at the Reserve Bank, where early on his views on the exchange and interest rates clashed with those of the then finance member, Sir P.J. Griggs. This was not unusual, as even in his role at the Imperial Bank, Smith had been vocal on the interference of the government in the day-to-day running of the bank, and the government was clearly unhappy with his efforts to run a loose monetary policy, which was counterproductive for British interests. Griggs decided that he needed to 'fix' Smith, and rumours about Smith's unsavoury character, including rumours of him being a womanizer, began circulating.[17]

Bakhtiar Dadabhoy's book, *Barons of Banking: Glimpses of Indian Banking History*, devotes considerable amount of attention to the first RBI governor, noting that the government went to extraordinary lengths to push Smith out, as his purpose of being an outsider was past its utility date, given that the appointment had already established the Reserve Bank's credibility as an 'independent institution', and the government was on the lookout for a 'suitable occasion and a favourable political environment in which it would pass without much fuss'. [18]

Unfortunately, Smith's relationship with his deputy James Taylor was also cold, and Sir Osborne spent a significant amount of his term 'travelling', as he received little support from his deputies for his policies. Smith also suspected that the government felt much more comfortable dealing directly with Taylor, who was happy to bypass Smith in favour of the government, to ensure support for himself in Delhi with the finance member. The run-ins came to such a point that Smith announced his resignation as early as the end of October 1936, just fifteen months into the job. However, he continued as the governor in principle till the end of June 1937, and was granted a leave of absence for the rest of his term by the board.

Sir Sikandar Hyat-Khan also left the bank a couple of weeks before Smith's departure, on account of his return to politics in his home state of Punjab. He would later go on to become the Premier of united Punjab, and died in 1942, in the middle of the Second World War. As RBI's official history notes, the post of the Indian deputy governor was highly valued, and Sir Sikandar's exit saw more than twenty people in the running to replace him. Eventually, the role went to Manilal Balabhai Nanavati, a veteran administrator from the princely state of Baroda, and an expert on agricultural finance and economics.

Nanavati's arrival at the RBI in December 1936 marked an important milestone in RBI's history, since the central bank's top echelons had till then been dominated by career bankers, bureaucrats and industrialists, and there was little room for specialization on agriculture. Despite the conservative approach of the RBI in its early days, Mr Nanavati managed to draw the attention of the central bank and the government towards agricultural credit. This manifested itself in regulation around cooperative banks through the agriculture credit department, which was initially set up by K.G. Ambegaonkar, an Indian Civil Services officer deputed to RBI, who later became the governor of the RBI, albeit for a very brief period.

James Taylor takes over

The selection process for Sir Smith's successor was relatively straightforward. Sir James Taylor, who had spent considerable time working within the government and shepherding the Reserve Bank bill, was seen as a natural choice, and he became the second governor of the Reserve Bank on 1 July 1937, having assumed organizational control roughly eight months earlier, in November 1936. Taylor was appointed for a five-year term initially, and had a profound impact on the foundation and organization of the Reserve Bank. Given his previous role in the finance ministry and closeness to Grigg, Taylor intimately understood what the government had set up the RBI for, and how the institution should be shaped as India was gradually approaching self-rule, followed by likely independence.

On taking over as the governor in July 1937, Taylor started scouting for a European deputy governor. However, the search remained elusive, and the central bank carried on with its operations with the governor and one deputy governor for the next four years. However, to alleviate rising concerns about personnel risk around Sir James Taylor, the government appointed Chintaman Dwarkanath Deshmukh, an Indian Civil Services officer working within the finance ministry, as 'secretary' to the central board in October 1939.

Given the poor relations between Osborne Smith and Grigg, Taylor was a breath of fresh air for the government. From the government's point of view, Taylor quickly made amends and found a common ground with the government on running a conservative monetary policy. This raised concerns among Indian businesses and political parties, who feared that with Sir Smith's departure, the institution was turning into an extension of the state machinery, despite the ample provisions made to ensure its independence. These fears were warranted, given that the contractionary policies adopted to sustain a high exchange rate were forcing India into deflationary territory, and economic conditions started deteriorating from 1938 onwards.

As the conflict between the government and the Reserve Bank ended, a new conflict was emerging between the central board and the government over monetary stance, with the governor of the RBI generally siding with the government. However, the conflict between the board the government continued, with several provincial governments[19] making the case for a weaker rupee/sterling rate, which was squashed by the government and by extension, the central bank. This conflict persisted for some time, but the economic scenario drastically changed as Germany invaded Poland in September 1939.

Banking during the Second World War

The Second World War had a significant impact on the Reserve Bank's operations, despite India not being part of the principal arena of war. Apart from a surge in the export of wartime supplies, the primary impact for the RBI came from its operations in Burma, the maintenance of the exchange rate with sterling, and eventually the move towards the issuance of fiat currency, delinked from any commodity.

The primary function of the RBI during the initial years of the war was helping the government manage its finances. Given the pressures of the war, the government of India was called upon to not only finance its own defence expenditure, but also help in meeting Britain's shortfalls through a combination of home charges and extra payments (recoverable post war). In such a scenario, an increase in taxes was inevitable, and even that was not enough to meet the shortfall.

At the same time, RBI was accumulating large sterling balances on account of a favourable trade balance, from which the monetary base of the country kept expanding. With Japan attacking British territories in Southeast Asia, commodity prices shot up, and inflation was becoming a major challenge. However, Governor James Taylor saw this as a shock to the aggregate demand led by government purchases, and along with his deputy, Governor Deshmukh, suggested shifting the sterling balances into gold or the US dollar. The problem of inflation persisted as the government deficit increased, the gold exchange standard was terminated, and the famine in Bengal worsened.

Operationally, the Reserve Bank had been preparing for the war even before it broke out, through the exchange control regulations and the 'sterling area' negotiations initiated by the Bank of England. A separate department was set up in the Reserve Bank called the 'Exchange Control

Department', which had the primary responsibility of controlling foreign transactions on behalf of the government. The Reserve Bank was allowed to issue licences to banks and others as 'authorized dealers' to undertake foreign exchange transactions. RBI also restricted the purchase or sale of gold externally without permission, fearing that its authority to manage the exchange control could be undermined if free exchange trade was allowed. These notices were issued shortly after the war broke out. At the same time, in 1940, RBI started issuing fiat currency, a significant change in approach, led by rising commodity prices.

Among its many jurisdictions, RBI was the central banker to Burma as well, and saw its operations getting disrupted as the Japanese occupation moved through Southeast Asia. Once again, the central bank had been preparing in advance and had already shifted a significant part of its operations from its Rangoon register to Calcutta. In 1937, when Burma had achieved self-rule, RBI had been appointed as the banker to the government in order to ensure the smooth management of currency operations. Over time, RBI started issuing currency notes meant only for Burma, but once the Japanese occupation began, RBI ceased to be the banking authority for the government, and its offices were closed in Rangoon in February 1942. It restarted its operations in Burma after the war ended in August 1945, but it proved to be a short-lived arrangement as the RBI ceased to be the banker to the Burmese government from 1 April 1947.

Taylor's unexpected demise

Even as the central bank was actively fighting many operational battles, tragedy struck closer to home. Sir James Taylor, a proponent of stable monetary and exchange rate policy through the war and a symbol of cooperation between the government and the RBI, died on 17 February 1943. His term had only recently been renewed for another five years in 1942. He was only fifty-two at the time of his death. Sir James Taylor, however, had prepared a strong bench, having handpicked Chintaman Dwarkanath Deshmukh, the liaison officer and later secretary of RBI as deputy governor in 1941, as a replacement for Mr Nanavati.

Over the years, C.D. Deshmukh had become close to James Taylor, and saw him as a facilitator of 'Indianization' within the RBI, even refusing to appoint a European deputy governor during his term. There was initially some apprehension over appointing Deshmukh, an Indian but an Indian Civil Services officer, to the position of governor. However, he had strong support from the central board, including Sir Purshottamdas Thakurdas, who spearheaded the push from the board, along with Brij Mohan Birla. In his biography, Deshmukh noted that while at one point the name of Sir Otto Niemeyer, a respected central banker in England, had been put forth, eventually there was broad consensus on backing Deshmukh.

The government eventually relented, but asked Deshmukh to appoint a British deputy and a Muslim to succeed him as deputy governor. Deshmukh readily agreed, and went on to appoint C.R. Trevor, a colleague from the Reserve Bank; Wajahat Hussain was picked to replace Deshmukh as the deputy governor. Once again, while Deshmukh had already been leading the bank for over six months, his appointment was only officially announced in August 1943.

An Indian governor

Chintaman Dwarkanath Deshmukh was born on 14 January 1896, and was only forty-seven years old when he took over the governorship of the Reserve Bank. A Sanskrit scholar par excellence, Deshmukh was known as the Indian Civil Services officer who had scored the highest percentage ever registered by an Indian in the qualifying examinations. Deshmukh's appointment as governor was widely celebrated, and it would have a fundamental impact on the bank's workings, especially in light of India's Independence and subsequent Partition in 1947. Deshmukh was a career bureaucrat in the British government, but was deeply nationalistic, and was advised by Bal Gangadhar Tilak to carry on in service in order to learn the art of governance.[20]

He had held several important posts before joining the RBI, including secretary of the second Round Table Conference in London in 1931, where he had spent some time with the leadership of India's freedom movement, including Gandhi. He had also played an instrumental role in designing India's federal structure in 1935, having drafted memorandums that helped shape the Government of India Act, 1935, which provided for autonomy of governance to provinces.

Deshmukh took over the governorship of the RBI at a time when the government in India was running large deficits, inflation was high and the famine in Bengal was at its peak. To support the war against the Japanese, the government relied heavily on using food stocks to feed its army, which further exacerbated the economic situation and the food shortages domestically. Deshmukh pursued a policy of maintaining monetary and exchange rate stability. Despite such large challenges, he played a key role in shaping the RBI into an institution that would serve the needs of India post-Independence.

Early on in his term, Deshmukh was asked to assist the government in developing the post-war rebuilding plans and the international monetary system that would follow, culminating in the Bretton Woods agreements. However, Deshmukh quickly realized that the central bank was ill prepared to deal with the data intelligence and gathering that would be needed during negotiations.

Some steps to improve RBI's research and data intelligence capacity had been taken early on during James Taylor's term itself. RBI had hired R.K. Madan, the then economic advisor to the government of Punjab, as the director of research in 1941, and by 1943, the central bank had expanded the section in order to better understand the implications of war and famine on India's economy. J.V. Joshi was hired initially on a secondment from the government, but went on to become a full-time economic advisor to the RBI. Both Mr Madan and Mr Joshi went on to become deputy governors of the RBI post-Independence. The appointment of J.V. Joshi was later made permanent when in August 1945, a separate department of research and statistics was set up, headed by J.V. Joshi. The department also had noted economist Dr B.R. Shenoy as an important member. Over time, stalwarts such as M. Narasimham, J.J. Anjaria, Anand Chandavarkar, V.V. Bhatt and Deena Khatkate joined the bank through this department.

Deshmukh wows Keynes at Bretton Woods

Even before the Bretton Woods meetings began in 1945 to discuss post war reconstruction and establishment of multilateral institutions such as

World Bank and IMF for developmental assistance, the government and the Reserve Bank were studying proposals by Lord Keynes, who was in favour of an international monetary arrangement to facilitate economic growth after the end of the war. While the initial proposal prepared by Keynes was sent to the government, as the war was drawing to an end, the Reserve Bank was asked to give its opinion.

The Keynes plan was straightforward. He favoured setting up an international clearing union based on a currency called Bancor (for accounting purposes), whose value would be fixed in gold. Member nations could then benchmark their currency against Bancor, which would act as a substitute for gold. Another programme, proposed by the Americans, was called the 'White' plan and called for a similar union, but required its member countries to use gold as an instrument of barter, with strict limits on a country's surplus.

While India was not yet independent, it was apparent that Deshmukh was thinking ahead, as independence was in sight, and most of India's suggestions were made keeping this in mind. The first set of official proposals from Keynes came in 1943, which were assessed largely within the finance department at the RBI. Both Deshmukh and Taylor were sceptical of Keynes's plan, deeming it to be inflationary in nature. In fact, Deshmukh recalls Taylor's disdain for Keynes is his personal memoirs, where Taylor said, 'I agree with you about Keynes—a monetary quack preferring a monetary panacea of the worst inflationary type for what is fundamentally an international political problem'[21], which indicates that while on a personal level, there were disagreements over the evolving monetary arrangement, the Reserve Bank still worked hard to get an effective deal from Bretton Woods.

Before the meetings, the Reserve Bank prepared a detailed memorandum for the government, in which it stated that while Keynes's plan would be expansionary and probably more desirable for the member nations, the revised plan submitted by the Americans was perhaps more practical. This view was put forth in the memorandum by Governor Deshmukh himself, as the American plan made provisions for war reparations and payments to be cleared, which was significantly in India's favour.

India's delegation to Bretton Woods was led by the finance secretary

Sir Jeremy Raisman and included senior officials of the RBI, including Governor Deshmukh, research head B.K. Madan, R.K. Shanmukham Chetty and others. In his memoirs, Deshmukh recalls meeting and developing strong relationships with several commonwealth central bankers, even though the Bretton Woods discussions were not going as per plan. Other countries were reluctant to give India its desired quota in IMF and World Bank's fund raising in spite of the fact that India's strong external balance put it in a favourable position to contribute generously to the IMF'ss coffers. This was almost a deal breaker and India at one point had decided to withdraw from the talks.

However, in the end the deal went through, and India managed to secure the sixth largest quota among member countries and a position on the board of governors, with the power to nominate an executive director to the International Monetary Fund (IMF), a position that would in coming years become a training ground for future RBI governors. Deshmukh recalls in his memoirs how even the British officers of the Indian delegation fought honourably to get India a larger role in the fund. Eventually, post war, Deshmukh went on to serve as the chairman of the board of governors of the IMF for its annual meetings in Paris in 1949.

Chapter 2

Preparing for independence

As Britain was winding down its World War II operations, it was simultaneously preparing to exit India. There were three clear pressure points for the Reserve Bank during this period, namely, the partition of the country and subsequently of the central bank and its operations. This was followed by the path for the nationalization of the Reserve Bank itself, a long-standing demand, especially of Indian parliamentarians. The third pressure point came through in the design and passage of the Banking Regulation Act in 1949, but that was more of an afterthought rather than an immediate concern.

As early as the Bretton Woods negotiations, there was some discussion on bringing Deshmukh to Delhi to work with the finance ministry, and reappointing a Briton as the governor in a direct swap. Deshmukh was sounded out on the proposal, but he politely yet firmly turned down the offer. His focus remained on institutionalizing several internal departments, including one on research and statistics, which till today have served the RBI well. However, given Deshmukh's rising clout in India's economic policymaking, a proposal for Deshmukh to join the executive council of the Viceroy Lord Wavell was soon made. Deshmukh turned down the offer while batting for a renewal of his term as governor, in order to ensure 'greater continuity'.[22]

The 1946 demonetization

The war had proved to be very costly for the British government, and it was desperate to raise funds. Following actions seen in France, Belgium and the United Kingdom, the government was exploring the possibility of demonetizing high value currency notes in order to 'fight against black money and tax evasions, which have now assumed enormous proportions.'[23] The RBI's official history notes that while the deliberations within the government may have begun in 1945, it was not until later that year that the Reserve Bank was looped into the conversation, and the central bank was at best reluctant to implement an 'ordinance' to withdraw high value currency notes without being at the onset of an inflationary spiral.[24]

Governor Deshmukh was circumspect, expressing doubt on the 'effectiveness of the measure to even raise 10 crores' through illicit money declaration, and pushed back on the plan. However, the government prevailed and issued an ordinance on 12 January 1946, withdrawing currency notes of five hundred rupees and above. This impacted currency issuance worth around ₹144 crore, of which almost ₹135 crore came back into circulation, thus extinguishing currency notes worth ₹9 crore. There was an echo of this measure felt in 1948,[25] when in September, Prime Minister Jawaharlal Nehru had to reassure the legislature and the public that the government had no plans to demonetize hundred-rupee notes, or freeze bank accounts.

As Deshmukh observed later, the measure was not 'revolutionary' and 'even its purpose as a minatory and punitive gesture towards black-marketing was not effectively served.'[26] Deshmukh also said that there was no foolproof method for RBI to differentiate between fair and illicit income, and ultimately, the measure was 'more of "conversion" at varying rates of profits and losses than "demonetisation".'[27]

The imminence of Partition

The interim government of India took control of India's affairs on 2 September 1946. The vice president of the viceroy's executive council, Jawaharlal Nehru, became the interim prime minister, and Liaquat Ali Khan, who would go on to become Pakistan's first prime minister, was appointed as the finance minister. With the bloodbath of the Direct Action Day[28], just behind them, the political leadership of India and the Muslim League led by Mohammad Ali Jinnah could not reconcile its differences to keep the country united, and focus turned to partitioning the country and its resources quickly. For the RBI, a decade-old institution that was serving the interests of two nations (India and Burma), Partition proved to be a tricky period.

For his part, Deshmukh tried to play a constructive and bipartisan role to ensure the orderly transfer of monetary control to authorities in Pakistan. The initial plan called for the transfer of power to a civilian administration run by Indians by June 1948, but the timeline was abruptly shortened as communal violence erupted following the announcement of the Radcliffe line, which demarcated the boundaries of the two nations. Looking to cut their losses, the British government, led by the labour administration in Britain, brought forward the date of handover to 15 August 1947, throwing the Indian administration into a tizzy.

While there was a special cabinet committee within the interim government that was looking into the division of resources, it was replaced in a hurry by a 'Partition Council' on 1 July 1947. One of the expert committees set up to divide resources and institutions between India and Pakistan was looking into matters of currency and coinage arrangements, the division of the central bank and its balance sheet, the formulation of an exchange rate mechanism, along with holdings at the International Monetary Fund and the World Bank. The Reserve Bank was only present within this committee in an advisory role, providing data and technical expertise. Deshmukh had requested both sides to keep the RBI in an advisory role, and delegated staff to help the committee with its requirements.[29]

The discussions had to be wrapped up within a limited time, but they were far from cordial. The committee submitted its report on 28 July 1947, and added supplementary notes in the first week of August. The eventual conclusion was to keep a common currency within India and Pakistan until March 1948, after which, for the next six months, only overprinted notes would be issued in Pakistan, but the Indian rupee notes remaining in Pakistan would continue to be legal tender until September 1948. This would be a period of transition, and the RBI would cease to be the monetary authority in Pakistan from 1 October 1948, transferring all liabilities of the overprinted Pakistani notes to the new authority. Before October, all profits of the central bank were to be divided between the two countries, and following the transfer, all RBI-related property would be transferred to the new monetary authority.

The RBI was also asked to make provisions for relocating staff from one side to another if they so desired, and it was also asked to recruit adequate staff in Pakistan. During the transition, RBI also agreed to depute staff as needed. Pakistan was split into two geographical halves by India in 1947. Dhaka did not have a central bank office, which the RBI set up. This branch in Dhaka would eventually become the Bangladesh Bank in 1971, at the same address.

While the administrative arrangements were largely agreeable to Deshmukh and his deputy governors, they took strong exception to Pakistan's suggestion to nominate a Muslim deputy governor for the period when RBI would serve as the central bank to Pakistan. There was also disagreement over Pakistan's proposal to nominate two directors to the central board, and its demand for giving the new government the authority to increase currency in circulation, if deemed necessary. The RBI was agreeable to the last point, but only if limits were set on the increase for both countries, and if the temporary increase could be settled against the transfer of assets between the two nations through the Reserve Bank. This would later become a highly contentious issue, and would result in RBI's premature withdrawal from the country.

Central banker to Pakistan

The Reserve Bank of India took control of Pakistan's monetary system under the Pakistan (Monetary System and Reserve Bank) Order 1947, issued on 14 August 1947, which provided for the RBI to operate as the currency and monetary manager for Pakistan until 30 September 1948. As agreed, Pakistan was not allowed to nominate a deputy governor, but the Reserve Bank was open to nominated members on the board who could put forward Pakistan's case, if needed. However, the names suggested by the new government in Pakistan ran into trouble.

While Sir Syed Maratib Ali, who was already a member of the board, was allowed to represent Pakistan, the nomination of John Turner, a Bank of England official working as an advisor to the government of Pakistan, was deemed inappropriate. Other nominations also ran into trouble; Pakistan wanted to nominate Nazir Ahmed Khan, who by his position in the constituent assembly of Pakistan, was unable to secure the position on RBI's board for a long period, as he was disqualified in March 1948 from his directorship. Despite these hiccups and the flaring tempers on both sides, the Reserve Bank describes its time serving the government in Pakistan as 'smooth' in the initial months. As Deshmukh highlights in his memoirs,[30] the RBI tried to act in a fair and non-partisan manner, and provided adequate funds, as per the agreements, to the new country.

One factor that brought both India and Pakistan together was the negotiations with the British government on war repayments and with the International Monetary Fund/World Bank on the division of the quotas that a pre-Partition India was holding on to. In these negotiations, India and Pakistan did find some common ground, with Shanmukham Chetty negotiating for India and Liaquat Ali Khan negotiating for Pakistan in 1947. The negotiations did not bear any material results, and another delegation was sent in 1948 with Chetty, Deshmukh and Thakurdas on India's side, and Ghulam Muhammad, Pakistan's first finance minister, negotiating for Pakistan. Both countries pressed Britain to continue its war repayments and provide adequate sterling for two years to help tide over the burgeoning economic stress in India.

With regard to RBI's employees, a large number of transfers between the two countries had been done by May 1948, and Deshmukh ensured that staff in Pakistan was adequate both in number and quality, while provisioning for training of new staff recruits. However, the relationship between the Reserve Bank and Pakistan's government was becoming dysfunctional, and the trust deficit widened significantly after Pakistan's invasion of Kashmir in late 1947.

In January 1948, Pakistan's government requested the Reserve Bank to release advance funds, which could be offset later against transfers due from India to Pakistan. The RBI, however, declined to give advances against the government of India's dues, but nonetheless agreed to provide a ways and means advance to support financing. This was agreeable to the Pakistanis, but when Deshmukh asked for information about the ability of Pakistan to repay the funds, the government took it as an affront and accused RBI of acting in a partisan manner. This allegation was vehemently opposed by Deshmukh, who decided to leave the decision to the central board, which had convened an emergency meeting on 14 January 1948.

Deshmukh was in favour of the payments being made,[31] on account of the promise that had been made to Pakistan by the government before the Kashmir conflict broke out. He advised the government along the same lines, but was shot down.

In a heated board meeting, the Pakistani representative put forth a memorandum for release of funds from the RBI, which was promptly voted down by the other members of the central board. The Pakistani members were also reminded in a resolution that while the RBI was a banker to both India and Pakistan, it had no authority to transfer funds to one country on behalf of another, without requisite orders. Meanwhile, the issue was picked up by Sardar Patel in Delhi, who made it clear that without a resolution on Kashmir, no payments would be made to Pakistan. However, Mahatma Gandhi, who was unhappy over these events, undertook a fast to ensure Pakistan got what it was promised, forcing the government and Prime Minister Jawaharlal Nehru to honour the agreement on 15 January itself, despite objections from Patel. This gesture by Mahatma Gandhi probably aggravated communal sentiments, and may have had something to do with his assassination, but that question remains imponderable in our history, as Deshmukh noted later.[32]

An unplanned exit

Even as the funds were provided, the relationship between the RBI and the government of Pakistan never recovered. A few days after the emergency board meeting, Pakistan decided to go ahead and float short and long-term loans, for which it asked RBI to make adequate preparations. The Pakistani government also wanted to understand whether these loans could be procured in India, but it quickly dropped the idea. However, despite RBI's misgivings on the timing of the loans, the government went ahead. While the funds were being raised, Pakistan's finance minister Ghulam Muhammad invited Deshmukh for talks on RBI's support to the fundraising exercise, but Deshmukh declined on account of the recent accusations made by the Pakistani government. The government was taken aback, and sent a sharp retort through the finance secretary.

Amid this war of words, the Pakistani government, through its high commissioner in India, Zahid Hussain (who went on to become the first governor of Pakistan's central bank, State Bank of Pakistan), asked RBI to stop issuing notes in Pakistan from 31 March instead of 30 June 1948, as previously agreed. While the decision came as a surprise, RBI was more concerned about the removal of India's current surplus notes in Pakistan, which had not been appropriately destroyed or returned to India. On receiving adequate assurances, RBI went ahead and signed an agreement with the government of Pakistan to terminate their relationship, and Pakistan assumed control of its finances from April 1948.

However, even in the midst of a premature departure, RBI was able to convince the governments of India and Pakistan to sign off on a payments agreement between the two countries, whereby both the Indian rupee and the Pakistani rupee would be treated at par, and no changes in the currency valuation would be undertaken without prior notice and consultations. On 1 July 1948, the State Bank of Pakistan was inaugurated. Its first governor, Zahid Hussain, was a respected figure, and was notably close to Mohammad Ali Jinnah. He was also a vice chancellor at the Aligarh Muslim University, and went on to serve the State Bank of Pakistan for five years.

The exchange control arrangement, however, proved to be short-lived, as Pakistan refused to devalue its currency in 1949, following the sterling devaluation. Indeed, even with the State Bank of Pakistan taking charge, there was to be no exchange control between the two countries for one year. The agreement was extended in June 1949 for another year, but in September, India decided to follow the sterling in devaluing its currency, a step Pakistan refused to take. India had promptly moved to devalue its exchange rate after Sir Stafford Cripps informed the commonwealth governments at the IMF meetings of 1949 that the sterling was going to be depreciated by 30 per cent. Deshmukh, who had completed his term as governor, but was still the representative for India at the IMF, agreed with the proposed devaluation, and also advised Pakistan's finance minister to follow suit, but the Pakistani government refused. For the payment system to be maintained, devaluation was necessary, but with Pakistan refusing to follow India's 30.5 per cent devaluation, the exchange rate was now skewed to 100 Pakistani rupees equalling 144 Indian rupees.

The Indian finance minister defended India's actions, but trade relations were affected, with confusion over the prevailing exchange rate. RBI decided to suspend transactions in the Pakistani rupee. The government of Pakistan still wanted their sterling payments to be made under the earlier agreements, but the Indian government refused to comply. In the market rate, it took a while before the devaluation started being passed on, which led to a temporary disruption in the remittances market as well. The exchange controls were as such strictly enforced from September 1949 onwards, but it was only after Pakistan's notification of its exchange rate in the IMF from mid-1950 that trade started to normalize between the two neighbours.

The Pakistan episode was a brief but major hurdle for the RBI, which it crossed effectively. The bigger challenge before the institution was the integration of the various monetary systems and currency arrangements that were prevailing under British rule, predominantly in the princely states. From both an administrative and regulatory perspective, the Reserve Bank was inadequately placed to deal with the various demands and expectations of a young country.

The bank was faced with two regulatory shortfalls. First, it had successfully managed to avoid nationalization so far, but in order to play a bigger role in India's financial system, the Parliament felt nationalization was urgently needed. Second, while commercial banking had been a flourishing business for some time now, the Reserve Bank did not have any legal backing to control the banking system as such, and the Imperial Bank of India continued to play a dominant role in influencing the financial system even with RBI's presence.

Nationalization of the RBI

RBI's departure from Pakistan was hasty, but it was not necessarily opposed by the government of India. Reeling under the loss of Mahatma Gandhi, who was assassinated on 30 January 1948, a wounded nation and its Parliament wanted to quickly move forward with its economic agenda. The nationalization of the Reserve Bank of India was deemed important in this regard.

Right from the time of the Hilton Young Commission, Indian politicians had argued for a government-owned central bank, which would work in harmony with the government of India and in the Indian interest. As Bakhtiar Dadabhoy notes in his seminal work,[33] this issue became a major hurdle post the Hilton Young Commission, where despite agreement on the need to set up a central bank, no consensus was reached on the ownership and operational control of the Reserve Bank. While Indian leaders such Lala Lajpat Rai, Pandit Madan Mohan Malaviya and R.K. Shanmukham Chetty opposed a private shareholders' bank, the British government actively pursued the idea, for it wanted to retain control of the Indian monetary system, and stuck to the idea of a private bank on the grounds of the independence of the RBI. This impasse led to several years of delay, and once the central bank was set up in 1935, it was largely on the principles of coordination with, rather than subordination to the government. However, the British government did not necessarily practice this principle.

Once the interim government took power in India in September 1946 to prepare for Independence, the nationalization of the Reserve Bank was back on the table. Following the culmination of the Second World War, central banks were being nationalized globally. In the lead-up to the formation of the interim government, central banks in France, England and the Netherlands had been converted into state-owned entities.

While the Reserve Bank was likely to be nationalized someday, Deshmukh argued against a hasty nationalization. Meanwhile, the research department at the Reserve Bank prepared an internal note outlining that while state control was indeed spreading as far as other central banks were concerned, the case for state control had to be more thoroughly justified in India. The note went on to give examples of the RBI's role having proven adequate and sympathetic to state requirements, and pointed out that in no instance had the RBI been found 'wanting'. This viewpoint was challenged as conservative, and there was already criticism of RBI's 'acquiescence' in the inflationary situation that had prevailed during the war years due to significant currency expansion.

The Reserve Bank strongly refuted these charges, but the die was cast for nationalization, and all that Deshmukh and RBI's position as central banker to two countries could do was delay the process. When asked for his opinion by R.K. Shanmukham Chetty in January 1948, Deshmukh highlighted that while one could not be 'dogmatic' in arguing for or against state control, the institution had served the country to the best of its nascent abilities, and initially, the larger impact of state control was likely to be on the central board run by experienced businessmen of the institution, and not on its role in monetary matters. He also indicated that one should wait and see how the Indian economy shaped up in the initial years, and then judge whether lack of state control was proving to be an impediment to higher growth, before moving towards nationalization.

Even before Independence and Partition took place, Finance Minister Liaquat Ali Khan, under pressure from certain members of the Parliament, had announced in his 1947/48 budget speech that nationalization of the RBI was a desirable step,[34] but the timing and manner in which RBI was brought under state control could be deliberated upon at a later stage. After that, as the political situation in the country deteriorated, the urgency to bring RBI under the government was somewhat lost. However, with tensions subsiding, the debate on nationalization gathered steam again. Despite stiff opposition from the central board, the government signalled its intention to press forward with the nationalization of the RBI in a note to the central board in April 1948.

In an act of foresight, the central bank had already prepared a memorandum detailing the process and provisions for its own nationalization. This provided the basis of a draft bill, which argued for minimal changes in the structure of the Reserve Bank and indicated that state control should largely be a symbolic transfer of ownership, while the day-to-day functioning of the Reserve Bank should remain unaffected. This draft bill was approved by the central board on 26 May 1948, and submitted to the government for comments.

In order to ensure that the credibility of the institution remained intact despite the change in ownership, Deshmukh was keen for the bill to explicitly indicate that the results of any actions taken by the RBI based on directives of the government were to be incumbent on the government itself. However, Finance Minister R.K. Shanmukham Chetty did not believe that such strong language was needed, and suggested diluting it to more conciliatory terms. Deshmukh was agreeable to the suggestion, and changed it to the provision that the Ministry of Finance would have to undertake prior consultation with the governor of the RBI before issuing any directives. In the meantime, Deshmukh was awarded a year's extension to continue as governor of the RBI from August 1948, primarily to facilitate the nationalization process.

Once the draft bill was agreed upon, it was placed in the legislative assembly on 2 September 1948, and was approved the next day. However, there were immediate demands following the introduction of the bill that the RBI, which some members saw as 'the slave, the maid of the old Lady of Thread Needle Street—The Bank of England',[35] should ensure that Indian interests, particularly in the agricultural sector, were taken care of. After being given satisfactory assurances, the legislature passed the bill. The RBI then pressed forward to complete the formalities of the transfer of ownership and compensation for existing shareholders, and on 1 January 1949, the RBI became a state-owned institution.

The Banking Regulation Act

Banking services in India expanded significantly during the war years. This expansion was seen both in terms of deposits and branches, but branch expansion was much larger than perhaps warranted. As such, bankruptcies were common, and the RBI had limited ability to intervene or regulate the banks' activities.

Financial services were first licensed only in 1913[36] under the Indian Companies Act, but there was no separate act that provided statutory control and regulation for banking. The Indian Companies Act 1913 made no strong distinction between banks and other companies. This made it difficult for the RBI to undertake punitive action against commercial banks, which in any case were not critically dependent on the Reserve Bank during their formative years. While a separate chapter on banks was incorporated in the Indian Companies Act 1936, from the point of view of RBI coming into its own, there was a need for a separate banking act to provide RBI with the legal provisions to supervise the banking system, but no concrete steps were taken initially, given RBI's own turbulent start.

During the Second World War, as banking services grew rapidly, RBI sought for itself legal rights that would allow it to control the banking network as well as the branch expansion programme, which was already underway, contributing to the instability of the small banks. This expansion was facilitated not only by RBI's own actions of increasing money supply to finance the war effort, but also by liberalizing remittance facilities, which helped non-schedule banks and cooperative banks to deal with RBI and its agent, the Imperial Bank of India, with relative ease.

Some progress on finding a better control mechanism over banking services was made under Governor James Taylor, who dictated that banks with a paid-up capital and reserves over ₹5 lakh could be included in the second schedule, which would allow them to transact directly with the Reserve Bank. Having suffered through the failures of the Travancore and Quilon banks in 1938, the RBI was conscious of increasing confidence in banking services across the country. As such, in 1940, the government introduced an amendment to the RBI Act, which gave RBI some powers to undertake surveillance and serve a notice to defaulting banks to stop accepting deposits. While this was still not an enabling legislation for any punitive action, RBI was given more control of the scheduled banks themselves.

The granting of additional powers did not distract the Reserve Bank from seeking a commercial banking act in itself. The RBI had prepared a draft bill as early as June 1939, having studied the banking laws of various countries such as Canada and the United States. The bill was largely prepared from the point of view of the depositor, and proposed strict norms on capital requirements, liquidity ratios and proposed liquidation of the bank, if needed. Among the more controversial requirements suggested was holding 30 per cent of deposits in cash or invested in government securities, a practice that continues today as the statutory liquidity ratio (SLR).[37]

The bill received a mixed reaction from various interest groups, but was largely opposed by the smaller banks, which saw their business being negatively affected by this new proposal. There were fears that such an act would strengthen the government's control over the banking system, and that the high capital requirements would put several banks out of business. Even as the RBI mulled over the suggestions and criticisms that the draft bill evoked, it knew that the passage of a banking act was not a top priority for the government, which was too distracted by the war. As such, while some changes were made to the RBI's role in relation to commercial banking in 1941 and 1943, the issue largely stayed on the backburner.

By mid-1943, Deshmukh, who had taken over the management of the RBI, decided to make another push for a banking bill. According to RBI's official history, Deshmukh noted that while the war could continue for another few years, managing the large number of banking establishments that had come up during the war years was critical, especially if the economy began to contract. As such, in early 1944, Deshmukh supervised a new bill for banking to be placed before the central board, which had added the role of inspections for the RBI, departing from the previous position advocated by James Taylor. After due consultations, the bill was sent to the central government in June 1944, and was introduced in the legislative assembly in November 1944. Among the criticisms and demands made in the assembly, there was a clamour to bring the Imperial Bank under the provisions of the new act, and the desire to nationalize the banking industry itself. Given the differences, the bill could not be passed, and it was relegated to a select committee for further deliberations.

Deshmukh's fears of an impending banking crisis came true, as from 1946 onwards, once the war ended, small banks started coming under pressure, particularly in Bengal. To give the RBI more powers, the government passed the banking companies (inspection) ordinance in 1946, to carry out its due diligence into banking operations. The government also approved an enabling bill to restrict branches, under the Banking Companies (Restriction of Branches) Act in October 1946, giving RBI the power to restrict the branch network of banks. While issues arose during the drafting of both the bills, the RBI largely got the powers it desired.

The crisis in Bengal was tempered by early 1947, but the larger challenge of getting a banking act in place remained. Even as the government was distracted by the violence that ensued in the lead up to the Partition, it handed RBI temporary special powers to give emergency funds against securities to keep banks in solvency. The RBI was criticized for being too conservative in its recognition of securities, as small bank failures continued. The comprehensive banking bill was reintroduced in 1946 in the legislative assembly, and by early 1947, the board wanted the RBI to have the power to vet a banking institution without requiring any clearance from the government. In terms of evolution, this was a significant departure from the original bill of 1939.

The bill was not a high priority one, as the country was dealing with the Partition, and so was the RBI. After several rounds with a select committee, several key provisions were approved through an ordinance in 1948. However, the bill was still held up, and in November 1948, it was referred to a select committee again, whose report was submitted to the legislative assembly in February 1949. The select committee had made recommendations largely in favour of the banks, with some relaxation on shareholding patterns and liquidation role of the RBI. Even at such an advanced stage, consensus on the banking act was not achieved. Several members, including future finance minister T.T. Krishnamachari, submitted dissent notes, particularly on limiting dividend payments from banks to their shareholders. The bill was finally approved on 17 February 1949, and it came into effect from 16 March. However, within a brief period, the bill had to be amended to incorporate regulations around the amalgamation and liquidation of banks in 1950.

Deshmukh leaves RBI

Chintaman Deshmukh had agreed to extend his term at the Reserve Bank for a year, largely to oversee the nationalization process. Once his objectives were achieved, he stepped down on 30 June 1949, ending what was a transformative decade at the bank. Now in its teen years, the responsibility of governorship was passed on to Sir Benegal Rama Rau, a career civil servant like Deshmukh.

Deshmukh's role in India's economic management was far from over. He remained involved in public policy as a 'financial ambassador' for the new government. Deshmukh negotiated with Americans to supply India with two million tons of wheat. He also accompanied Nehru to Washington for meetings with President Truman, and other engagements. In 1950, Nehru appointed him to be a member of a new institution called the Planning Commission.

Concurrent to his appointment as a member of the Planning Commission, Deshmukh was appointed as the finance minister by Nehru. Deshmukh's predecessor, John Mathai, had resigned largely due to his opposition to the Planning Commission. Deshmukh was not keen on joining politics, but accepted the position after Nehru, following Sardar Patel's recommendation, goaded Deshmukh into saying yes. Deshmukh's appointment as the finance minister added to the RBI's reputation, and the central bank now had a very strong supporter in Delhi.

Chapter 3

Dismantling imperial structures

The Reserve Bank was quite preoccupied with addressing the immediate problems of Partition and legal provisions in the aftermath of the Second World War. But by the early 1950s, these issues started to settle down, and focus started shifting towards the larger and much greater challenge of nation building. For Prime Minister Nehru, who was converted to the idea of state planning, the Reserve Bank's role was rather limited to securing funding for projects, especially from foreign donors, and helping to build new institutions, while converting the old ones into state entities, as needed. Nonetheless, for several years, RBI was allowed to focus on its core role of policymaking, and the years between 1950 and 1957 were largely about that.

In June 1949, when Chintaman Deshmukh retired from the Reserve Bank, Sir Benegal Rama Rau took charge of the bank. Rama Rau came from a prestigious family. One of his brothers, Sir Benegal Narsing Rau, was widely renowned for the role he had played in framing the Indian Constitution. Another brother, B. Shiva Rau, was an eminent politician and journalist. Benegal Rama Rau himself had been an officer in the Indian government for a long period, and had served as India's ambassador to the United States.

Under Rama Rau, the Reserve Bank was a young national institution with new powers and great responsibility. However, it also faced intense competition. Under Nehru's vision of an industrialized economy driven by state planning, several institutions were being crafted and remodelled. The Planning Commission, Imperial Bank of India and the Reserve Bank were in a sense competing institutions for mindshare and thought leadership, despite having different mandates and roles in the Indian context. As such, for the Reserve Bank, cooperation with these institutions for a meaningful dialogue was critical to its evolving role in the first decade after Independence.

As the second volume of the history of the Reserve Bank summarizes, there were four key pillars of the Reserve Bank's evolution between 1950 and 1960. First, the bank adopted a new monetary framework, which had remained largely dormant and focused on exchange rate stability prior to independence. Financing deficits became a critical component under this new framework, which would only be undone several decades later. Disagreements over the monetary policy stance also led to the resignation of Rama Rau in 1957, an episode that somewhat undermined RBI's autonomy as an institution.

Second, the Reserve Bank was able to strengthen its regulatory framework for commercial banks, managing key hurdles like the nationalization of the Imperial Bank of India and the consolidation of the princely banks. Third, promotion of agricultural credit and a push for a rural banking system in an institutional manner was a unique feature for a central bank. Finally, creation of new industrial financing institutions to support the planning process was a key feature of RBI's role in helping secure development financing.

Fighting for monetary control

An immediate challenge the Reserve Bank faced was establishing its dominance over the monetary system in India. While RBI had been in existence for roughly fifteen years, it still faced considerable competition, even if not intentionally, from the Imperial Bank of India, which remained in private hands post-Independence. While a brief history of the Imperial Bank has already been discussed, it is worth looking back at the evolution of the bank.

For more than a century, the Presidency Banks had occupied a special place within India's monetary system. They were the dominant financial institutions in British India, and were merged to form the Imperial Bank in 1921, on the recommendations of the Chamberlain Commission. While the power of currency issuance was taken away from the Presidency Banks in 1862, they still had an inordinate influence on India's finances, given their large role and reach. After their merger, the Imperial Bank controlled almost 40 per cent of total deposits and more than one-third of all bank branches in India by 1926.

Before the Reserve Bank came into existence, the Imperial Bank of India was the sole banker to the government, a privileged position accorded to it at the time of the merger. This restored its pre-1862 status, and despite its private ownership, the government exercised significant control over the bank, as most of the key officers were directly appointed by the government, and it could also instruct the bank to undertake any transaction it deemed fit.

During the deliberations of the Hilton Young Commission, some of the Indian members put forward many arguments in favour of converting the Imperial Bank into a fully fledged central bank, given that it was already performing several functions that the proposed Reserve Bank was expected to perform. However, the Imperial Bank had started playing a critical role in tightening the India Office and Bank of England's control over India's finances, and hence Lord Montagu Norman, the influential governor of the Bank of England, argued against the move.

As the RBI came into being in 1935, the question of the Imperial Bank being converted into a central bank ceased to exist. However, in order to placate the influential institution, the Imperial Bank was appointed as the agent of the Reserve Bank where the RBI had no centre and continued to perform its treasury function. Moreover, as the RBI was hampered by internal leadership quibbles in its initial years, the Imperial Bank maintained its financial dominance, both in terms of branches and influence, partly due to its British leadership and closeness to the government.[38]

As India achieved independence, there were demands for rapid changes to the status, function and objectives of multiple institutions in the financial sector. While the RBI avoided nationalization for some time, it had to undergo a change in ownership in 1949. Similarly, a demand for the nationalization of the Imperial Bank was also made, and along with its intention to nationalize the Reserve Bank, the then finance minister Shanmukham Chetty declared that the government was agreeable to nationalization in principle. However, unlike the RBI, the Imperial Bank was able to avoid nationalization for a longer period, given its complicated merger with princely banks.

Pushing for the nationalization of the Imperial Bank

The arguments in favour of state control of the Imperial Bank were strong and largely valid. For a bank that had thrived on state patronage, the leadership and ownership of the Imperial Bank was largely foreign. The push for 'Indianization' was weak within the bank itself, and unlike the Reserve Bank, the Imperial Bank continued to have foreigners manning critical positions after Independence. The push for developing Indian leadership at the Imperial Bank had been present since its inception, but it had found little favour within the bank itself. In 1946, J.R.D. Tata, who had been a member of the central board of the Imperial Bank, resigned over this very issue. In fact, the first Indian to hold a major position at the Imperial Bank was S.K. Handoo, who became a deputy managing director only in 1950.

As such, with the Reserve Bank being firmly on the path to nationalization, the Imperial Bank was expected to follow suit. However, the board and Imperial Bank leadership put up a much stronger fight than the Reserve Bank. After Shanmukham Chetty had promised to look into nationalization in February 1948, Deshmukh managed to convince him to put the matter on hold after the Imperial Bank's managing director A.R. Chisholm and his board passed a resolution in April 1948 that the nationalization was not justified. Deshmukh cautioned the government that it was biting off 'more than we can chew'. The government heeded this advice and agreed to retain the commercial nature of the Imperial Bank. As things settled down, the Ministry of Finance continued to study the subject, with K.G. Ambegaonkar examining the matter. As Finance Minister John Mathai took charge in 1949, he reneged on Chetty's promise of nationalization of the Imperial Bank, largely owing to ongoing banking troubles in the economy. However, Mathai did promise to look into some of the 'unsatisfactory' areas within the operations of the Imperial Bank.

In November 1949, Mathai's promise manifested itself in the form of a Rural Banking Enquiry Committee (RBEC), led by Sir Purshottamdas Thakurdas, who despite his reservations on the committee's scope, agreed to lead it. The committee also included people like B. Venkatappiah, who was a key proponent of the nationalization of the Imperial Bank, and would go on to work within both the Reserve Bank and the State Bank of India.

The committee was asked to focus on the possibility and mechanisms of improving availability of banking services in semi-urban and rural areas, and to suggest ways in which government treasury services could be provided in places where banking services were not easily available.

The committee saw a lack of banking penetration in the country, particularly in the rural areas. However, Sir Purshottamdas Thakurdas, who had previously advocated against nationalization, tried to find a middle ground along with RBI governor Rama Rau. They tried to convince Chisholm to persuade the board of the Imperial Bank to give the government a say in the appointment of senior leadership at the bank, a practice that had been discontinued after 1935. Initially, Chisholm agreed that a non-executive chairman should be appointed with government approval, a solution that both the RBEC and Chintaman Deshmukh, who had become finance minister by that time, were comfortable with. As stated in the second volume of the RBI's history, in May 1950, the recommendations of the RBEC were largely along the lines of this informal agreement, and it presented a case for government control on senior leadership appointments, but with scope for operational autonomy.

However, Chisholm did not keep up his end of the bargain, and the Imperial Bank board repudiated the findings of the committee in a resolution, which the RBI described as 'dismissive, even derisive'.[39] The resolution argued that the Imperial Bank could not extend operations in areas where there was no demand for banking services and asked the government to focus on creating opportunities in rural areas instead. The resolution even said that the business the Imperial Bank got from the government was not profitable, and that '[...] we would willingly consent to our being deprived of government business if we could do so without causing embarrassment to government'.[40]

The condescending tone of the Imperial Bank's memorandum evoked an exhaustive thirty-four-page response from B. Venkatappiah, who was an executive director at the Reserve Bank at the time. Point by point, Venkatappiah broke down the reasons for greater state control, and this response would later play a significant role in the recommendations of the rural credit survey, which paved the way for the nationalization of the Imperial Bank. Venkatappiah stressed on state patronage and subsidies, and highlighted the need for 'Indianization' to correct management bias towards European businesses. In Venkatappiah's view, the role of central banking after 1935 was effectively split between the Reserve Bank and the Imperial Bank, and he was of the view that nationalizing the Imperial Bank would help the Reserve Bank gain proper control of the monetary system. Venkatappiah concluded by providing the alternative solution of having a government nominee on the board of the Imperial Bank who would have the power to delay decisions that had a national impact.

The memo from Venkatappiah formed the backbone of the note from Governor Rama Rau to the government in December 1950, which argued for an amendment of the Imperial Bank's constitution to put it on par with other commercial banks and place the appointment of the chairman under government approval. This alternative recommendation was widely debated within the RBI, but was reluctantly accepted to avoid outright nationalization of the Imperial Bank. While legislative changes were expected to take some time, the entire episode had put significant focus on the role of banks in provisioning credit in rural areas.

After convening an informal conference of experts on rural finance and cooperative bank representatives, RBI appointed a new committee in August 1951 called the All India Rural Credit Survey Committee (AIRCS), which was to undertake a comprehensive survey on rural credit. The committee was empowered not only to undertake a statistical exercise, but also to 'direct the planning, organization, and supervision of the survey', along with interpretation of results, and to make recommendations on steps needed to improve credit conditions. The committee included Venkatappiah as a member, but it was headed by A.D. Gorwala and also had D.R. Gadgil, P.S. Narayan Prasad and N.S.R. Sastry as its members.

Rural credit surveys and the State Bank of India

The AIRCS was one of the most comprehensive studies undertaken at the behest of the central bank, and its final report and recommendations were submitted in three volumes in August 1954,[41] almost three years after it was constituted. The survey was conducted in seventy-five districts across the country, and covered 1,27,343 families in six hundred villages.[42]

The survey findings confirmed the issues pertaining to poor availability of financial services in rural areas that had been raised in the legislature.

It found that for farmers, only 4 per cent of financing came from official institutional sources, while the rest came from non-institutional sources such as moneylenders and local credit agencies. The committee also observed that credit conditions had barely changed in rural areas since the Indian Central Banking Committee findings in 1931, and even within cooperative banks, the focus seemed predominantly on large farmers, rather than small and medium ones. The committee also observed that while it would not be easy to find an alternative to the cooperative financing structure, the government could provide the requisite help in amending the institutional deficiencies plaguing the rural credit conditions.

The report concluded that since cooperatives depended on bank financing, it would be desirable to create a 'State Bank of India' through a merger of the Imperial Bank and ten large state-associated banks and four minor state-associated banks. The ownership of the state bank was to be directly managed by the RBI on behalf of the government. The ten large state-associated banks were the banks in former princely states. They were the State Bank of Saurashtra, Bank of Patiala, Bank of Bikaner, Bank of Jaipur, Bank of Rajasthan, Bank of Indore, Bank of Baroda, Bank of Mysore, Hyderabad State Bank and Travancore Bank.

Deshmukh, despite several antagonistic steps taken by the board of the Imperial Bank, had put the prospect of nationalization on the backburner. The AIRCS recommendations were prepared in the early months of 1953, largely by Venkatappiah and Gorwala. Venkatappiah, who had been a strong advocate of the nationalization of the Imperial Bank, largely followed his instinct in the report and bypassed the views of Governor Rama Rau who was in favour of taking a more gradual approach towards nationalisation, who later heard 'certain rumours' about a nationalisation proposal on a trip to Delhi.[43] While Rama Rau sought a joint meeting with the AIRCS members to understand the latest proposals, the official history of the RBI notes that it was unclear whether such a meeting took place.[44] As such, despite some opposition from the governor of RBI, it was the RBI's executive director viewpoint that trumped Governor Rau's viewpoint in influencing the decision on the nationalization of the Imperial Bank.

Despite his initial apprehensions, Deshmukh agreed to the recommendations after they were backed by Governor Rama Rau. Deteriorating relations between the board of the Imperial Bank and the government probably played a large part in convincing Deshmukh to support the nationalization. He put forward the recommendations in Parliament on 20 December 1954 and offered to compensate the shareholders on market value. Although the management at the Imperial Bank protested the decision, the government did not change its intent to proceed with state ownership.

On 22 April 1955, A.C. Guha, the minister for revenue and defence expenditure (Deshmukh was indisposed at that time), moved the bill for the nationalization of the Imperial Bank, and it was passed on 30 April. While there was some confusion over the location of the headquarters as B.C. Roy, chief minister of West Bengal, objected to Bombay, the issue was resolved and the State Bank of India was inaugurated in Bombay on 1 July 1955. The former finance minister John Mathai was appointed as the first chairman, while Gorwala was appointed as the government nominee on the central board.

The State Bank of India and its associates

Along with the Imperial Bank, the ten state-associated banks were also supposed to be merged. At the time of Independence, as the erstwhile princely states were merged with the union, some fifty-four banks fully or partly owned by the royalty came under state control. These banks functioned as a government department, and in areas where the Imperial Bank did not have a presence, they performed treasury services. These banks were of all sizes. Some, like the Bank of Baroda, were very large with deposits totalling several crores, while others, such as a bank in Barwani (a small town in modern-day Madhya Pradesh), had deposit bases of not more than a few thousand rupees. Once the modern constitution of India came into effect, the Reserve Bank split these banks into two groups. The first group consisted of small banks that needed to be either wound up or merged with other institutions, while the second group consisted of fourteen large banks with a functioning business model and some scale.

From 1949 onwards, several small banks were either converted or merged into new entities, and a few of them were allowed to continue as cooperative banks. In 1952, the government encouraged these banks to come under the purview of the Banking Companies Act, which a majority of the institutions were agreeable to. However, there were legal hurdles in several banks such as the State Bank of Hyderabad, which prevented the Reserve Bank from having any regulatory say in their affairs. Further, with the rise of sub-nationalism within the country, several state governments were not agreeable to making changes to their local financial institutions.

The Indian State Finances Enquiry Committee of 1949 and the Rural Banking Enquiry Committee of 1950 had both recommended a gradual rundown of these state-associated institutions where possible, and providing the Reserve Bank with some regulatory oversight powers for those banks that could operate on their own. In 1954, the AIRCS submitted a forceful argument for the amalgamation of these institutions with the State Bank of India. However, Governor Rama Rau made a case for a gradual implementation of the recommendations in relation to the state-associated banks. Within the Reserve Bank, the Department of Banking Operations and the Department of Banking Development got into an exchange of memos, with banking operations arguing against a merger, and banking development making pro-merger arguments.[45]

At the central board meeting in February 1955, Governor Rama Rau again argued for a gradual approach, and did not favour compulsory mergers. He also opined that as the State Bank of India found its feet, it could manage the other state banks as its subsidiaries. The Reserve Bank called for a transfer of only completely state-owned associated banks like the State Bank of Saurashtra, the Bank of Patiala, and the State Bank of Hyderabad, in which the state government was the majority stakeholder.[46]

The government accepted the governor's suggestion to defer the proposal, but did not necessarily agree with the approach suggested by him on the issue. In fact, the Ministry of Finance saw it as another example of the Reserve Bank's preference for the private sector in banking, and he prepared a memo arguing for the government to 'compulsorily'[47] acquire and integrate the state banks. Even as the Ministry of Finance and the Reserve Bank had differences, the government decided to postpone a forced merger after Rama Rau spoke to Finance Minister Deshmukh. Whether it was because of the state movements in various parts of the country as the state reorganization commission was meeting simultaneously or an inclination to preserve the identity of the state-associated banks, Deshmukh continued to rely on the advice of RBI on the treatment of these princely banks, overriding the advice from within his own ministry.

The fight between the RBI, led by B. Venkatappiah, and the Ministry of Finance for a speedy takeover continued even after the State Bank of India was inaugurated. While operational difficulties were quite likely, after much deliberation, the union cabinet in May 1956 approved in principle the decision to take over the banks in Hyderabad, Patiala and Saurashtra.

Meanwhile, with Deshmukh resigning as finance minister in 1956 on the back of the Bombay agitation[48], the argument for a state takeover of the state-associated banks strengthened. The new finance minister T.T. Krishnamachari constituted a committee to look into the matter again. This committee comprised largely of State Bank staff and takeover sympathizers. As such, the committee recommended handing control of more state-associated banks to the State Bank of India. The list of associated banks kept growing longer. From 1959 onwards, the State Bank turned the banks in Hyderabad, Bikaner, Jaipur, Indore, Travancore, Mysore, Saurashtra and Patiala into associate banks.

In present times, while some of the associate banks have finally been merged, the real problems of associate banks and their own management styles have largely persisted since the 1960s. This has now culminated in a final round of mergers with the much larger State Bank of India, which will perhaps be a fitting end to the issues of fragmentation in the Indian banking system that prevail today. Ironically, this fragmentation has been a by-product of the attempts to streamline and consolidate the banking services in the 1950s.

A planned economy and the RBI

Along with a drive to convert old institutions founded by the British into state entities, there was also a strong push to create new institutions in a 'mixed economy' set-up. While the Indian state did not necessarily trust foreign private capital, the regime in the first decade post-Independence was largely open, and regulations were not stringent. Restrictions on private ownership of capital were not prohibitive, and once India came out of the significant inflationary phase seen during the late 1940s, the economic environment was largely benign and conducive to focusing on the arduous task of nation building. As such, India needed more institutions, and as Nehru favoured centralized planning to deploy India's frugal resources, on 1 March 1950, his finance minister decided to appoint a Planning Commission with a view to making an assessment of India's factors of production and to determine their best use and order of priority.

As part of a mixed economy model, Prime Minister Nehru was convinced that India needed to industrialize rapidly and private investment was not the right way to build the much-needed economic capacity. Even before Independence, India's future economic policymakers and industrialists had agreed to an economic agenda, which popularly came to be known as the 'Bombay Plan'. This detailed agenda was signed by people such as J.R.D. Tata, Ghanshyam Das Birla, Purshottamdas Thakurdas and the future finance minister, John Mathai.

The Bombay Plan had two simple objectives. The first was to double the agricultural output and achieve a fivefold increase in industrial output within fifteen years, which would lead to a doubling of the per capita income. The second was to protect Indian businesses. The argument put forth was that India could not grow without more government regulation and intervention, and that Indian businesses needed protection from foreign business interests. While the Bombay Plan was widely criticized,[49] it sparked a discussion over the role of the state in businesses, and while Nehru did not see much merit in the numbers projected in the Bombay Plan, the approach of the Planning Commission, and more importantly of the first five-year plan, was broadly modelled on the Bombay Plan.[50]

Deshmukh, who after becoming the finance minister stayed on as a member of the Planning Commission, was in agreement with the institution's statistical approach to growth planning, and said that while details were flimsy, it was largely down to lack of information rather than intent. The Planning Commission gained traction as the economy showed signs of improvement, and the initial years of the planning process saw a sharp drop in inflation as supply constraints eased. This considerably increased the influence and heft of the Planning Commission, and from 1952 onwards, a significant push was made to add an array of new institutions which strengthened central planning to India's economic structure. However, as I.G. Patel describes, Deshmukh felt vulnerable given his lack of political heft within Nehru's cabinet, and hence the first five-year plan was relatively cautious and prudent, so as to maintain broader economic stability, and prevent any major risks in the economic management of the country.[51]

The Reserve Bank had little input in the structure and priorities of the Planning Commission, but it became an important ally for the institution and helped design and set up several agencies to aid the process of industrialization. Among the notable ones were the Industrial Finance Corporation of India, which was set up in 1948. The government set up a National Industrial Development Corporation of India in 1954, and this was followed by the setting up of the Industrial Credit and Investment Corporation of India in 1956, which later morphed into ICICI bank in 1994.

The first policy change, and the first five-year plan

One area where the RBI did play a greater role in the planning process after 1950 was its new monetary policy framework and subsequent practice of deficit financing. Given the planning process and utilization of funds from the Reserve Bank, which was the custodian of the sterling balances, the general thrust of fiscal policy was expansionary. Further, given that India was coming out of a severe inflationary cycle in the aftermath of the Bengal famine and the Second World War, the Reserve Bank faced the challenge of balancing short-term price pressures and long-term investment requirements.

With the context set, the Reserve Bank took baby steps during the first plan period (1951–1956) by lending ₹260 crore to the government's first five-year plan, which was worth ₹1,960 crore.[52] Even though the amount of deficit financing was relatively small, the Reserve Bank was still cautious in its approach. As such, it started contemplating steps to somewhat dampen any inflationary effects of this effective monetization of debt. While informal discussions had been going on between Finance Minister Deshmukh and Governor Rama Rau, the RBI still had an internal note prepared by P.S. Narayan Prasad, the then economic advisor to the Reserve Bank, arguing for a higher bank rate, which he believed was necessary to counterbalance this expansion and 'apply restraint at both points.'[53] Narayan's report was prepared in October 1951, and on 15 November, the Reserve Bank raised its bank rate to 3.5 per cent, after keeping it at 3 per cent since 1935. It also closed the repurchase window for government securities for commercial banks, adding more firepower to its monetary operations.

The increase in rates was a momentous occasion for the Reserve Bank, which was still trying to find its feet as far as control of India's financial system was concerned. RBI's own history notes that until the 1950s, the Imperial Bank was effectively competing with the Reserve Bank in providing accommodation to commercial banks, rendering RBI's bank rate ineffective at times. The abandoning of the 'cheap money' policy also gave a big boost to the public perception of the Reserve Bank, as it had earlier been called a follower of the Bank of England, and had been an object of suspicion for several political leaders.

As the first plan progressed, its efficacy and implementation credentials improved. The government's confidence in the state planning approach, particularly Prime Minister Nehru's, grew as well. Growth had improved significantly during the first five-year plan period relative to the pre-Independence years, while inflation was low. However, despite the initial success, the Indian National Congress made a strong shift towards a socialist economic model in January 1955 at its party session in Aavadi, Tamil Nadu.[54] In their declaration, the Congress announced that the government would pursue a socialistic model of society, and the industrial policy that accompanied the second five-year plan was significantly expansionary, while also raising the stakes on deficit financing.

The second plan and the socialist model

By the end of the first five-year plan, growth was starting to stagnate, inflation had started rising, and the external position was deteriorating. Naturally, the Reserve Bank was concerned with the magnitude of deficit financing planned for the second plan period (1957–1961). Curiously, despite their reservations regarding the quantum of deficit financing, the Reserve Bank under Governor Rama Rau approved a 'minor change'[55] in the deficit monetization mechanism, which later on would create significant headaches for the central bank. In January 1955, the Reserve Bank received a note from H.S. Negi, then a deputy secretary at the Ministry of Finance, to create ad hoc treasury bills in such a manner that it would prevent the weekly end of balance of the government in the ways and means advances from falling below ₹50 crore, and on a daily basis maintain it at a minimum of ₹4 crore.

While it was initially pitched as a temporary arrangement to tide the government over during periods of mismatch in cash flow, by May 1955, both the Ministry of Finance and the Reserve Bank endorsed the mechanism, and Governor Rama Rau and his deputy Ram Nath issued standing instructions to create ad hoc bills as required before the weekly closing of the books. This was a significant departure from the previous arrangement of the ways and means advances, which allowed the Reserve Bank to lend money to the government for a period of three months only. The long-standing nature of the new arrangement proved far costlier as we will see later, given that the Reserve Bank became a cheap source of funding for the government.

Despite such significant accommodation, the Reserve Bank tried to fend off any signs of inflation. However, the government's ambitious investment programme required significant fiscal expansion, which would have had a considerable impact on the external balances. Given that India's currency system was still based on a pre-war proportional reserve system, a sharp fall in foreign exchange reserves would have had negative consequences for the money supply. The government then pushed the RBI to look into adopting a fiduciary cover system, or consider lowering the proportional cover or even doing away with a statutory requirement for a currency reserve.

The Reserve Bank's response was measured, but it agreed to move to a minimum currency reserve, without a proportional reserve cover. This move, however, did not work out, as India's external finances deteriorated sharply on the implementation of the second five-year plan. At the same time, as activity improved, demand for currency improved as well, creating a shortage of assets for the Reserve Bank to hold against currency issuance. However, the problem was solved in a rather convenient manner wherein the government agreed to issue ad hoc treasury bills as and when needed, in order to satisfy the shortage of assets for the Reserve Bank.

The Rama Rau and Krishnamachari episode

In early 1956, as the state reorganization committee submitted a proposal to reorganize states on the basis of language, the government moved a bill in the Parliament to carve out Gujarat, a Gujarati-speaking state, from the Bombay Presidency, while the rest of the Presidency and Marathi-speaking parts of Hyderabad were to be merged into Maharashtra. This sparked a significant backlash from backers of a united Maharashtra project, and the movement quickly led to widespread violence.

Chintaman Deshmukh, who was largely seen as a non-political technocrat, resigned from the cabinet in mid-1956, after a police shooting ordered by the Morarji Desai government to quell protests over the proposal to make the city of Bombay a Union Territory killed 105 people in Bombay.[56] While Nehru kept delaying the resignation, Deshmukh eventually left, and was replaced by Tiruvellore Thattai Krishnamachari (or better known as T.T.K.), a sharp-tongued politician from Tamil Nadu. Apart from being a two-term finance minister, Krishnamachari was also known to have founded the TTK business group, famous for its 'Prestige' brand pressure cookers. Deshmukh's departure had an enormous impact, even if it was unspoken. For the Reserve Bank, Deshmukh had been a strong advocate for almost two decades, first within the bank itself, and then as the finance minister.

As the government wanted to press on with industrialization with the state leading the way, the focus on deficit financing increased, and the new finance minister had little time for bureaucrats or procedures. Thus, the period 1956–57 saw increasing tensions between the government and the Reserve Bank. There are two versions of what followed, one narrated by the RBI and another by B.K. Nehru, who apart from being Jawaharlal's cousin, was an important joint secretary in the Ministry of Finance at that juncture.

As per the RBI's official version,[57] T.T.K. had been a long-standing critic of Rama Rau, opposing his selection as governor from the beginning, and had also been a long-standing supporter of the nationalization of the Imperial Bank. As Deshmukh left the Ministry of Finance in July 1956, T.T.K.'s appointment was perhaps an unsavoury moment for Rama Rau, who by 1956 had spent almost seven years as the governor of the

RBI. Rama Rau himself was not necessarily the most actively involved governor. His tenure at the Reserve Bank was relatively benign, and he was described by his subordinates as aloof and distant.[58] Within weeks of taking charge, Krishnamachari started interfering with RBI's mandate to manage credit policy, and unilaterally decided to make an announcement contrary to RBI's own viewpoint and stance.

Upon this public show of hostility by the new finance minister, Rama Rau wrote to Nehru, accusing the new finance minister of behaving towards him with 'personal rudeness', using 'very rude language', passing 'rude remarks', and indulging in 'rude behaviour'.[59] While Rama Rau wanted to resign, Nehru convinced him to stay on. However, this arrangement did not last for long. Krishnamachari kept escalating the row with Rama Rau, and decided to go ahead and impose a stamp duty on bills of exchange to mobilize revenues, which the RBI had been using as an instrument of policy for some time. This was a direct subordination of the policy process, and Rama Rau, who had personally championed the development of the bills market, felt obliged to vigorously protest this proposed measure.

In Parliament, Krishnamachari called the proposal a 'fiscal measure with a monetary intent', which infuriated the Reserve Bank governor, evoking a strong response in a memorandum submitted to the Reserve Bank's central board. He wrote that 'two authorities who would operate the Bank rate—the Reserve Bank in the usual manner under Section 49 of the Act, and the Government by variation of the stamp duty by executive order of the Finance Ministry'.[60] This dual control was unacceptable to Rama Rau, but for T.T.K., 'subordination' was a bigger issue, and in an informal cabinet meeting, he apparently asked Governor Rama Rau to only address specific questions and not to present the bank's general views.

As the matter pressed on, the relations between the two men deteriorated to such an extent that Krishnamachari called the RBI 'a section of the finance ministry', and B.K. Nehru noted that on their next encounter after the cabinet meeting, Krishnamachari confronted Rama Rau publicly in the Ministry of Finance, and 'let fly in no uncertain terms and in the loudest of the voices',[61] who was in charge. Rama Rau, a man of gentle and mild persona, wrote a long letter (over 3,500 words) to Prime Minister Nehru on 29 December 1956 outlining how the current finance minister had made it impossible for him to continue at the RBI.

Nehru, who had so far managed to convince Rama Rau to stay put, surprisingly backed away from supporting the governor and in his reply dated 1 January 1957, criticized Rama Rau for his 'agitational approach'. Nehru also defended Krishnamachari's assertion that the RBI's role was subordinate to that of the finance ministry, saying that the use of references such as 'department' or 'a section' needed to be seen in a wider context. With a gentle but firm rebuke, Nehru ended his response with 'since you feel now that it is absolutely impossible for you to continue in office, I do not know what further advice I can give you. If you so wish, you can submit your formal resignation to the Finance Ministry.'[62]

Rama Rau sent his resignation to the Ministry of Finance and the prime minister on 7 January 1957, and it was promptly accepted. On 14 January, deputy governor K.G. Ambegaonkar took over as acting governor of the RBI and was in charge till 28 February 1957. Rama Rau had served as governor of the RBI for almost seven and a half years, and remains till date the longest serving governor of the Reserve Bank.

K.G. Ambegaonkar's term turned out to be the third shortest among all the governors, and was uneventful. He was replaced by Haravu Venkatanarasimha Varadaraja Iyengar, or H.V.R. Iyengar, who like Rama Rau and Deshmukh, came from the Indian Civil Service. He had also served as Nehru's personal secretary for some time.[63] Prior to his appointment as the governor of the Reserve Bank, Iyengar was leading the newly founded State Bank of India, and had worked previously with Krishnamachari, which made him T.T.K.'s personal choice for the role. Iyengar was different from his predecessor, and would actively seek out discussions with his juniors.[64] He was known to be very sharp, but his interventions on behalf of the Reserve Bank were rather limited.

An unfortunate consequence of the spat between the Ministry of Finance and the governor of the RBI was the disillusionment experienced by Sir Purshottamdas Thakurdas. He had been a founding board member of the Reserve Bank since its inception in 1935, and was appalled at the treatment meted out to Rama Rau and the institution. He decided to sever ties with the institution given the increasing government interference, and in a letter to Rama Rau, expressed his shock at the 'extraordinary, one-sided and unprovoked' events, and asked Rama Rau to ensure that he was not nominated to the board again in a letter dated 8 January 1957.

The Mundra scam, and the RBI loses face

Krishnamachari's attacks on the Reserve Bank continued even after Rama Rau's departure. While the new governor, H.V.R. Iyengar, was seen as someone who would be able to manage the finance minister T.T.K. much better, T.T.K. was of the view that rural credit, which was critical for the revival of India's agricultural sector, should be administered by the Ministry of Finance through other agencies, and not the RBI.

However, this assertion of finance ministry over the RBI would prove to be short-lived, as Krishnamachari found himself in the middle of a political scandal, which unfortunately led to doubts being cast on RBI and Governor Iyengar as well. In late 1957, after business confidence was weakening, Finance Minister T.T.K. decided to instruct the newly formed Life Insurance Corporation of India or LIC, to buy shares in the Mundra Group of Companies, which was undergoing financial troubles.

The RBI was aware of the problematic transactions, and after the Parliament raised a hue and cry, the government was forced by the Parliament questioning to set up a new committee under Justice M.C. Chagla in December 1957. The RBI soon became a party in the Chagla Committee investigations. Even Governor Iyengar appeared as a witness, but his testimony was widely believed to be only partially correct, and it was suspected that he was holding back information.[65] Iyengar's testimony helped protect T.T.K., but it did bring great disrepute to the office of the RBI governor, according to B.K. Nehru. Eventually, Krishnamachari resigned, and the episode dimmed Iyengar's lustre both within the RBI and in the financial community at large. In fact, even the next governor of the RBI, P.C. Bhattacharya, who was then the expenditure secretary and a close confidante of Krishnamachari, was consulted extensively in the Mundra affair and chose to align himself with the minister, as it 'would have displeased and even compromised the minister.'[66]

After this episode, the RBI went from a developing institution with a range of powers to one that was just seen as a 'section' of the wider financial apparatus in the country. The following governors made considerable efforts to uphold the Reserve Bank's autonomy, but the dismissal of Rama

Rau and then the Chagla committee investigations set the institution back by several years, in terms of its emerging dominance over India's financial system. Between 1957 and 1969, the RBI experienced a reverse takeover, with governors being transferred from the State Bank of India, which was owned by the RBI itself.

Chapter 4

Crisis and consolidation

After the departure of Benegal Rama Rau in acrimonious circumstances, the stature and importance of the Reserve Bank in the sphere of economic policy suffered a setback. The Indian state, which was entering its teen years, was starting to see the initial excesses of the planning process, and external factors such as wars with China and Pakistan along with droughts had a debilitating impact on India's economic conditions. In between, India saw a series of small bank runs, significant shortfalls in food supply and a gradual deterioration in the external balances, which resulted in high inflation through the 1960s and a sharp devaluation of the rupee in June 1966. The political economy of the country also became more fractured, following the deaths of Nehru and Lal Bahadur Shastri, and the advent of Indira Gandhi at the helm in Delhi. The Reserve Bank played a role in firefighting on these issues mostly as a support player, rather than leading from the front. However, as far as institution building is concerned, several key steps were taken and powers acquired between 1955 and 1967.

The second five-year plan and currency troubles

India's external position had been one of its strengths when it gained independence. Right from the beginning, the exchange rate was kept unduly strong to benefit the British government, especially during the war years. This meant that on the eve of Independence, India's sterling balances amounted to over 1.1 billion pounds, or ₹1,512 crore. The general consensus within the political class was to deploy this fund for rapid industrialization and economic growth, and the Reserve Bank was appointed as the custodian of the sterling reserves. India was still a part of the sterling area, and in September 1949, had to follow through with an almost 30 per cent devaluation in order to preserve the sterling value of the balances. While India contemplated diluting the arrangements it had in the sterling area, it maintained them essentially because of the large sums of money the British owed to the government. Nonetheless, India was slowly diversifying its reserves away from sterling towards the US dollar, and this created significant tensions between the Reserve Bank and the Bank of England in the mid-fifties.

Even as the Reserve Bank negotiated with the British government on the adequate use of the sterling balances, the advent of planning and eventual use of deficit financing would prove to be detrimental to the external position. However, the deterioration was not immediate, but rather a long drawn out one. Although the government's ambitions rose after the relative success of the first five-year plan, the second plan was to create conditions for a major setback over ten years. Between 1957 and 1966, India experienced two balance of payments crises, but of different intensities. The changing political economy of the country amplified this, along with hostility from neighbouring countries.

The very expansionary nature of the second five-year plan immediately created problems on the external front. India expected to run a deficit of ₹1,120 crore in the second plan period, of which it expected to fund roughly ₹200 crore from its reserves. Governor Rama Rau was not convinced, as the over ₹800 crore of foreign assistance earmarked for the plan was four times what India had received in the previous plan, and hence the pressure on the external finances could be more severe. The government, however, did not pay much attention to these suggestions of too much reliance on foreign funding, and as a result, in fiscal year 1955–56, India's foreign reserves fell from ₹902 crore to ₹681 crore. As the history of the RBI notes,[67] India spent the total planned reserve withdrawal in the first nine months of the plan period, justifying RBI's scepticism.

The Ministry of Finance and the Planning Commission engaged in a fight over the arithmetic. But the Reserve Bank still had to go ahead and impose stringent import controls in 1957. This was not enough to prevent a further slide in foreign exchange reserves, and at the end of the plan period, the total drop was almost three times the amount that had been anticipated by the Planning Commission, notwithstanding the higher foreign aid. The Reserve Bank played a significant role in averting what could have been a much larger crisis for India by aggressively bargaining for multilateral assistance at the International Monetary Fund and its sister organizations.

India approached the IMF for short-term financing only in early 1957, when it was becoming clear that imports were not slowing down. While officials in Washington were sanguine about India's request for drawdowns, the US Treasury remained unconvinced about the short-term nature of India's shortfalls. India's executive director to the IMF, P.S. Narayan Prasad, managed to negotiate a deal with the Fund despite the Treasury's reservations that India was seeking development assistance in the garb of balance of payments shortfalls. Thanks to the deft manoeuvring by Prasad, India was given a US$200 million facility, consisting of both drawing down of its quota and a US$72.5 million standby facility. This would turn out to be one of the many drawings India made in the coming decade.

Even with the IMF's support, India still had a large shortfall to meet on its external financing for the success of the second five-year plan. Indian politicians were reluctant to draw the West into India's development agenda, but they still had to bargain for large-scale development assistance. As such, framing the negotiations within a technical point of view rather than as a political process was key. Hence the process was largely delegated to officials from the Ministry of Finance and the RBI, who shared a good relationship with the president of the World Bank, Eugene R. Black, who favoured development assistance to India.

Reserve Bank officials along with Governor Iyengar visited several European countries to raise funding for India's government securities between 1957–58, with mixed success. India also organized an 'Aid India' meeting in August 1958 with the World Bank's support, as it thought approaching individual creditors was 'most undignified and politically impossible.'[68] The meeting was a success, and the World Bank, in conjunction with the United States, Britain, Canada, Germany and Japan, agreed to commit US$302 million, which rose to US$332 million at the end of the second plan. This helped India tide over its balance of payments difficulties until 1961.

Doubling down on foreign support

Being bailed out by donor support in 1958, India's sights for the third five-year plan moved even higher. Under the illusion of continued support from Western capitals, the government was toying with the idea of a funds outlay of almost ₹10,000 crore, which made several donor countries nervous. Even though the environment for foreign aid was conducive, India's external position at the end of the second five-year plan was a bit precarious, with only ₹304 crore of foreign exchange reserves left. The government, however, encouraged by Western academics and confident bureaucrats, moved ahead with a large plan outlay, and immediately, India's external balance was found wanting.

India returned to the IMF in July 1961 for a withdrawal of US$250 million, which was seen by some other countries as a roll over of its earlier withdrawal. However, it was allowed, but its benefits were not seen for long. There was hardly any improvement in India's external balances, with the Reserve Bank's foreign assets declining sharply. In June 1962,[69] the new governor of the Reserve Bank, P.C. Bhattacharya, in a committee of economic secretaries, argued for import curtailment to arrest the deteriorating trend. At his insistence, the committee also recommended curtailing all unauthorized travel by both government and private citizens, and issue of import licenses, unless there was aid available for it. According to the official history of the RBI, the government had also considered devaluation of the rupee, but the measure was quickly ruled out.

With some of the recommended steps implemented, India's external position started to recover gradually through 1962, but after the war with China in October 1962, the trend of deterioration resumed. This problem was compounded by a relatively agnostic World Bank under the new president George Woods, and back-to-back droughts in 1963–64, which hurt India's growth significantly, especially following the war on its eastern borders. At the same time, donor interest in India was waning, as the large developed countries started dealing with their own external positions. Meanwhile, Jawaharlal Nehru passed away on 27 May 1964, and was replaced by Lal Bahadur Shastri as the prime minister. Western countries started considering India's debt repayment problems, amid declining foreign reserves, which fell to ₹237 crore.

As the foreign reserves kept falling, the Reserve Bank was called upon to provide technical support and compile projections, and between 1964 and 1965, the bank provided personnel support to the government. Further, Governor Bhattacharya became a key member of the team of bureaucrats directing India's external policies.[70] The role was enhanced when J.J. Anjaria, who was then India's executive director at the IMF, wrote a letter to the RBI governor about the Fund's uneasiness over India's economic situation and the rupee's valuation.

The RBI immediately swung into action but soon discovered that refinancing its debt through other options was not feasible. B.K. Nehru, who was by then India's ambassador to United States, suggested suspension of a statutory currency cover, but the advice was dismissed by both RBI and the Ministry of Finance. Meanwhile, L.K. Jha, who was secretary to the prime minister and would later go on to replace P.C. Bhattacharya at the RBI, had negotiated a deal with the Bank of England, which was later sealed by Bhattacharya himself. However, the funds were never drawn down, due to other, extraneous circumstances.

The situation continued to deteriorate as a payment of US$100 million came due in March 1965, which the IMF was reluctant to roll over without some payment being made. The finance minister, in a speech to the Parliament, revealed that the foreign reserves stood at just ₹78 crore in February 1965, and India had to transfer confiscated and domestically mined gold to RBI's issue department to shore up its foreign assets. The Reserve Bank pushed up the bank rate in February 1965 by 1 per cent to 6 per cent, as part of its firefighting efforts. However, despite all efforts, most senior officials including L.K. Jha, P.C. Bhattacharya and I.G. Patel agreed that currency devaluation was starting to look imminent.[71]

Bargaining for time

While the decision to devalue the rupee was taken by Indira Gandhi, the foundation of the move was laid during the Shastri administration by his closest advisors and the Reserve Bank itself. Shastri was considering devaluation as a feasible solution to India's persistent external problems. In the summer of 1965, rumours around a possible devaluation gained steam with the visit of Bernard Bell, an American economist who had come to India to conduct a study on Indian finances for the World Bank. Bell was no friend of India, and I.G. Patel recalled a memorable meeting over drinks between Bell, RBI governor Bhattacharya and himself, which ended unpleasantly over a big disagreement.[72]

In June 1965, Governor Bhattacharya, along with L.K. Jha and I.G. Patel, submitted a report making a case for further import restrictions and checks on outflows, which was widely seen as the first official response to the Bell report and the campaign led by George Woods (president of World Bank) for a devaluation of the rupee. The Indian response cut no ice with the Bell mission, and Bernard Bell recommended a devaluation nonetheless, along with fundamental changes to India's system of economic management.[73]

While the Indian response to the Bell mission report from T.T. Krishnamachari was dismissive, it did not necessarily reflect the thinking within the government. The Reserve Bank was at the same time advised by the IMF to consider introducing multiple exchange rates, which was another way to avoid a simple devaluation. As time passed, Governor Bhattacharya, his executive director Bhoothalingam and Shastri's secretary L.K. Jha saw the futility of stopgap measures and concluded that a simple devaluation was perhaps more desirable.

Shastri ensured that his argumentative finance minister Krishnamachari was eased out of the Ministry of Finance, and he was replaced by Sachindra Chaudhari,[74] a lawyer from Calcutta, who was described as an 'economic illiterate, political lightweight, but a thoroughly pleasant and agreeable professional' by Patel.[75] He was also a friend of Governor Bhattacharya's, who thought the finance minister would not just be agreeable to the prime minister, but also a pliant friend for the RBI. As soon as this handover took place, Bhattacharya, accompanied by I.G. Patel, flew to Washington to inform the IMF of its intention to devalue, but unfortunately, Shastri passed away in early January 1966.

Indira Gandhi and the 1966 currency devaluation

Understanding the political economy of India in the 1960s is imperative to understanding the timing and nature of the devaluation India undertook in

June 1966. After Nehru's death in May 1964, Shastri proved to be a non-ideologue leader, who was willing to barter for technology and aid in return for market access.[76] However, with the breakout of the India-Pakistan war in August–September of 1965, Western economic aid to both countries was suspended. This had a devastating impact on India, and Shastri's sudden death on 11 January 1966 in Tashkent complicated the situation further.

After intense wrangling within the Congress Party, the senior leaders in control of the party (called the 'syndicate') chose Indira Gandhi, Nehru's only child, as the next prime minister, and she took charge of the country on 24 January 1966, with elections due in just one year in February 1967. According to Katherine Frank's biography of Indira Gandhi,[77] she was nominated due to the inability of senior Congress leaders to find a consensus candidate from among their ranks. She won the election for the leadership against Morarji Desai, and became the prime minister two weeks after Shastri's death.

Indira Gandhi took charge of India at a challenging time, with war, drought and a worsening external situation all coming together at the same time. Undermined at home, Gandhi focused on external relations first and went to the United States in March 1966, just over a month into her term. While keeping up the charade of a 'goodwill tour', Indira's real purpose was to secure both food and foreign exchange aid from the Johnson administration, which was initially sympathetic to India's situation. Indira Gandhi managed to charm President Lyndon Johnson, and the United States agreed to grant the aid needed, provided India met a few conditions: the devaluation of the rupee, adoption of a new agricultural strategy to boost output and the establishment of an Indian American education foundation.[78]

Behind the scenes, Indira Gandhi had already asked her team to establish contact with the IMF and the World Bank on the potential for external assistance. RBI governor Bhattacharya met officials in February in Washington, and found the multilateral institutions to be more supportive than he had anticipated. While it was in Bhattacharya's remit to inform the Fund of the government's intention to adjust the exchange rate,[79] he left it to IMF executive director Anjaria to inform the Fund verbally of the impending change, given Anjaria was managing the dialogue with the Fund in Washington.

Back home, political opposition to a possible devaluation was mounting. Nonetheless, the RBI and Ministry of Finance officials were locked in negotiations to find the 'right level' for the rupee. Initially, it was felt that the IMF might be happy with a rate of ₹6 against the US dollar, up from ₹4.76. However, the policy thinking was in those days driven by discretion, and B.K. Nehru in his memoirs is quoted as saying 'Fixation of an exchange rate is a matter of complete guesswork [...]Pierre-Paul Schweitzer [then head of the IMF] had wanted Rs10 but I thought Rs7.50 would be about right. He [Govindan Nair, economic secretary] said that gave a rate of Rs21 to the pound, which meant that the value of a rupee would be less than a shilling. That he said was psychologically bad. [But] I said [...] Rs7.50 was a nice round figure.'[80] It is also reported in RBI's official history that Pierre-Paul Schweitzer, who was head of the IMF at the time, told Indira Gandhi that 'six rupees to the dollar would be good [...] seven and a half would be fantastic,'[81] which may also have influenced the government's thinking.

The decision to devalue the rupee was announced on 6 June 1966, with significant political criticism. The cabinet was informed only on 5 June, and it was largely critical of the decision. The rupee was devalued by 36.5 per cent. Within the RBI, only Governor Bhattacharya had known of the impending decision until late May, when he chose to confide in two senior officials. Even right-leaning political parties who supported free enterprise criticized the decision, resenting the overarching impression of the government giving in to pressure from foreign institutions.[82] Senior politicians like K. Kamaraj blamed the government for the devaluation, calling it 'a sell out to the Americans.'[83]

Alongside the devaluation, India also initiated trade reforms, particularly the scrapping of import entitlement schemes and export levies, in order to boost the impact of the devaluation in promoting exports and reducing imports. Indira Gandhi was blunt in her assessment, and in a speech addressed to the nation on 12 June, termed the devaluation as 'stronger medicine [...] necessary to restore the nation to economic health.'[84] This boldness from Indira, however, had little impact on both the political posturing and the general public sentiment, which was reeling under double-digit inflation, food shortages due to consecutive droughts and now the devaluation under foreign pressure.

The 1966 drought dealt a body blow to the liberalization instinct, and by the third quarter of 1966, the impulse to decontrol the economy was lost. The RBI in its official history notes that the 1966 devaluation 'failed'[85] due to the under-delivery of economic aid from Western economies. But it was perhaps the lack of political follow-up and a lurch towards populist policies that sealed the fate of the devaluation. The negative effects of the drought and higher defence spending were evident in the 1967 elections, when the Congress Party saw its share of votes decline to 41 per cent and Indira Gandhi had to turn to socialist policies in order to retain popular support, including nationalization of private banks, coal, oil and insurance companies.

As such, within a short span of two decades, India went from having a significant source of funding through its foreign sterling reserves, to a significant foreign exchange crunch and a high dependency on external aid. While this could be pinned down to poor policy management, especially the planning process, the two wars and the droughts had substantial negative effects, which the government was unable to recover from. The Reserve Bank played a largely technical role in the negotiations, having little bandwidth to materially influence the decision-making process, and operated as an extension of the government's economic planning process.

The Palai Bank failure

Despite the RBI's apparent lack of independence as displayed in the bitter exit of Governor Rama Rau, the period between 1957 and 1967 saw considerable ammunition being added to the bank's regulatory and supervisory armour so it could better manage the fragmented banking structure that prevailed in India even a decade after its Independence. However, the powers to regulate banks on licensing, returns, capital adequacy, branches and eventually mergers came only in the wake of bank failures between 1945–1960.

Following the end of the Second World War, many of the banks that had mushroomed during the war years started going out of business. After 1947, the exchange of people across new boundaries of India and Pakistan meant that small regional banks in Punjab and Bengal especially got into trouble, and 205 banks went out of business between 1947 and 1951. A majority of the banks were in West Bengal, which was reeling under the pressures of Partition and the famine. The passage of the Banking Companies Act in 1949 helped, but did not prevent bank failures, and the situation only stabilized somewhat by the end of 1951. The continued bank failures in spite of the passage of a banking regulation act undermined confidence in the Reserve Bank initially. However, once the Banking Regulation act was passed, the Reserve Bank was given the power to licence banks, but its ability to change behaviour or influence incentives was still modest.

By 1951, about 566 banks were in business in India,[86] with most of them being small and financially unviable over the longer period. However, the process of consolidation required a crisis, and the large one came only in 1960. After the banking crisis in West Bengal in the early 1950s, the Ministry of Finance and the Reserve Bank had a run-in over whose responsibility it was to liquidate an unviable bank. While the RBI had no legal basis to participate in any liquidation, political opinion, particularly in Calcutta, favoured some obligation on the part of the RBI to ensure a smooth and orderly process. This gave way to some consolidation, and the United Bank of India was set up as an amalgamation of four local banks in West Bengal. Even as an internal committee recommended a more active role for the RBI in November 1952, the government moved slowly, and only gave more powers to the RBI to collect information and execute liquidation as per an amendment in 1953.

While the Banking Companies Act of 1949 had given the Reserve Bank the power to licence a bank, the process of licensing for existing banks was an arduous one. Small banks had flourished in the fragmented political set-up before Independence, and after 1947, the status quo was maintained for several years. In its early years, the Reserve Bank was conservative on licensing and by 1954[87] had licensed only thirty-three banks, while several requests for licensing had been turned down. As some institutions continued to grow despite the lack of a banking licence, the Reserve Bank's supervisory role was relatively weak for these unlicensed deposit-taking institutions. This fundamentally changed with the Kerala banking crisis in 1959–1960, and once that bank run was settled, the RBI acquired significant powers to control banks and their behaviour.

While the epicentre of the 1960 bank run was in Kerala, it started with a relatively small scheduled bank called Laxmi Bank in Akola, Maharashtra.

In May 1960, the bank was asked by the RBI to begin winding up through a court appeal. This lack of confidence in banks spilled over for no apparent reason to Kerala, where a large scheduled bank, the Palai Central Bank, was asked by RBI to stop its business in August 1960, leading to significant political backlash. The Palai Bank's failure was the biggest in independent India and followed the failure of two other major banks, the Travancore National Bank and the Quilon Bank in Kerala in 1938.

While the RBI seemed steadfast in its decision to close the Palai Bank, the news of a large bank failure triggered minor runs on banks in Delhi, Madras and of course in Kerala.[88] Kerala's banking structure had always been fragmented, with numerous rural banks serving small communities. Of these, five small banks came under immense pressure, and simultaneously, the State Bank of Travancore, which was the princely bank under the State Bank of India, saw a noticeable rise in deposits. As a precautionary measure, the Reserve Bank assured support for all functioning banks on 9 August 1960, but the matter spun out of control in a week's time, when several banks in Kerala applied for emergency funds. The RBI provided some funds, but mainly to support the scheduled banks.

Meanwhile, the public outcry on the state of the nation's banking affairs inevitably led to demands for de-facto nationalization of the troubled banks. Many suggested that the State Bank of India should take over the smaller banks. While the Reserve Bank governor Iyengar was not opposed to the suggestion, the State Bank chairman P.C. Bhattacharya was. The government acted decisively, and in September 1960, passed an amendment to the Banking Companies Act that gave RBI the powers to impose a moratorium on deposits and to compulsorily amalgamate banks, if deemed necessary.

Armed with its new statutory powers, the Reserve Bank, along with the government, moved ahead to reorganize the banking sector in Kerala. Despite the urgency to prevent a full-fledged bank run, no solution was found between September and December 1960, and on 8 December, a significant upsurge in deposit withdrawals was observed. As political pressure from Kerala's chief minister Pattom Pillai increased on the Reserve Bank, on 18 December, five local banks were granted a moratorium on their deposits once they filed for it. While banking services were disrupted, in June 1961, the banking crisis in Kerala came to a close with three troubled banks being merged with the State Bank of Travancore, while two were merged with Canara Bank. A sixth bank was taken over by the South Indian Bank.

The Kerala crisis resulted in significant powers being granted to the Reserve Bank to intervene in the banking sector, and allowed for a smooth reorganization of the banking system in general. In the 1960s, as the situation evolved, RBI was able to successfully manage the mergers or takeovers of 204 banks over seven years. It also paved the way for a deposit insurance facility, which at that time only the United States was offering.

RBI sets up deposit insurance

RBI had been flirting with the idea of starting a deposit insurance scheme in the wake of multiple bank failures in the post-war years. The idea was being considered during the Bengal bank runs in the late 1940s, but Governor Deshmukh suggested avoiding the implementation of such a measure without first understanding the state of the banks. Both the Rural Banking Enquiry Committee and the Shroff Committee on finance for the private sector also proposed deposit insurance as a needed policy, but it was held back due to the Reserve Bank's insistence on ensuring the correct sequence of rollout for banking sector consolidation and deposit insurance schemes.

In reality, there was a lack of consensus among various departments within the Reserve Bank, which held back the introduction of deposit insurance. The banking operations department, which was responsible for the day-to-day operations and supervision of banks, argued against implementing the scheme as it would unnecessarily add to the cost burden on banks. The banking development department along with the banking research group, however, favoured a deposit protection scheme, arguing its potential to boost confidence in India's banking system and as such attract more funds to the banks.

With banking sector growth being strong in the 1950s, Governor Rama Rau sided with the banking operations group and argued for a voluntary consensus among commercial banks for such a scheme in a central board meeting in June 1954.[89] But as government policy started moving towards more direct state control, the government asked the

Reserve Bank to consider the viability of a deposit insurance scheme in 1956. Both sides within the bank argued their cases passionately, and to avoid confrontation, the Reserve Bank favoured the scheme but asked for more time for consultations with commercial banks, as a delaying tactic. However, with the banking crisis in Kerala, the fifteen-year push for a deposit insurance scheme materialized in almost fifteen months.

As the Palai Bank was on the verge of failing, the department of banking research once again raised the issue of deposit insurance, to boost depositor confidence. It also correctly highlighted that a voluntary scheme would not work unless the Reserve Bank was directly involved in it. Governor Iyengar received positive feedback from the Indian Bank's association , and on 18 August, constituted a working group of Reserve Bank officials to prepare an operational design for the scheme. The report proposed an initial cover of ₹1,000 for the individual depositor, which would protect almost 80 per cent of account holders[90] for a nominal fee of 0.02 per cent of the deposit base. The Ministry of Finance and the Indian Bank's association informally agreed to the proposal, but in their formal response, the bankers stated that the scheme was encouraging of unsound behaviour and the similar treatment of 'good' and 'bad' banks. Surprisingly, as the Palai Bank crisis and the following bank run started to lose traction, the Ministry of Finance backtracked from its earlier support for the Reserve Bank's proposal in October 1960, which drew an acerbic response from Governor Iyengar.

As pressure started to mount again, the Ministry of Finance agreed to shepherd the bill, and in February 1961, a draft bill was sent from the Reserve Bank to the government. The cost of insurance had been raised marginally to 0.05 per cent, but eventually, the limit of protection was raised to fifteen hundred rupees. The bill moved forward with little difficulty, and was signed into law in December 1961. The Deposit Insurance Corporation came into existence on 1 January 1962, just two months before Governor Iyengar retired on 28 February 1962. In 1968, as social control over economic policy increased, the deposit insurance cover was raised to ₹5,000,[91] and eventually the law was extended to cooperative banks as well, but with more regulatory oversight for the RBI.

In hindsight, while the period between 1957 and 1966 was challenging for India and also for the Reserve Bank, institutional character was not diluted as significantly as one would have feared following Rama Rau's dismissal. Governor Iyengar and his successor Bhattacharya steered the Reserve Bank and also helped manage many crises with a steady hand, and the institutional structure that India's financial system enjoys today has its roots in several steps undertaken in the 1960s, despite the turbulence of war, famine and external crisis that the country went through.

Chapter 5

A sharp left turn

Institutional independence was significantly attacked under Indira Gandhi's rule, and no organization felt this more than the Reserve Bank. The decline began soon after the Congress Party, reeling from a failed exchange rate devaluation, witnessed its worst ever electoral performance in the February 1967 general elections. Despite winning a comfortable majority,[92] the sharp decline in its seat count left the Congress leadership shaken, with questions being raised over the political leadership of Indira Gandhi. Congress also lost control of several key state assemblies, such as Madras, marking a significant shift in the country's polity.

After the formation of the government in March 1967, Indira Gandhi was pressured by the 'syndicate' to accommodate senior leaders such as Morarji Desai, who was appointed as deputy prime minister and then finance minister in the second cabinet post 1967. However, the relationship between Indira Gandhi and Morarji Desai remained frosty, and the tussle for control of India's economy continued.

At the Reserve Bank, the fallout of the political bickering was initially limited. After spending five years as the governor, P.C. Bhattacharya retired on 30 June 1967 and was replaced by Lakshmi Kant Jha, a civil servant like his predecessors, who had also served as principal secretary to prime ministers Lal Bahadur Shastri and Indira Gandhi for a brief period. Unsure about his loyalties, Indira Gandhi shunted L.K. Jha to the Reserve Bank after her uncle, B.K. Nehru, refused Morarji Desai's offer to take up the position of governor of the RBI.[93] B.K. Nehru in his memoirs noted that, 'The reason why I had so far refused was the lack of independence of the Governor. I explained to him [Desai] that the great battle between T.T.K. and Rama Rau, which the latter lost, had made it clear that the Governor was a subordinate of the Ministry of Finance. Even as Joint Secretary, I used to issue orders to the Reserve Bank. I did not cherish the idea of my juniors ordering me about.' As such, while the position of the governor of the Reserve Bank was in principle an important one, its sheen had rather worn off since the ugly episode between T.T. Krishnamachari and Sir Benegal Rama Rau in 1957.

The lingering demand for bank nationalization

India's economy started to recover gradually after the devaluation of June 1966. Better weather conditions, improving agricultural output and better economic sentiment helped lift activity. Meanwhile, Indira Gandhi replaced L.K. Jha with Parmeshwar Narayan Haksar, or P.N. Haksar, as her principal secretary, a position that Haksar held for six years, emerging as Indira Gandhi's key strategist. Haksar, a Kashmiri Pandit and an Indian Foreign Service officer, was friends with her husband Feroze Gandhi, and was handpicked to turn her prime ministership around. A socialist by nature, Haksar can be deemed partly responsible for the sharp left turn that India's economic policy made during the late sixties, as he helped Indira Gandhi navigate through the treacherous waters of the Congress Party.

As the Indian economy started to recover during 1967–1968, the clamour for a better agricultural credit facility picked up again. The usual demand for the nationalization of the banking infrastructure resurfaced, even though both Governor Jha and Finance Minister Morarji Desai were opposed to the idea. However, there was an urgent need to pacify the growing disenchantment with India's banking apparatus, which had multiple conflicts of interest, including ownership, management by industrialists and the nature of their operations.

In its 1967 election manifesto, the Congress Party had advocated 'social control' over the banking system to enable it to serve the interest of economic growth more effectively. While institutions to focus on industrial credit and retail savings such as IDBI and Unit Trust of India were established in the early 1960s, lack of institutional credit to agriculture and small businesses was still seen as a critical hurdle. After the Congress Party's poor electoral performance in February, the May 1967 meetings of the Congress working committee brought the fissures between Morarji

Desai and Indira Gandhi out in the open. However, as a compromise, the party agreed to first tighten the Reserve Bank's control over the banking system, while Morarji Desai made the case for social controls to be tightened. According to RBI's official history,[94] Indira Gandhi was not an active participant in the debate, but was probably biding her time to implement more stringent measures.

To kick-start the process of implementing 'social controls', Desai commissioned V.A. Pai Panandikar, an advisor to the Ministry of Finance, to examine how banks could be brought under social control. He received little support from within the ministry itself,[95] but nonetheless went about preparing his report. His only contribution would be introducing the term 'social control' to the policy debate.

In the meantime, on 18 June 1967, Morarji Desai called an informal meeting of the Ministry of Finance and the Indian Banks' Association, which was attended by several large bank owners and industrialists. As per D.N. Ghosh's memoirs, meeting notes were not kept,[96] but attendees included L.K. Jha, who was about to take over as the governor of the RBI, as well as I.G. Patel and S.S. Shiralkar, both bureaucrats in the Ministry of Finance.

In the meeting, Desai made the case for banks to reform voluntarily, rather than being forced to. He asked for credit distribution to be made more equitable to serve the needs of the agricultural sector. The banks were naturally apprehensive and highlighted the existing extensive controls that the Reserve Bank had over private banks in India. However, Desai understood the zeitgeist and encouraged the banks to reform their management and reduce ownership control. While there was general agreement on the issue, the banks chose to promote existing senior managers to chairman of banks, while reporting compliance to the RBI. As such, not much changed in the behaviour of the private banks, which would have dramatic consequences later on.

Panandikar submitted his report in August 1967, and it was on the lines of Morarji Desai's thought process. The report advocated strengthening banking laws, while giving the government more say in the appointment of directors. It also advocated for the creation of a banking commission to oversee the organization and structure of India's banking system. The report concluded by pitching for a National Credit Council (NCC) under the auspices of the Ministry of Finance, a proposal the RBI was not sanguine about, although former RBI employee M. Narasimham recommended it.

The Reserve Bank rightly felt that an alternative credit control body could undermine the Reserve Bank's own policies. Further, the RBI was incensed by the Panandikar report's criticism of the RBI's role in credit generation, particularly at the sectoral level. The Reserve Bank wrote a strongly worded memorandum highlighting the need for the NCC to be under the Reserve Bank's control, but also welcomed the proposal to improve banking regulation laws.

The social control experiment

Eventually, despite reservations, the Reserve Bank agreed to formulate regulations that would enable the government to tighten its grip on the banking system. But the Panandikar report was another instance in which the government, trying to further its own agenda, unintentionally ended up hurting the Reserve Bank. Nonetheless, the Reserve Bank went ahead and drafted the changes to the Banking Regulation Act, and in December 1967, Desai announced the changes in Parliament. However, in order to enable such a dramatic step, changes were also needed in the RBI and the SBI Acts. With the economy recovering, there was no urgency to push the bill through, and after a due consultation process under a select committee, the bill was finally submitted to the Lok Sabha on 6 May 1968. However, it took another two months to pass the bill, and the changes came into effect from February 1969.

The contours of 'social control' over banks required existing banks to reconstitute their boards so that more than half of the board of directors had extensive experience, with adequate representation for the rural sector. It also gave the Reserve Bank the power to change auditors if deemed necessary, while reducing the ability of banks to make loans to their directors or their inter-group holdings in cases of conglomerates. Finally, the most critical power given to the government through the RBI was its ability to acquire any bank business if it was considered necessary to protect depositor interest. Interestingly, as the RBI's history recollects, Desai initially wanted to merge any misbehaving private bank with the

SBI, but changed his mind after Governor Jha convinced him to leave the SBI alone.[97]

Meanwhile, the government notified the creation of the National Credit Council in February 1968. However, apart from Governor Jha and Deputy Prime Minister Morarji Desai, few were enthusiastic about the newly set up body when it met for the first time in May 1968. Perhaps the body politic of the day and the intensifying political battle between Morarji Desai and Indira Gandhi doomed the NCC. It met only twice more, once in July 1968 and then again in March 1969, before the events of July 1969 and the subsequent nationalization of major commercial banks left the NCC defunct.

Indira Gandhi and the quest for control of the Congress Party

Grasping the politics behind the nationalization of banks is critical to understanding the whole episode. The political war that had been brewing ever since Indira Gandhi took over as prime minister in 1966 culminated in bank nationalization, which by all accounts was well received by the country's largely poor population.

Indira Gandhi was forced to accommodate Morarji Desai as deputy prime minister after the Congress Party's poor showing in the 1967 elections. However, the truce was temporary, and while Gandhi favoured drastic steps to recalibrate India's economy, she was biding her time till her opponents made mistakes. After a tough beginning, Indira Gandhi prevailed in getting Dr Zakir Hussain, the then sitting vice president, appointed as the third president of India in May 1967, despite reservations from Morarji Desai and the Congress president K. Kamaraj. However, tensions escalated again with the new Congress president, S. Nijalingappa, working with the syndicate to oust Indira Gandhi. The fight spilled out in the open when Nijalingappa and Gandhi publicly traded verbal blows through their respective speeches on the government's economic policies and the country's economic status at the seventy-second session of the Congress Party, held at the end of April 1969.[98]

Determined to end the feud conclusively in her favour, Indira Gandhi had made up her mind to undertake a course correction on economic policy. An opportunity presented itself when the sudden demise of

President Dr Zakir Hussain on 3 May 1969 led to an unexpected opening, which both the syndicate and Indira Gandhi were determined to leverage.

In the interim, V.V. Giri, who was then the vice president of India, took office as the acting president until fresh elections could be held. The syndicate within the Congress Party had decided to nominate Neelam Sanjiva Reddy, who was then the speaker of the Lok Sabha and was also the first chief minister of Andhra Pradesh in 1956. Indira Gandhi did not agree with the choice, and instead proposed the name of veteran leader Jagjivan Ram. In the 9 July meeting of the Congress working committee,[99] the business of choosing the next candidate was to be expedited. However, Indira Gandhi decided to throw a spanner in the works and drafted a note pitching for the nationalization of major commercial banks in the country.

Indira Gandhi proceeds with bank nationalization

The Congress Party was heading for a split. The sudden proposal to reconsider nationalization came as a shock to Morarji Desai, who had designed the entire apparatus around 'social control' over banking. Even Indira Gandhi had publicly backed the idea, calling for the experiment to be given at least two years and restraining 'young Turks' like Chandra Shekhar Singh from demanding outright nationalization (Chandra Shekhar later went on to become prime minister). However, with political realities changing, Indira Gandhi had little choice but to move ahead with an ideological fight over India's economic future.

The proposal for reconsidering nationalization disrupted the Congress working committee meeting, with tempers running high during the week-long event. Indira Gandhi was unhappy at being thrown down the gauntlet by the syndicate on the issue of nationalization. As the resolution noted, the party in an effort to almost challenge Indira Gandhi virtually asked the government to go ahead with nationalization if it was in the interest of the nation. Not one to back down, Indira turned to her trusted aide Haksar, who was instrumental in engineering what followed next.

On 16 July, the prime minister decided to take control of the Ministry of Finance by relieving Morarji Desai of the portfolio. He retained the position of deputy prime minister, but without any departments to look after, pushing him to promptly resign. At the same time, Haksar was convinced that immediate nationalization of banks would win Indira Gandhi public support and thus sideline the syndicate within the party. There are two versions of what followed.

The first story is well known, and is the one that was recounted by I.G. Patel in his memoirs.[100] Indira Gandhi told Patel that, 'For political reasons, it has been decided to nationalize the banks. You have to prepare within twenty-four hours the bill, a note for the cabinet, and a speech for me to make to the nation on the radio tomorrow evening.'[101]

The second version was recounted more recently in the memoirs of D.N. Ghosh, who was a junior bureaucrat in the Ministry of Finance at the time. On the advice of his friend and deputy governor of the RBI, A. Bakshi, Haksar decided to summon Dhruba Narayan Ghosh, a deputy secretary managing the banking division in the Ministry of Finance, on the evening of 17 July,[102] before Patel found out about the impending nationalisation, as Haksar and Indira Gandhi saw Patel as being closer to Morarji Desai.

The choice of summoning Ghosh instead of economic affairs secretary I.G. Patel or L.K. Jha, the governor of the RBI, was perhaps strange but not surprising. The prime minister and Haksar chose secrecy over dialogue, and it was well known that Governor Jha was not in favour of nationalization. Haksar's instructions to Ghosh at his residence on the evening of 17 July were simple. According to Ghosh, Haksar was keen to understand the administrative feasibility of pulling off such a move, and was looking at the possible nationalization of enough banks to control eighty to eighty five per cent of the banking system.

Time was of the essence, and a decision had to be made quickly as Parliament would be convening in three days. Ghosh suggested using an ordinance prepared under Finance Minister Krishnamachari to nationalize five large banks in 1963 as the blueprint. Bakshi, who joined the meeting late, after returning on a special plane from Madras, was wary about the ability of the government to run the entire banking system. He flagged the administrative issues that arose with the nationalization of the State Bank of India, and suggested a gradual approach.[103] However, Haksar had by then made up his mind, as Indira Gandhi's political survival depended on this action. Governor Jha was ironically in New Delhi on 17 July, and had met with Prime Minister Indira Gandhi to give a long presentation on how social controls were becoming more effective.

On the morning of 18 July, Haksar asked Ghosh to go ahead with drafting the regulation, for which he commandeered his services from the Ministry of Finance, without letting out the real reason. There is some confusion over how Indira Gandhi agreed to go ahead with fourteen banks, while leaving out National and Grindlays Bank, the only foreign bank that had a deposit base greater than ₹50 crore at that point. While Ghosh claims to have convinced Haksar, the official history of RBI and I.G. Patel's memoirs maintain that it was Patel, the then economic affairs secretary in the Ministry of Finance, who convinced Indira Gandhi to leave the foreign banks alone. Ghosh claims that after a brief meeting with Indira Gandhi in the morning, Haksar moved forward with the proposal, inviting both Reserve Bank governor Jha and I.G. Patel to meet him at the earliest.

By that afternoon, Morarji Desai had, after a meeting with Indira Gandhi, decided to resign from the cabinet, and Haksar got the ball rolling by informing Patel of the impending nationalization. He also asked RBI executive director R.K. Seshadri and joint secretary in the Ministry of Law S.K. Maitra to join in the drafting of the ordinance. The team shifted base to the Reserve Bank office on Parliament Street on the suggestion of Governor Jha, who had by then returned to Delhi. Through the night of 18 July, the team, including Governor Jha, worked on the draft, with a focus on two issues: compensation in lieu of nationalization and the administrative set-up of the new national banks. After a long night of deliberations, the draft was ready and agreed upon by all members of the team.

The basic contours of the Banking Companies (Acquisition and Transfer of Undertakings) Ordinance allowed the government to take over the assets and business of fourteen large private banks with deposit bases greater than ₹50 crore. The move was justified 'in order to serve better the needs of development of the economy in conformity with national policy and objectives and for matters connected therewith or incidental thereto.'[104]

The ordinance empowered the government to appoint a chairman if deemed necessary, who would work with an advisory board appointed by the government. Regarding compensation, the government agreed to pay bank shareholders the difference between their computed assets and liabilities, a formula similar to the one proposed when the Imperial Bank was nationalized, and a proposal that would run into legal trouble later.

The drafting of the model ordinance was only the initial challenge; getting it approved was the next one. On 19 July, Indira Gandhi met with her cabinet at 5 p.m. to update them on the situation and her decision to immediately nationalize fourteen large banks. Barring a few issues raised by Defence Minister Sardar Swaran Singh and Law Minister P. Govinda Menon,[105] the ordinance was quickly approved by Acting President V.V. Giri. Indira Gandhi then proceeded to address the nation at 8:30 p.m.

The failed backlash against bank nationalization

For Indira Gandhi, the decision to nationalize the banks was a political one, not an economic one. She justified her actions by advocating the step for nationalization was one of the many that had been taken by successive governments to establish 'control over the commanding heights of the economy'.[106]

Patel, who drafted Gandhi's speech, also linked the move to previous measures, to blunt its revolutionary edge. In his memoirs, Patel recalled inserting the sentence, 'This is not the first step in a new wave of nationalisation. This, in fact, is the culmination of the process which began with the nationalisation of life insurance corporation and the Imperial Bank, to occupy the commanding heights of finance.'

The reaction to the decision was largely predictable. The nationalization drew the support of large sections of the Congress Party, with even syndicate leader Kamaraj supporting the move. Even within the opposition, the communist party, along with some socialist parties, welcomed the move. The reaction from the business community was inevitably one of disappointment, with the head of the Federation of Indian Chambers of Commerce and Industry (FICCI), Ramnath Poddar, calling it a 'hasty step'. Former RBI governors Chintaman Deshmukh (who unsuccessfully ran for the post of president of India in 1969) and H.V.R. Iyengar were largely in favour of social controls over nationalization.

Within Parliament, most welcomed the move, but it was criticized by a few. Atal Bihari Vajpayee, who was then an opposition leader, questioned the urgency for an ordinance. C. Rajagopalachari argued that the move was unconstitutional and a breach of private ownership rights. Eventually, legal petitions were filed against the ordinance, especially by Minoo Masani, a right leaning liberal who was a leading parliamentarian of the Swatantra Party, and an interim stay order was granted for two weeks. The bill was eventually passed with limited changes on 4 August in the Lok Sabha and on 8 August in the Rajya Sabha.

The Reserve Bank managed the process of nationalization with efficiency. While the governor was clearly not a strong proponent of the move, several RBI personnel including deputy governor Bakshi and executive director R.K. Seshadri had played a critical role in drafting and shepherding the bill. Even after the process of issuing the ordinance, the Reserve Bank served as the coordinator between the government and the fourteen commercial banks that were being nationalized.

In fact, some of the research commissioned by the National Credit Council along with the Reserve Bank on banking statistics and banking penetration would prove to be the guiding evidence that the government used to win the case against its actions in the Supreme Court.

The RBI was working in the background to operationalize the takeover, and on 18 August, Governor Jha declared that there was no intention on the part of the government or the RBI to merge these nationalised banking institutions, and they would rather be preserved as separate entities. This proposal was welcomed by Nani A. Palkhivala, who was a member of the central board at the RBI, but was also fighting the case against the ordinance on behalf of Rustom Cavasjee Cooper, a chartered accountant from Bombay and a shareholder in several banks. This case would ultimately lead to a critical twenty-fifth amendment in the Constitution of India, which curtailed the right to property, and stated that compensation would be determined by the government or public bodies and not the owner.

The RBI continued to engage with the new public sector banks to rationalize branch expansion policies and to introduce new credit disbursal criteria, while operationally, a new department called Department of Banking was created in the Ministry of Finance to manage the commercial banks. P.N. Haksar would eventually handpick his friend and former deputy governor of the RBI Ardhendu Bakshi to run the department. However, this was not achieved without some courtroom drama.

Nani Palkhivala's case and the defence presented by the then Attorney General Niren De are well documented in the book by D.N. Ghosh. As per Ghosh, Palkhivala had a captivating presence in the courtroom, and the case built by him focused on the narrow definition of banking as described by the Banking Regulation Act. Supported by a director of the credit planning cell, A. Raman, Ghosh recalls spending a significant amount of time with De to meticulously break down Palkhivala's arguments and provide justifications from ministry of finance's point of view for nationalisation.[107] Given the sensitivity and importance of the petition, a full twelve-judge bench was hearing the case, led by Chief Justice J.C. Shah.

Somehow, even with the solid arguments for private citizen rights, the lack of banking services and perhaps the overwhelming public support for the move swung the decision towards the government. On 10 February 1970, the Supreme Court upheld the legislative competence of the Parliament, but struck down the Act because of some offending provisions. This had an insignificant impact on the nationalization itself, as the government passed another ordinance on 14 February 1970, which was approved by the Parliament by March 1970.

For the Reserve Bank, the nationalization episode could have led to a temporary loss of autonomy as it was contemplated that the bank should report to the newly created Department of Banking, a proposal that led to a significant backlash within both the RBI and the Ministry of Finance. Patel, who was economic affairs secretary, was already peeved at losing operational control of banking, and he raised the issue with the cabinet secretary, who eventually ruled that the Reserve Bank would continue to remain under the purview of the economic affairs department[108]and not the new Department of Banking. The latter, however, the department of banking would continue to work alongside the Reserve Bank, guiding the RBI on credit channels and also on sectoral deployment of funds.

After the nationalization, there was a notable change in India's body politic. The Congress Party split in November 1969, after several members broke ranks and voted for V.V. Giri in the presidential elections, instead of Neelam Sanjiva Reddy. Indira Gandhi was expelled for indiscipline. The syndicate was rebranded as Congress (Organisation), while Indira Gandhi set up a new party called Congress (Requisition). Many MPs chose to stick with Mrs Gandhi, and she managed to save her government with support from some socialist and communist parties.[109] Eventually, armed with her 'Garibi Hatao' (remove poverty) slogan, Gandhi come back with a thumping majority in 1971, rendering the Congress (O) irrelevant.

RBI avoids subjugation to the Department of Banking

For the prime minister, bank nationalization was just a political necessity for survival. However, for the Reserve Bank, there lay ahead the arduous task of implementation. The biggest and quickest impact of the nationalization was felt in the branch licensing policy. The Department of Banking's key performance indicator was proliferation of banking services.

To meet this objective, Secretary Bakshi wanted to see rapid increase in banking services but Governor Jha was in favour of a gradual approach, to prevent concentration of bank branches. He proposed that branch licensing should remain under RBI's domain, and that the interests of the State Bank of India and other smaller private banks had to be preserved given the new licensing policy. However, with nationalization done, political pressure from both members of Parliament and state governments was rising, who wanted banking services to be expanded in their own areas, while also batting for local banks to be given preference. Push came to shove, the RBI was perhaps a bit too liberal in giving branch licences, and as the official history notes, concerns around profitability soon arose, with even public sector bank heads pushing back on the Ministry of Finance's constant demand to increase branches.

By the end of the nationalization episode, Governor Jha was asked by the government to leave office to take up a new position as the Ambassador of India to the United States. Jha quit on 3 May 1970, and was replaced temporarily by B.N. Adarkar, who was then the deputy governor of the Reserve Bank. He served as governor (the ninth) for a brief period of forty-two days, till a suitable replacement could be found.

As the official history of the RBI notes,[110] the wide speculation was that S. Jagannathan, a civil servant and then the serving executive director of India at the International Monetary Fund, was being considered for the position of governor, and this eventually came true. Jagannathan took over RBI as the tenth governor on 16 June 1970 and was handed a five-year term. His international experience came in handy during the oil shocks that followed, but the next ten years from 1970 to 1980 turned out to be a difficult time for the central bank, as political discretion increased and interference was common. This was also the period when the Department of Banking had significant sway, which it used to push the Reserve Bank around for some time.

Chapter 6

Under shock therapy

The beginning of the 1970s marked not just a tumultuous period in the history of India, but also led to significant changes in the Reserve Bank. It lost some autonomy and had to follow various diktats from New Delhi as fiscal profligacy demanded accommodative monetary conditions. At the same time, profound changes were taking place in the global monetary order, which began with the collapse of the Bretton Woods currency arrangements and culminated in multiple shocks in commodity prices, particularly crude oil.

Back home, after the nationalization of banks, Indian politics and its fulcrum began revolving around the cult of Indira Gandhi, and she became the supreme leader of India. Her position was further solidified after India's triumphant win against Pakistan in the war of 1971 in December, and her authority over the country and its institutions was unmatched. With her focus on domestic and regional developments, external policies, particularly those economic in nature, were largely left to bureaucrats, which gave the Reserve Bank some space to operate in the background, but not necessarily without interference from the Ministry of Finance.

After the bank nationalization, Indira Gandhi proceeded to cancel the privy purses of erstwhile royal families.[111] The result was a big surge in her popularity, and in an election held before schedule in March 1971, Indira Gandhi returned with a thumping majority of 351 seats out of 525, which gave her a two-thirds majority and control of both the houses.

Buoyed by the election results and sustained by improving economic performance, particularly in the agricultural sector, the government continued its expansionary fiscal stance in what has been described as a 'mood of euphoria' by Joshi and Little.[112] However, several exogenous shocks came in a short period, which had a debilitating effect on India's economy.

The gold standard collapses

The first exogenous shock to hit India was the collapse of the Bretton Woods system. After the devaluation of 1966, India's external position started to improve gradually, with imports declining and exports gradually picking up. The position improved to a point where even with the devaluation of the sterling in November 1967, India decided not to follow through given the recent adjustments. But the global imbalances were rising rapidly, preceded by very strong growth in the sixties, led by the United States.

As economic policy turned expansionary in 1969 and 1970, 1971 brought severe challenges on exchange rate management. It started in May 1971, when the par values of the Deutsche mark along with other European currencies were suspended, and ended with the convertibility of US dollar being suspended on 15 August 1971, amid a burgeoning payments crisis.[113] For India, the suspension of conversion between the US dollar and gold was significant, and for a temporary period, the government, on the RBI's advice, decided to shift its peg to the US dollar, at a rate of ₹7.50 to a dollar, to take advantage of a depreciating dollar. However, the RBI also advised changing the sterling value of the rupee daily, in accordance with the London foreign exchange markets.

An anecdote recounted in the RBI's official history highlights the bank's lack of preparation in relation to the exchange rate volatility.[114] In a board meeting, a board member, Arvind N. Mafatlal, asked Governor Jagannathan what his thoughts were on a simultaneous devaluation by the United States and the United Kingdom. Governor Jagannathan brushed aside such a possibility, but indicated that the government and the RBI may need to initiate some action.

After the August episode, the central banks and finance ministers of the Group of Ten (G10) nations met in Washington on 8 December at the Smithsonian Institute. They agreed to a proposed devaluation of the US dollar against gold by 7.89 per cent,[115] with the US removing its import surcharges. The move for such a large multilateral currency adjustment was the first in history and came to be known as the Smithsonian agreement. The Reserve Bank followed suit, and on 20 December, repegged the rupee to the pound sterling, but weakened the exchange rate marginally to ₹18.97 to the sterling from ₹18 previously. This was done while allowing modest appreciation against the dollar, with the rate moving up to ₹7.27 from ₹7.50 previously. This was also done keeping in mind the 2.25 per cent margin allowed by the IMF to enable a marginal boost to exports amid manageable inflation.

As discussions resumed on finding a more enduring solution, the calm was broken on 22 June 1972. After weeks of pressure building on short-term capital outflows, the Bank of England allowed the sterling to float and imposed capital controls across the 'sterling area', bringing an end to the long-standing arrangements under it. The sterling depreciated sharply against the US dollar, but the Indian authorities through the RBI maintained the exchange rate, allowing a modest appreciation against sterling two weeks after the incident. India also flirted with the idea of switching the peg back to the US dollar, but decided against it.

The fall in sterling put a big question mark over the Smithsonian agreement, and the search for another solution began, but was again upset by a sudden depreciation in the US dollar against the SDR (Special Drawing Right) by 10 per cent, on 13 February 1973. While most of the European nations accepted the move to devalue the dollar, India decided to keep its fixed exchange rate system intact against sterling, but stopped the spot and forward purchases of the dollar and forward purchases of sterling to prevent any negative impact from any further depreciation.

Through the currency shock, the Reserve Bank and Governor Jagannathan continued to defend its traditional policy of a peg against the sterling, on account of stability. The central bank took steps to diversify its foreign reserves and did well to protect its value through a policy of acquiring the French franc and the Deutsche mark while reducing US dollar holdings through the Bank of International Settlements (BIS). However, after the sterling was floated and the Reserve Bank saw the currency depreciating against the US dollar, it reversed course. As the dust settled, the pound remained the weakest among the major currencies.

The collapse of the par value system triggered introspection about the feasibility of continuing with the sterling peg. By 1975, the rupee had depreciated significantly against most major currencies, with the effective fall coming close to 23 per cent.[116] Keeping in mind India's rising vulnerability, the Ministry of Finance officially abandoned its sterling peg and moved it to a basket of currencies of major trading partners on 24 September 1975. The government took advice from Dr Vijay Joshi, a well known academic who was appointed special adviser in the Ministry ofFinance in designing the basket, which had five currencies.[117]

The government was initially reluctant to give the Reserve Bank complete freedom to run the basket. It took a while before the rates could be given out to the market, which entailed delays in the rupee reflecting correct exchange rates. T.C.A. Srinivasa Raghavan recounts the anecdote of Janakiraman,[118] a senior Reserve Bank official who flew to Delhi to ask Dr Manmohan Singh, then the chief economic advisor, to obtain the clearance for RBI to set the rates. Manmohan Singh refused to take a call, and took Janakiraman to meet Morarji Desai's finance minister Hirubhai Patel, who Raghavan recalls was visibly upset at being disturbed late at night. Janakiraman asked that the Reserve Bank be authorized to decide the daily fixings. From then on, the Reserve Bank remained the custodian of the basket.

The first oil shock and sleeping behind the wheel...

While the external problems played out from 1970 to 1975, domestic problems were compounding quickly. Although the war effort against Pakistan in 1971 was successful, India saw a very large influx of refugees and asylum seekers (approximately ten million), which drove up government spending. Along with that, defence expenditure was quickly climbing to fund the war.

The government also saw its aid from the United States reduced because of the war, which the Nixon administration saw as an 'act of aggression'.[119] Finally, after several years of normal weather, India also faced droughts in 1972 and 1974, which compounded domestic inflation. However, it was the sharp rise in oil prices during 1973–74 that led to a complete unravelling of the macroeconomic stability that had come about between 1968 and 1972. The Reserve Bank had to undertake a series of swift monetary policy shifts over a short period.

Coming into 1972, India was already running an expansionary fiscal policy, due to the various factors listed above. Simultaneously, the Reserve Bank was slow to tighten monetary conditions,[120] leading to a significant expansion in money supply. Inflation started climbing due to inadequate food supply, and the government's response was slow given the over-optimistic projections regarding the harvest. With money supply and net credit to government growing in double digits,[121] headline wholesale price index (WPI) inflation rose by 10 per cent in fiscal year 1972–73[122] and by 20.2 per cent and 25.2 per cent in the years following that.

Between January and May 1972, inflation had climbed marginally from 4.4 per cent to 6.2 per cent. However, as the monsoon started failing, fear of food shortages increased, leading inflation to rise to 8.4 per cent by August. At this point, the RBI was slow in taking remedial action, but raised the SLR by 1 per cent to 29 per cent. Even then, the growth in money supply continued, albeit to support the government's fiscal spending. The ongoing rise in money supply and inflation led to considerable backlash from several economists (including V.K.R.V. Rao and C.T. Kurien) and parliamentarians, with demands for a probe into the workings of the central bank.

Amid strong criticism, the Reserve Bank took little action to correct perceptions as its ability to prevent government borrowings was non-existent. By its own admission, the Reserve Bank's ability to influence monetary policy was 'severely abridged'[123] given the ever-increasing government borrowing requirements. Despite some objection from Governor Jagannathan, the government continued to expand its borrowing programme and by the end of fiscal year 1972–73, the government had borrowed ₹478 crore instead of a budgeted ₹215 crore.[124] To finance this, the SLR was eventually raised to 30 per cent in November 1972.

By early 1973, some in the government started taking cognizance of the rampant inflation and credit growth. Credit rationing began and on 30 May 1973, the Reserve Bank raised the cash reserve ratio (CRR) from 3 per cent to 5 per cent, and the bank rate to 7 per cent from 6 per cent. This, however, had little impact and inflation continued to rise in double digits. More stringent measures followed in July, but none of them addressed the key problem of deficit financing. The second round of measures focused on the corporate sector debt, which led the then SBI chairman R.K. Talwar, a celebrated banker, to write a 'private' letter[125] to Governor Jagannathan arguing for a reduction of government deficit rather than private credit.

Criticism continued to mount and despite some remedial measures, inflation remained in the double digits. Another dose of monetary tightening was delivered on 14 August, when the RBI raised the CRR to 7 per cent while raising the net liquidity ratio (NLR) to 40 per cent. Further, Governor Jagannathan proposed keeping a ceiling on credit ahead of the busy harvest season. However, by that time, war was approaching in the Middle East and on 6 October 1973, a coalition of Arab nations led by Egypt and Syria launched a pre-emptive attack on Israel. The United States provided reinforcements to its Middle Eastern ally, which led to an oil embargo from 20 October, resulting in a quadrupling of oil prices over a short period of five months from approximately US$3 a barrel to US$12 a barrel.

For India and the Reserve Bank, the exogenous shock of higher oil prices was a body blow. This led to an abandoning of gradual measures and by the end of November, the SLR was hiked to 32 per cent and a slew of measures to restrain bank credit were also taken, including raising the minimum lending rate. However, with the cost of oil and raw materials shooting up, credit demand remained high and inflation shot up to 26 per cent by January 1974, rendering the measures relatively unsuccessful.

Meanwhile, the rising import requirement for food, a weak sterling and rising oil prices meant India's current account deficit started widening. While the foreign reserves position of the RBI was adequate, the situation deteriorated quickly as imports in US dollar terms soared, largely due to an adverse terms of trade shock. Despite stringent import controls on non-essential goods, India's current account widened sharply in 1974–75, leading to a further tightening of monetary and fiscal policy, but not before significant time had been wasted on deliberations.

Public sentiment took a turn for the worse and student protests broke out in Gujarat under the Nav Nirman Andolan, which would eventually give shape to the people's movement under Jayaprakash Narayan.[126] Gujarat's chief minister Chimanbhai Patel was made to resign given deteriorating social conditions on 9 February 1974.

By that time, the economic conditions continued to remain dire as more rationing was forced upon the country. A rail strike by over two million employees began in May 1974 for twenty days and was forcibly broken only in by end May 1974. The government's hand was finally forced and three ordinances[127] were passed on 7 July 1974, undertaking some of the most severe measures to control income and raise taxes, prices and interest rates.[128]

The government raised excise duties, froze government salaries and asked all income tax payers to deposit anywhere between 4 to 10 per cent of their taxable incomes with the Reserve Bank. At the same time, dearness allowances of government employees were partly frozen and new taxes on dividend distribution and interest income of commercial banks were introduced. The government raised the prices of railway and other administered services as well.

According to its official history, the Reserve Bank was not consulted before these fiscal measures were undertaken, which were largely decided upon by the prime minister's core advisory body consisting of her secretary P.N. Dhar, economic advisor Dr Manmohan Singh and cabinet secretary B.D. Pande along with G. Ramachandran. [129] The Reserve Bank, however, was accorded the blame by the press as it was seen as lagging on monetary policy. As such, on 19 July, the Reserve Bank went along with the tightening by raising SLR to 33 per cent and the bank rate to 9 per cent from 7 per cent. Minimum lending rates were also pushed higher to 12.5 per cent from 11 per cent.

By this time, the oil embargo in the Middle East had ended, but oil prices remained sticky. The measures taken by the Reserve Bank to tighten credit and restrict money supply started working and by the end of 1974, inflation was showing signs of abatement. However, the draconian steps taken to bring down inflation were brewing widespread resentment against Indira Gandhi and her government and even though economic conditions were coming under control, the political situation was turning hostile. What started as the Bihar Movement gave rise to the Gandhian 'Sampoorna Kranti' (Total Revolution) movement of Jayaprakash Narayan, which culminated in the disqualification of Indira Gandhi as a member of Parliament by Supreme Court judge, Justice V.R. Krishna Iyer, and the imposition of an emergency on 25 June 1975, just as India was escaping another balance of payments crisis.

The Emergency era begins

Jagannathan was a benign personality who kept things steady but had little appetite for conflict or confrontation. He enjoyed travelling and relished attending the BIS meetings. Once there, he had a penchant for entertaining other central bankers. Narasimham recounts one particular evening when Governor Jagannathan, finding himself with no invitation to any parties, impulsively invited other central bankers who had also not been invited to any parties. Narasimham called this the Jagannathan law of entertainment—if you are not being entertained, you do the entertaining.[130]

The pattern of making the Reserve Bank follow the government's bidding had been well established, especially after the Rama Rau episode. However, from the time of the currency devaluation in 1966 until I.G. Patel took over as governor of the Reserve Bank, institutional credibility and independence were perhaps at their lowest. In fact, even under Governor Jagannathan, the Reserve Bank was made to follow instructions from mid-level officials in the Ministry of Finance, especially from the Department of Banking, which had been created after the bank nationalization.

During the Emergency, perhaps the biggest impact on the Reserve Bank came in the form of the appointment of K.R. Puri, the then head of the Life Insurance Corporation (LIC) of India, as the governor. However, the back story to his appointment needs to be seen in the context of S. Jagannathan's early departure from the RBI, which was a precursor to an even bigger exit of R.K. Talwar at the State Bank of India later during the Emergency years.

The run-ins with Sanjay Gandhi

Even as Indira Gandhi reigned supreme, the internal dynamics of the Congress Party were changing through the 1970s. As a young man doing his apprenticeship at the Rolls-Royce plant in Crewe, England, Sanjay Gandhi, Indira Gandhi's son, had nurtured a dream to manufacture indigenous cars in India. The idea was not new, for even in the 1950s the government had toyed with the idea of giving priority to manufacturing of 'small cars', which would be cheap and fuel-efficient. However, despite several committees being set up to deliberate on the subject, the idea never took off. When Sanjay returned from England, having left his apprenticeship midway,[131] the government had made up its mind to give the project to the private sector.

Despite receiving bids from several renowned carmakers such as Renault, Toyota and Volkswagen, it was Sanjay Gandhi's Maruti that won the contract to produce 50,000 small cars in November 1970. Haryana's chief minister Bansi Lal offered Sanjay a large plot of land for the project at throwaway prices, to please Mrs Gandhi. In 1971, a public sector company called 'Maruti Limited' was formed, with M.A. Chidambaram, a noted industrialist and uncle of P. Chidambaram, as its chairman.[132]

The funding requirements for producing a car prototype had clearly been miscalculated. Despite creative solutions such as 'dealership deposits', Sanjay Gandhi soon found out that the math of selling a car for six thousand rupees was not going to work. Even with a price hike, the company soon racked up large loans, especially from Punjab National Bank and Central Bank of India. This invited the attention of the deputy governor of the Reserve Bank R.K. Hazari, who instructed the nationalized banks to stop lending to Maruti till the company had repaid its earlier loans.

By early 1975, as the political sun of Sanjay Gandhi was on the rise, tensions were simmering between the government and the Reserve Bank over raising the credit limit for Maruti,[133] which had already been faltering in its repayments. The RBI stood firm, refusing to increase the limit. However, for Governor Jagannathan, who had spent his working life in the government, the writing was on the wall. Although he was due to retire on 15 June 1975, Jagannathan made an early exit on 19 May, perhaps being in a hurry to move on to his next assignment as India's executive director at the IMF.

Deputy governor R.K. Hazari was a clear frontrunner to replace Jagannathan, but the government, which was already under pressure from Jayaprakash Narayan's movement, was wary of appointing an 'insider' to the governor's chair. As a temporary arrangement, N.C. Sen Gupta, who was the head of the Department of Banking in the Ministry of Finance, was appointed as the governor for a brief period of three months. During this time, the Emergency was imposed and the focus shifted from the economy to politics.

Sen Gupta's appointment was brief but not without irony. As the erstwhile head of the Department of Banking, Sen Gupta now found the 'boot to be on the other foot' as he faced criticism from the government for not consulting it on the announcement of the credit policy for the slack season.[134] The RBI's official history also notes that it was outgoing governor Jagannathan who had in an act of defiance announced the credit policy, leaving Sen Gupta to sort out the mess. The government sent Dr Manmohan Singh to the Reserve Bank's headquarters in Bombay to deliver a stern message, 'bluntly informing the Bank's top executives that the government felt that there could have been "prior consultation" with them before announcing the credit policy on May 8.'[135]

The appointment of Governor Sen Gupta was an interim arrangement and came about due to the differences between Finance Minister C. Subramaniam and Indira Gandhi. While Subramaniam wanted a senior economist such as I.G. Patel, S.R. Sen or M.G. Kaul to be appointed to the position, Indira Gandhi was adamant on appointing K.R. Puri, chairman of LIC, as the governor of the RBI. Indeed, after the Emergency, the government moved ahead and appointed Puri, who had no prior experience in banking. He took over as governor of the RBI on 20 August 1975.

The appointment of K.R. Puri further dented RBI's credibility. In one of his first acts after becoming governor, Puri, without consulting any senior officials of the RBI, introduced a new credit policy for working capital limits,[136] raising the limit to ₹2 crore from ₹1 crore previously. The move came as a surprise for Reserve Bank officials. As a deputy governor noted in the official history, the move was made keeping Maruti and Sanjay Gandhi in mind.[137] Maruti had recently applied for additional grants, but had been turned down by the Central Bank of India, a decision that the RBI's credit planning cell concurred with. However, the bypassing of the senior RBI officials was not a surprise.

For K.R. Puri, it seems that loyalty to the government of the day, especially to Sanjay Gandhi, was more important than loyalty to the institution. In a telling anecdote, the late journalist Vinod Mehta recalls in his book that K.R. Puri was a frequent visitor to 1 Safdarjung Road, where Sanjay Gandhi lived with his mother. On one of his visits, after waiting for an hour, Puri asked R.K. Dhawan, a close confidante of Sanjay, whether he could see Sanjay 'if Mr Gandhi is free now'. Dhawan curtly told Puri to wait a little longer, as 'after all you have nothing much to do in the office.'[138]

The Talwar episode

During the Emergency, it was not just the Reserve Bank that came under pressure. Even state-owned banks were overstretched and the discretionary and often vindictive nature of rule affected major institutions such as the State Bank of India as well. The SBI had come into its own between the 1960s and early 1970s, undergoing massive expansion in both banking services and branches. The institution was being credibly led by Raj Kumar Talwar, a postgraduate in mathematics from the Government College University in Lahore, and a State Bank employee from 1943. He had been at the helm of SBI from 1 March 1969, taking over at the age of 47,[139] and had been renewed for a three-year term in 1974 after serving for five years in his first stint.

A banker par excellence, Talwar was a competent leader, but he butted heads with Sanjay Gandhi soon after the Emergency was imposed. In early 1976, Talwar blocked an extension of a loan to Jaipur Udyog, a sick cement company run by Alok Jain, who was close to Sanjay Gandhi. When Sanjay asked the finance minister to consider the issue, Subramaniam asked Talwar to make an exception, but Talwar refused. Not one to back down, Talwar also refused to meet Sanjay Gandhi, saying that Sanjay Gandhi had no constitutional authority to summon Talwar.[140]

An infuriated Sanjay asked the finance minister to sack Talwar. Wary of making such a monumental change, Subramaniam offered Talwar the chairmanship of the Banking Commission, which was in the process of being formed. Talwar refused the position, upon which he was informed by Subramaniam that he was 'undesirable' at the SBI and would be put on leave unless he resigned. Sanjay meanwhile asked the Central Bureau of investigation (CBI) to look into Talwar's matters. While some doubts were raised over his frequent trips to Pondicherry (Talwar was an ardent devotee of Sri Aurobindo and the Mother), no major issues were found. Talwar could not be dismissed without cause, as the SBI Act protected the chairman against removal without substantial cause for dismissal.

At that juncture, the government ran out of patience and on Sanjay Gandhi's instructions, proceeded to amend the SBI Act so that Talwar could be removed without substantial cause. On 11 June 1976, the amendment sailed through the Parliament given the lack of an opposition (most opposition leaders were in jail), and on 4 August, the government put Talwar on a thirteen-month leave, to finish out his term. Not perturbed, Talwar explored legal options but was advised by Nani Palkhivala to let the matter rest.[141] Talwar retired eventually in the Auroville Ashram in Pondicherry, barring a brief stint as chairman of IDBI in 1979.

As a postscript, the seventies turned out to be a period of difficult economic times, questionable economic decisions and lack of autonomy for the Reserve Bank. While governors L.K. Jha and S. Jagannathan showed moments of leadership, it was bankers like R.K. Talwar who showed the temerity to stand up for sustainable banking in India. R.K. Talwar might have made a very credible governor for the Reserve Bank, but independence of thought or action was not seen as a positive trait by the government of India in those days.

Chapter 7

Out of the frying pan and into the fire

On 18 January 1977, Prime Minister Indira Gandhi announced fresh elections in March and released all political prisoners. The Emergency, which was in its nineteenth month, had been a relatively peaceful time for economic policymakers, but it certainly did not mean that institutions such as the RBI had much discretion in policymaking.

Under K.R. Puri, the Reserve Bank moved to a new 'needs-based' credit policy,[142] which would ensure credit was available to those who needed it the most. This policy would later encourage cronyism. The Reserve Bank also struggled with the Ministry of Finance's widening powers and a new governor whose appointment was largely seen as political.[143] During the Emergency, several positive innovations were also started under Governor Puri, one of them being allowing non-resident Indians to hold foreign currency deposits with Indian banks, which the RBI would later deploy for crisis management several times.

The Emergency period also saw the RBI maintaining a prudent monetary stance amid improving economic conditions. Perhaps in the eagerness to achieve Mrs Gandhi's twenty-point programme[144], the Ministry of Finance was trying to assert more control on the monetary policy than was warranted. Buoyed by negative inflation in fiscal year 1975–76 amid a bumper harvest,[145] Finance Minister C. Subramaniam was not in favour of keeping money supply and credit conditions tight but went along with the Reserve Bank after much cajoling. However, fiscal policy remained relatively loose, but its impact on inflation was not felt immediately amid high growth and an improving balance of payments position.

Getting rid of K.R. Puri

Eventually, by early 1977, Indira Gandhi, along with her son Sanjay Gandhi and the Congress Party, decided to highlight the 'innumerable benefits' of the imposition of emergency, which included higher industrial growth, foreign reserves being at an all-time high, large buffer stocks of food and low inflation.[146] However, the electorate did not buy the economic narrative and in a shocking election result, the Congress Party for the first time in independent India lost the national election to a united opposition in March 1977.

Morarji Desai, who had been Indira Gandhi's bête noire since the death of Lal Bahadur Shastri, became the new prime minister, with Hirubhai Patel, a senior but retired civil servant, taking over as the finance minister. Although hoping for a change in approach, the Reserve Bank was disappointed. The new government was keen to show results as well and was being asked by its supporters to reverse the decision of maintaining prudent money supply growth and credit rationing. Within a month of taking power, the government, through the Department of Banking, sent the Reserve Bank a request for a three percentage point reduction in the bank rate, followed by a relaxation of the credit squeeze, particularly the removal of the additional 10 per cent CRR on incremental deposits, which was a constraining factor for credit growth.

In an anecdote recounted in the RBI's official history,[147] the letter of request was sent via telex, which caused the Reserve Bank a lot of concern, given its open nature. The bank was also surprised by the omission of the department of economic affairs from the discussion and defended its policies to keep rates steady. However, the sudden nature of concern changed Manmohan Singh's tune, then the economic advisor, and said it was not the government's intention to consider changes in interest rates at that point of time.

Within days of the Janata Party government coming to power, both the prime minister and the finance minister Hirubhai Patel wanted Governor Puri to step down, which was communicated by Banking Secretary M. Narasimham to Governor Puri. Puri was shocked but agreed to resign with a slight delay at the end of April, as advised by his 'Guru'.[148] Patel left the country to attend the interim meetings of the IMF, and upon his return, was surprised to find that Puri had still not resigned, despite his wishes. Puri finally quit on 2 May 1977, but not before asking a flustered finance minister for another posting.

With Puri out, the government needed to appoint a temporary governor, as their preferred choice, I.G. Patel, was not available immediately, being on assignment with the United Nations Development Programme.[149] The government considered appointing a senior deputy governor to the post, but was reluctant to appoint R.K. Hazari as he was reputed to be a leftist intellectual and close to the Congress leadership. Hence as a compromise, the government appointed M. Narasimham, who was then the banking secretary in the Ministry of Finance and a grandson of Dr S. Radhakrishnan,[150] a former president of India, as the stopgap governor for seven months until 30 November. Narasimham remains till date the only RBI cadre officer to become the governor of the apex bank.

Indraprasad Gordhanbhai Patel became the governor of the Reserve Bank on 1 December 1977 and was appointed for a full term of five years. His reputation as a seasoned bureaucrat and competent economist was well established, but the government perhaps failed to match his wavelength. He was also the seventh RBI governor to be appointed during a short, seven-year period between 1970 and 1977, underlining the frequent change in leadership and policies during the seventies at the RBI.

The 1978 demonetization

The Janata Party government and its members had inherent conflicts on ideology and approach and governance did not come naturally to many members of the government. The Reserve Bank under Governor Patel immediately announced steps to improve banking services and increase branch penetration, but the government was more keen to display 'social justice' and on 17 January 1978, it issued an ordinance to demonetize high denomination notes of rupees 1,000, 5,000 and 10,000.[151] The decision was taken in remarkable secrecy, like the exercise in 2016, but the magnitude of currency notes converted into legal tender was relatively small at around ₹146 crore.[152] This was the second demonetization India had witnessed since the more successful exercise in 1946 under Governor Deshmukh.

The original suggestion to demonetize high denomination currency notes was given by the Wanchoo Committee, which had been set up to look at measures to curb the black economy had in its interim report in 1971. However, the idea was shot down by then Prime Minister Indira Gandhi, who is quoted to have asked Finance Minister Y.B. Chavan, 'Chavanji, are no more elections to be fought by the Congress Party?' The finance minister got the message and the suggestion was promptly shelved.[153] However, the Janata government decided to implement the measure to reduce 'illicit transfer of money for financing transactions which are harmful to the national economy.'[154]

The Reserve Bank only found out about the demonetization shortly before the government's announcement. On 14 January 1978, Janakiraman, a senior official at the RBI, was asked to come to Delhi to discuss an important policy matter. He was accompanied by M. Subramaniam, a senior official in the exchange control department. On reaching Delhi, they were apprised of the government's decision and were asked to prepare an ordinance to go ahead with the exercise. President Neelam Sanjiva Reddy approved the ordinance on 16 January, and it came into effect on 17 January.[155]

Although Governor Patel went along with the move to demonetize large denomination currency notes, he was unconvinced about its effectiveness. In his memoirs, he observed that the move was political in nature and that he was not in favour of the exercise. He recalls that when the finance minister, Hirubhai Patel, informed him of the impending decision, he pointed out to the minister that 'such exercises seldom produce striking results' and that 'the idea that black money or wealth is held in the form of notes tucked away in suitcases or pillowcases is naïve.'[156] The exercise was, however, carried out relatively peacefully and barring long queues and some trouble for tourists, about 85 per cent of the total demonetized tender, i.e. about ₹125 crore, came back to the Reserve Bank.

The gold auctions

In his budget speech on 28 February 1978, Finance Minister Hirubhai Patel announced that the demonetization was not an isolated move, but part of a series of measures to try and reduce unlawful activity, which included illegal smuggling of gold. High inflation, uncertainty around the rupee and a growing population had kept demand for gold high and hence prices had remained elevated. Going into the gold auctions ordered by the government, gold was trading almost 30 to 40 per cent above international prices, which encouraged smuggling. To curb this problem and to take advantage of 'the excellent market for Indian gold jewellery,'[157] the government announced its plans to allow gold imports or sales through the government, to lower prices.

The government intended to sell gold from its confiscated reserves and from the government-owned mines at Kolar, Karnataka. However, the Reserve Bank was not entirely convinced about the move's effectiveness. India's foreign reserves position had improved significantly, adding to flexibility and resilience to external shocks. The government formed a committee to decide the norms of the auction, and it was decided that the Reserve Bank would conduct auctions every two weeks, with rules around minimum and maximum bids. Despite Governor Patel's views about gold being an unproductive asset, RBI went along with the government's plan. Later, in his memoirs, Governor Patel indicated that he had tried to dissuade the finance minister from pursuing the path of gold auctions, but said that 'he [Hirubhai Patel] was obviously under pressure and had to do something.'[158]

The auctions began on 3 May 1978. They were initially well received but failed to bring down the price of gold. The government threatened to tighten the rules and put a ceiling on prices, but the threats were largely empty in nature. By August, after multiple auctions had been conducted, the government was starting to get more desperate as prices continued to rise. This led to a serious questioning of the efficacy of the policy, and on 14 October, Hirubhai Patel announced[159] that the government would decide on whether to import gold to continue the auctions, but also added that the objective of curbing the smuggling of gold had been achieved.

By then, Morarji Desai had to step in, and on 19 October, he announced that the government would be stopping the auctions, given falling stocks. The last auction was conducted on 23 October, but the controversy around the gold auctions continued even after the Janata Party was no longer in power in 1980, and the Congress returned triumphantly in 1980 elections.

In response to demands made by Sanjay Gandhi in the Lok Sabha, the Congress government under Indira Gandhi formed a one-man commission in February 1980 under former RBI governor K.R. Puri to look into any irregularities around the gold auctions. Opposition member Dr Subramaniam Swamy raised questions around the propriety of appointing Puri to investigate a government that had dismissed him from his role at the RBI,[160] but the new government did not pay any heed.

K.R. Puri submitted his report in 1981 and was very critical of both Governor Patel and Finance Minister Hirubhai Patel. He observed that the RBI had appeared in 'undue anxiety' to carry out 'the government's wishes' without any legal authority.[161] The government chose to study the matter further and appointed a four-member committee comprising R. Venkataraman, Pranab Mukherjee, P.V. Narasimha Rao and Shiv Shankar, all senior cabinet ministers under Indira Gandhi. Initially, the government appeared firm on pursuing a case against Morarji Desai, but as time passed, the committee failed to find much evidence and Venkataramanan in his speech in the Lok Sabha closed the issue by calling it 'just an error of judgement.'

While the incident did not create embarrassment for the government, for the Reserve Bank, a former governor leading the charge against a sitting governor certainly left a bad taste in everyone's mouth.[162] In his memoirs, Deputy Governor Ramakrishnayya, who was heading the gold auction committee, recalls that Puri 'gave [...] the impression of a man who had made up his mind even at the start and was only searching for evidence to confirm that gold was cornered by a few parties [...].'[163] However, Governor Patel in his memoirs also recalls that in his interactions with Puri during the questioning, 'he [Puri] was scrupulously courteous and professional and not confrontational at all.'[164]

The Iranian revolution and the second oil price shock

The Congress came back to power in 1980 largely on the back of policy mistakes made by the Janata Party government, along with some exogenous shocks to blame. As in the period before the 1973 oil price shock, India's external position was very strong when the Janata Party came to power in 1977. Foreign reserves were at an all-time high while reserve adequacy relative to imports had been comfortably placed at nine months before the shock was felt. The government's high handedness had been tempered as the collateral damage from strict protectionist policies and licensing was starting to become obvious.

Even within the Congress, efforts to raise foreign investment and funds had been increasing since 1975. At one point, the government had sent delegations led by senior bureaucrats and ministers to countries with large Indian diasporas to promote the idea of making the Andaman and Nicobar Islands a free port with a financial centre to compete with Hong Kong.[165] But the Congress lost the 1977 elections, and the Janata government inherited an economy that had recovered both in terms of high growth and manageable inflation.

When the Janata Party took charge, the government had a significant lack of experience. Barring some ex-Congressmen such as Prime Minister Morarji Desai and his deputy Jagjivan Ram, there was little ministerial experience in the cabinet. They were 'overwhelmed and overawed' by the task, especially those holding economic portfolios.[166] However, to establish economic socialism, the government started supporting measures to fuel the growth of small industries and introduced new rules for greater credit support for them.

The RBI was aware that expansionary policies coupled with strong balance of payments surpluses could bring back inflationary pressures. It resisted pressure from the Janata government to pursue an expansionary monetary policy but was unable to force banks to curb lending as the government expanded the list of products reserved for small-scale industries from 180 to 500—taken during the Janata government period of 1977–1980. Now it was the 'policy of the government that *whatever* can be produced by small and cottage industries *must only* be so produced.'[167]

The early signs of the evolving crisis started to emerge in the first quarter of 1979, when prices started to rise. While the availability of foodgrains was the prime reason behind the low inflation that had persisted for some time, the RBI had cautioned the government in its annual report against complacency. The RBI was coming under pressure from the government to lend more to priority sectors, especially small farmers,[168] but the bank refused to expand its lending. Even with some policy tightening, money supply grew by 17 per cent in fiscal year 1978–79, and the RBI was worried with inflation rising over 7 per cent by April 1979.

Meanwhile, trouble was brewing for the Janata Party government.

The investigations against Indira Gandhi and her son Sanjay Gandhi were going nowhere. The allies of the Janata government were also starting to lose faith in Morarji Desai, and eventually Desai had a political fallout with his deputy Charan Singh, who had also been appointed as finance minister in January 1979.

The government was divided, but to fight inflation, the cabinet decided to reduce bank lending to the commercial sector for goods prone to hoarding. The measures had little impact on money supply as by then, the government's borrowing from the Reserve Bank had increased substantially over a very brief period. The large expansion in fiscal deficit came from the government's reluctance to raise administered prices of various commodities, which had been rising globally through 1978. Indeed, subsidies were ballooning and the fiscal deficit for both 1978 and 1979 turned out to be much larger than initially anticipated.[169]

As the summer approached, political temperatures were also rising. Charan Singh replaced Morarji Desai as the prime minister in July 1979, and Hemvati Nandan Bahuguna was appointed as the finance minister. But with India experiencing one of its worst droughts in over a century, the change in leadership had little impact on the economy. The drought was confirmed in August 1979, and food prices were already increasing amid fears of food shortages. Then the oil crisis hit, unravelling whatever little the government had to offer in terms of resistance.

In the Middle East, a revolution led by a Shia cleric Ayatollah Ruhollah Khomeini was brewing in Iran against the excesses of the Shah Mohammad Reza Pahlavi in 1978. The Shah of Iran fled to the United States in early 1979. The global demand for energy was high and oil prices were rising in response to fears of supply disruption[170] and rising precautionary demand for oil. By mid-1979, oil prices had quadrupled and India's terms of trade caused the trade balance to deteriorate rapidly.

In response, the Reserve Bank asked banks to tighten bank credit. The government was still coming to terms with the extent of the economic shock. The RBI restricted its refinance facility for banks for food procurement and imposed restrictions on credit withdrawals by large borrowers.[171] However, inflation continued to grow and reached 17 per cent in August. The RBI had to take more dramatic steps and it raised maximum lending rates by 300 bps in September 1979.

By September, Charan Singh had resigned from the prime ministership after failing to prove his majority in the Parliament. However, the elections were not held until January 1980, which gave technocrats in the RBI and the Ministry of Finance some breathing room to take a few harsh measures to regain control of the economy. In January 1980, Indira Gandhi and the Congress were voted back to power, but the crisis was just starting to intensify.

Return of Indira and the second bank nationalization

Indira Gandhi rode back to power in 1980, but her approach to governance had changed somewhat during the period of her political isolation, and her economic policies turned less restrictive. In her new term, she appointed R. Venkataramanan as the finance minister, who had the difficult task of managing the burgeoning crisis.

However, in an ironic twist of fate, the Reserve Bank and Governor I.G. Patel advised Indira Gandhi to nationalize six more private sector banks as they were now large enough to be brought under state control. I.G. Patel in his memoirs recollects[172] that 'one of the first steps I had to recommend to Mrs Gandhi was that she should nationalise another swathe of private banks [...] some of them, like the Punjab and Sind Bank and Vijaya Bank, had become the personal fiefdoms of individuals who disregarded all rules [...]'. While Patel also recalls that Mrs Gandhi had 'no appetite' for further nationalization, she went along with the governor's advice and on 15 April 1980, an ordinance was issued to nationalize six more banks.

The response to the second round of nationalization was similar to the response to the first round, with financial press and industry bodies calling the second wave unnecessary. Nonetheless, the government stated that the purpose of nationalization was 'to further control the heights of the economy, to meet progressively and serve better the needs of the development of the economy, and to promote the welfare of the people in conformity with the policy of state'.[173] The ordinance, despite some brief exchanges in the Parliament, was approved in June 1980 and received the president's approval on 11 July 1980.

On the crisis front, by March 1980, the government realized the extent of fiscal mismanagement. The revenue deficit had tripled in two years, and the overall budget deficit had doubled on the back of rising subsidies, transfers to states and drought relief work. As such, the government needed to take some swift decisions, and there was an urgent need to reduce borrowing and control the money supply.

Despite the deteriorating capital account and external position, money supply had grown rapidly to finance the deficit. The government initially did little to address the fiscal deficit and placed the burden of finding resources on the Reserve Bank, which had already been borrowing through the IMF quotas.[174] In total, India borrowed about US$1 billion in two years, which helped reduce the loss of foreign exchange reserves.[175] While the government reinstated some of the Emergency era taxes, material fiscal consolidation was not on the horizon, so the burden of policy tightening fell on the Reserve Bank.

Governor Patel through 1980 insisted on maintaining credit restraints but growth in money supply remained high. In 1981, the government's fiscal borrowing was scheduled to go up even further and it had to formally approach the IMF for a loan facility to tide over the funds crunch. The talks were facilitated by M. Narasimham, the former RBI governor who had become India's executive director at the Fund.

The government was not keen on approaching the IMF, but M. Narasimham convinced Indira Gandhi, underscoring the need to raise domestic oil exploration and production to shelter India from oil shocks on a structural basis. The IMF was open to funding India, with Narasimham convincing Managing Director Jacques de Larosiere of India's past record of making prepayments on its programmes and the need to improve India's public sector efficiency.[176] Initially, the loan negotiations were for SDR 3 billion, but very quickly, Narasimham raised it to SDR 5 billion, raising eyebrows within the Fund.

Jacques de Larosiere promised to release the funds if the government kept its part of the bargain to reduce state control.[177] But soon, under pressure from the United States, where the Reagan administration had taken charge, the IMF changed its tune on the proposed loan. The United States was putting pressure on India to instead borrow money from banks. Especially, American banks led by Citibank were pushing the US government to get India to undertake commercial borrowings through financial institutions, rather than taking part in multilateral borrowings.[178] Even domestically, media institutions were opposed to the loan, and in a leak of the terms and conditions in October 1981, *The Hindu* and its editor N. Ram splashed them across the front page, leading to communists such as Ashok Mitra, the then finance minister of West Bengal, calling the loan a loss of economic sovereignty.[179]

With the IMF at a loss to explain the leak, the Indian government was furious. Official history suggests that the real reason behind the United States' vociferous opposition to the loan was not grounded so much in economic logic, but was more because India was said to be placing a large order for French fighter planes, the Mirage.[180] In the meantime, Governor Patel called his counterpart Paul Volcker at the Federal Reserve, who was sympathetic to the argument but was unable to change opinions. Governor Patel also reached out to influential people in the German and British governments, which helped as well.

Eventually, in November 1981, the IMF told the Indian government that it could make a drawing of up to SDR 5 billion over a three-year period in three instalments, which was the largest loan facility the Fund had ever granted. The IMF had put conditions on money supply growth and public finance indicators, which were barely altered through the life cycle of the loan facility. The government appreciated the support from the world community. The initial seeds of reforms were starting to be sown, with a focus on boosting growth and incomes.

Chapter 8

A unique responsibility

Unlike its counterparts in the Commonwealth, when the Reserve Bank of India was founded, it had a unique responsibility in supporting India's largely agrarian economy. Initially, the Reserve Bank tried to deliver on its obligation to support rural credit through the cooperative banking system, but until Independence, its monetary policy was designed to maximize the objectives of the British government. Post-Independence, the nationalization of the Reserve Bank in 1949 and the subsequent nationalization of the Imperial Bank of India were done with the key objective of taking banking and credit services to India's rural sector.

For a large part of the first fifty years of the RBI's existence, a special institution to direct farm credit was missing, unlike the industrial sector, which had specialized institutions such as IDBI, ICICI and IFCI dedicated to its credit needs. The agricultural sector too saw the adoption of a multi-agency approach from the late 1960s, but it did not serve its intended purpose and eventually led to formation of the National Bank for Agriculture and Rural Development (NABARD) in 1982.

The early efforts to promote rural credit through cooperative banks began before Independence itself, with one of RBI's early deputy governors, Manilal Nanavati, leading the study.[181] Manilal Nanavati was an expert in the field of rural finance and understood the benefits and shortcomings of the cooperative model quite well. Agricultural financing was kept within the ambit of the Reserve Bank's functions, despite several studies such as the Rural Banking Enquiry Committee (RBEC) under Sir Purshottamdas Thakurdas in November 1949, and the All India Rural Credit Survey Committee (AIRCS) under A.D. Gorwala.

The consistent narrative of each study and commission was the poor availability of financial services in rural areas. Even with the nationalization of the Imperial Bank, financial penetration in rural areas remained weak, notwithstanding the creation of a deputy governor's position to exclusively focus on rural credit in 1955. Innovations such as a National Agricultural Credit (long-term operation) fund,[182] an Agricultural Refinance Corporation[183] and strengthening of the cooperative banking system were pursued through the 1950s and 1960s to improve medium-term lending, but the malaise of poor credit availability persisted.

When Indira Gandhi took over as prime minister in 1966, her initial focus was not so much on the agricultural sector. The Green Revolution had arrived in India's farms, and despite the lack of credit, India's rural population experienced an improvement in incomes. Till then, RBI's primary support to the rural sector had been in the form of short- and medium-term loans through refinancing cooperative banks. As the prices of input commodities such as diesel, seeds and fertilizers fluctuated, farmers were at the mercy of the vagaries of the weather. This made farm loans an unattractive business for the largely private banking system, which eventually became one of the key reasons behind the enormous popularity of the bank nationalization of July 1969.

Agriculture Credit Board and the foundations of NABARD

In July 1969, as the government was preparing for nationalization, the All India Rural Credit Review Committee submitted its report just ahead of the defining event. The committee had closely studied the impact of a multi-agency approach in the industrial sector shepherded by the RBI, and recommended a similar approach for agriculture, with financing support through the commercial banks.[184] The committee's recommendations were quickly adopted and several agencies, such as the Rural Electrification Corporation (REC), Small Farmers Development Agency (SFDA) and the Agriculture Credit Board (ACB) were created.[185]

The ACB was formed to provide more effective management and disbursal of farm credit, and wished to empower state governments to take a lead on the matter. In between, the government had appointed a Banking Commission led by R.G. Saraiya in 1969, which apart from giving suggestions on deepening India's banking system, batted for improving the interface between commercial and cooperative banks and empowering primary credit societies.[186] The commission's report also advocated the setting up of new institutions called regional rural banks where cooperative and primary credit societies were weak.

The interim report of the National Commission for Agriculture in 1971 influenced the Banking Commission recommendations on rural credit in 1972, which ultimately suggested taking away the function of providing rural credit from the RBI and placing it under the auspices of a new bank for agriculture.[187] Naturally, the Reserve Bank was not thrilled with its findings and instead pushed for a consolidation of the cooperative banking system along with the setting up of special institutions that would help provide banking services to farmers where the cooperative system was weak.

The National Commission on Agriculture, which was constituted in September 1970, submitted its exhaustive report only in 1976. The final report was a treasure trove of data on India's rural sector and comprised sixty-nine chapters in fifteen volumes.[188] However, the commission was able to influence policy thinking along the way by providing twenty-four interim reports in the seven years of its existence. A key player in the recommendations of the NCA was its vice chairman B. Sivaraman, a long-serving bureaucrat and an expert on India's agricultural sector. Sivaraman was secretary of the Ministry of Agriculture during the Green Revolution and along with C. Subramaniam and M.S. Swaminathan, is widely credited for ushering in high-yield crops to raise farm productivity in the sixties.

While the final recommendations of the NCA came in the middle of the Emergency, the government had already taken note of the suggestions of the interim reports and was moving ahead with them. The culmination of the idea of opening new banks exclusively for the farm and other rural sectors came with the setting up of regional rural banks (RRBs). The government spearheaded the move to set up RRBs in 1975; the RBI had little role to play in the conception of the idea.[189]

Regional rural banks

Emergency had just been imposed, and in one of the first decisions taken by the government, stakeholders were informed of Prime Minister Indira Gandhi's 'desire' to set up new rural banks, which would generate employment in rural areas and help proliferate banking services. On 1 July 1975, the government constituted a committee under former RBI employee M. Narasimham, who was then posted to the Ministry of Finance. The committee submitted its report quickly on 31 July 1975 and proposed the setting up of 'regional rural banks'.

The government met with no opposition to the idea. In fact, within the Reserve Bank, there were some supporters of the idea. The agricultural credit department within the Reserve Bank had been pushing for the restructuring of cooperative banks into rural banks, with commercial banks providing support. B. Venkata Rao, a deputy officer, had written many technical notes on the concept[190] and would play a key role in the creation of NABARD. The Narasimham Committee took the recommendations one step further and advocated for commercial banks to take ownership of the regional banks and run them as subsidiaries. However, for both economic and political reasons, the government did not agree completely with the recommendations.

The government wanted the new institutions to be run based on economic viability, but at the same time wanted to avoid purely 'rural banks' with linkages to the cooperative banking model, which was a key recommendation of the Banking Commission set up by Morarji Desai in 1969 and headed by R.G. Saraiya. Eventually, the banks were modelled to combine 'the professional expertise of the commercial banks and the local feel of the cooperative banks'.[191]

Three months into the Emergency, the government issued an ordinance on 26 September 1975 to set up RRBs, and on Mahatma Gandhi's birthday celebrations, the government 'inaugurated' five regional rural banks. In a remarkable exchange of roles, it was the Department of Banking in the Ministry of Finance that asked RBI among other institutions to give its suggestions and comments on the bill. With K.R. Puri already at the helm of the RBI, the suggestions were minor and the government proceeded to set up more banks along with enacting a final act.

The RRB bill was introduced in the Lok Sabha on 16 January 1976 and was passed promptly. Under one of the provisions agreed upon, the government would directly manage the workings and the policy direction of the RRBs, given its large share holding of these banks both directly and indirectly, with the Reserve Bank likely to be consulted before any significant policy shift. However, for most of their initial years, RRBs continued to struggle,[192] and thus did not really help to improve banking services in rural India.

Setting up NABARD

By the time the NCA submitted its comprehensive report in 1976, India's farm sector was showing robust performance. The government welcomed the proposal given by the NCA to set up an integrated institution for farm credit and promptly constituted a committee to investigate the proposal under the ministry of agriculture.

Before the NCA submitted its report, the government had taken steps to transform the Agricultural Refinance Corporation into the Agricultural Refinance and Development Corporation (ARDC). This change was designed so ARDC could play a larger role in supporting other rural credit financing agencies, along with the Agricultural Financing Corporation, which was set up in 1968. The Reserve Bank continued to mount resistance against the idea, but the Congress was keen to follow through with it[193] and included the creation of an apex bank for agricultural development in its manifesto for the 1977 general elections.[194]

The 1977 elections changed everything. The proposal for an agricultural development bank was put on the backburner under Morarji Desai, despite strong demands by his government to ease up on credit controls and improve supply of funding in rural areas. The turning point came when Charan Singh, a peasant leader from Uttar Pradesh, became the finance minister in early 1979. Keen to prove his mettle, Charan Singh wanted 'to do something spectacular for satisfying the farm lobby.'[195] As deputy governor of the RBI, Ramakrishnayya, recalls in his memoirs, he was specially called back to Delhi from Karachi, where he was attending a conference, on the pretext of possible riots given the imminent execution of Zulfikar Ali Bhutto by the military government under President Zia-ul-Haq in January 1979. He later came to know that the newly anointed finance minister wanted to set up a new agricultural bank, which would be 'separate from the RBI.'[196]

The Reserve Bank did not wish to completely sideline the idea, so it proposed a short-term and a medium-term solution to address the problem of rural credit. First, the Reserve Bank agreed to provide cheaper credit to farmers through the ARDC and to guide a committee to consider the proposal of a new agricultural bank. The committee was chaired by B. Sivaraman, who was a member of the NCA and deeply knowledgeable about India's farm sector. The committee also included G.V.K. Rao to present the government's point of view, along with deputy governor of RBI Ramakrishnayya among others. On Governor Patel's advice, the committee expanded its mandate to include non-farm activities.[197]

The committee was named Committee to Review Arrangements for Institutional Credit for Agriculture and Rural Development. It was set up by the RBI on 30 March 1979 and submitted its interim report on 28 November 1979, when the government under Charan Singh was operating in the capacity of a caretaker. Sivaraman's views on agricultural credit and its operational control were known through the NCA's final report in 1976. The committee agreed that a 'separate' institutional arrangement was needed for RRBs and the overall management of farm and rural credit. However, to enforce stricter supervisory control, CRAFICARD agreed that the RBI should have the power to inspect regional rural banks.[198]

In its interim report, the committee thus advised the government to form a National Bank for Agriculture and Rural Development (NABARD), which would be jointly owned by the Reserve Bank and the government.[199] To grant the RBI some operational control, the committee also suggested that the chairman of NABARD should be one of the RBI's deputy governors, given that the bank would be the key financier of NABARD's operations initially. This solution was acceptable to both the government and the Reserve Bank, but under Indira Gandhi, who returned to power in 1980, the cabinet decided to limit this arrangement to fifteen years.[200]

Indira Gandhi, who supported the creation of a national bank for agriculture, asked the RBI to go ahead with the drafting of an act to set up NABARD in January 1980.[201] The bill was prepared by April 1980 and proposed to separate RBI's agricultural credit department and rural planning and credit department to be merged with the ARDC in line with CRAFICARD's recommendations. The bill also empowered the RBI to nominate three directors to the central board of NABARD, apart from its chairman.

Once the final report of CRAFICARD was submitted in 1981, the Reserve Bank began the operational procedures of setting up NABARD, with an initial corpus of ₹100 crore in paid up capital. The RBI contributed half of that amount, and on 12 July 1982, NABARD came into existence, with deputy governor of RBI M. Ramakrishnayya as its founder chairman[202] and its headquarters in Mumbai.

Ramakrishnayya recalls in his memoirs that the last two years of his term at the Reserve Bank were devoted to setting up NABARD,[203] with his focus on operationalizing the institution as swiftly as possible. However, when his term at the RBI ended in January 1983, the government did not move quickly to appoint a successor at NABARD, as it wanted to get rid of Ramakrishnayya before appointing a successor. Finance Minister Pranab Mukherjee in fact asked Ramakrishnayya to step down[204] as chairman of NABARD so that government could nominate its own candidate, which Ramakrishnayya refused given the statutory requirement of the existing chairman continuing until a successor was appointed.

Ramakrishnayya also recalls that once Dr Manmohan Singh took over as the governor of the Reserve Bank, the government tried to push M.M.K. Wali, the then chief secretary of Rajasthan, to succeed Ramakrishnayya at NABARD. However, the government wanted more operational control and chose to nominate R.K. Kaul, an additional secretary in the Department of Banking in the Ministry of Finance, as Ramakrishnayya's successor and a deputy governor at the RBI, despite Governor Singh's opposition.

At the same time, Finance Minister Pranab Mukherjee was threatening to rescind the RBI's power to licence bank branches, given an entanglement over a bank application of a Pakistani bank Bank of Credit and Commerce International (BCCI),[205], which wanted to set up operations in india and permitting Lord Swaraj Paul to buy shares of Escorts, which was not permitted as per RBI's guidelines at that point.[206] Eventually, Dr Manmohan Singh offered to resign as the governor in 1983 but was convinced by Prime Minister Indira Gandhi to stay on, and the matter was laid to rest, with R.K. Kaul becoming a deputy governor in a quid pro quo.

Labour troubles and I.G. Patel's exit

NABARD came into existence around the time when Governor I.G. Patel's term at the Reserve Bank was ending. After a long period of instability and frequent changes in leadership, the Reserve Bank had had a governor who had survived for the entire five-year term. Patel had previously served under the Indira Gandhi government during 1966–1970, but left to take up an assignment with the United Nations once policy started turning significantly leftwards. Patel indeed returned to India to take over RBI's governorship in 1977, but by 1980, when Indira Gandhi returned to power, the situation had changed, and she left institutions such as the Reserve Bank alone. She even listened to RBI's advice actively and helped pave the way for the second round of nationalization and the creation of NABARD.

However, she did not necessarily trust the present leadership at the RBI, and nor did Governor Patel have a strong inclination to serve a second term as governor of the Reserve Bank. In fact, close to the end of his term, Finance Minister Pranab Mukherjee politely suggested to Governor Patel that he could take up the role of executive director at the IMF, should he choose to do so.[207] Governor Patel noted in his memoirs that after multiple run-ins with the government, 'life would [...] increasingly become difficult and it did'. As Governor Patel entered the final months of his governorship, union trouble in Calcutta threatened to usurp his legacy, but given the support from the chief minister of West Bengal, Jyoti Basu, Governor Patel created the conditions for his exit by taking up the role of director of IIM Ahmedabad.

Governor I.G. Patel's term ended on 15 September 1982, and he was replaced by Dr Manmohan Singh, who had served in various capacities in the Ministry of Finance, including being the chief economic advisor. Governor Singh, having spent a considerable amount of time with the ministry, was largely expected to follow the tradition of the bureaucrat cooperating with the government while running monetary affairs.

The Sukhamoy Chakravarty Committee

In one of his first actions as the governor of the Reserve Bank, Governor Singh decided to initiate a thorough review of the RBI's conduct of monetary and credit policy, its role in India's economy and financial system, and the instruments at its disposal. Governor Singh in his first address at the Maharashtra Economic Development Council hinted at the formation of such a committee, and in December 1982, a committee was constituted under Professor Sukhamoy Chakravarty. Other members included Dr C. Rangarajan, a deputy governor at the RBI, along with R.K. Hazari, M.P. Chitale and F.A. Mehta, with J.C. Rao as the secretary.[208]

The RBI asked the committee to conduct a critical review of India's monetary system and its interface with fiscal policy, especially its relationship with debt financing and public debt management. This was a significant departure from the trend of the RBI playing the role of a backroom player, and it initiated a much-needed debate on debt monetization. The committee was also asked to examine what market instruments could be developed to improve credit policy transmission and strengthen policy formulation.

The general terms of reference given to the committee allowed it significant room to improvise. After a tumultuous decade of multiple crises, the Reserve Bank and the government were starting to recognize the shortfalls of their policies, and hence a thorough review of policies and instruments was welcomed. Further, it appears that the government was starting to see an improvement in financial savings, brought about by greater penetration of banking services. However, the low growth rate meant that the productivity of capital and the ongoing problem of deficit financing were seen as impediments to India's progress.

The committee submitted its report only on 10 April 1985, after Governor Manmohan Singh was moved to the Planning Commission in January 1985 by Prime Minister Rajiv Gandhi. The committee's report was exhaustive, and given the rather generic terms of reference, the policy document was more or less a blueprint for India's monetary and economic policy going ahead.[209]

The committee was of the view that India's monetary policy, while aligned to the overall economic policy, needed to balance multiple objectives. It touched upon the interface of monetary and fiscal policy, while regulating money supply and inflation and conducting policy through more flexible interest rates. Given India's problems with inflation in the period between 1960 and 1980, the committee identified maintaining price stability as an overarching objective and gave monetary policy the precedence on it. To ensure prudent policy, the committee recommended an ideal average annual increase in wholesale price index to be 'no more than 4.0 percent."[210]

To achieve price stability, the committee recommended the use of broad money, or M3, within an acceptable range, which was almost revolutionary to the extent it required considerable fiscal discipline, given the strong linkages between deficit financing and money supply growth. The committee suggested a money multiplier of 2x, which would imply 14 per cent growth in broad money, given an assumption of 5 per cent real GDP growth and 4 per cent inflation. The committee was also critical of fixed rate financing from the RBI and recommended revising up the discount rates to increase participation of non-banking sectors of the economy, and to increase the cost of financing for the government to enforce some discipline.

The committee also recommended improving the rate of return on government debt and made suggestions to improve credit channels through improvements in priority sector lending. The suggestions were taken largely on board, and incoming governor R.N. Malhotra put together a task force within the Reserve Bank to implement the recommendations.[211] Reforming the country was the zeitgeist within the Rajiv Gandhi government after his thumping victory in the 1984 elections, and the finance minister V.P. Singh was happy to accommodate monetary reforms. While some changes were implemented, the policy backdrop and the eventual unravelling of the fiscal position with mounting political problems would push the Indian economy towards its most difficult position since Independence.

Chapter 9

Broke and on the brink

Indira Gandhi's assassination on 31 October 1984 changed India's polity and brought her son Rajiv Gandhi to power under unusual circumstances, with the Congress winning more than three-fourths of the seats in the Parliament in elections held hastily in December 1984. Armed with a brute majority, the young prime minister Rajiv Gandhi was looking to rapidly change India's approach to both growth and poverty. He chose to pledge modernity, efficiency and a mass rebuilding of infrastructure. This was also in line with the initial easing of controls that was being attempted under Indira Gandhi's government, with a vision to accelerate reforms and improve economic growth.

Rajiv Gandhi takes charge

Rajiv Gandhi inherited an economy that was on the mend. Economic growth in 1983–84 and 1984–85 was 8.2 per cent and 3.8 per cent respectively, amid broadly stable inflation. While fiscal deficit was rising during this period, it was seen to boost capital spending, armed with the ongoing funding from the IMF. The government saw a rapid influx of 'professionals' from Doon School and Cambridge, where Rajiv had studied. This was a move to infuse a sense of urgency to the changes that Rajiv wanted to see in the government, and to fight against the vested interests both within the Congress and in sections of the bureaucracy.[212]

Rajiv Gandhi also chose to personally commandeer the steering wheel of the Indian economy by removing Pranab Mukherjee as the finance minister and replacing him with Vishwanath Pratap Singh, who had served briefly as the chief minister of Uttar Pradesh, before being made the commerce minister in 1983. The government also benefitted from having several reform-minded individuals, such as former RBI governor L.K. Jha, Montek Singh Ahluwalia and Rakesh Mohan, appointed to key positions in the government. Montek Singh had a formidable reputation as a market-oriented economist, having joined the World Bank after his stint in Oxford University, and returned to India in 1979 to work with the ministry of Finance. Rakesh Mohan was also trained at the world Bank before returning to India in 1980.

At the same time, the government decided to move RBI governor Dr Manmohan Singh to the Planning Commission as the organization's deputy head, a post that was seen as having no value under the new regime. As C.G. Somiah's book recounts, Prime Minister Rajiv Gandhi famously called the Planning Commission a 'bunch of jokers', who were bereft of any understanding of modern ideas of development.[213]

Deputy governor Amitav Ghosh took over as the governor of the RBI for a brief stint of twenty days, from 15 January to 4 February 1985. His stint would remain the shortest in the governor's chair, and he resumed his position as the deputy once the new governor was appointed. Ram Narain Malhotra, a long-time bureaucrat and former finance secretary at the Ministry of Finance, was appointed to replace Dr Singh on a long-term basis.

A liberalizer's instinct

The first two years under Rajiv Gandhi saw significant liberalization of industrial policy. The first budget in fiscal year 1985–86 lowered direct income tax rates[214] for corporates and individuals, while lowering the income tax slabs from eight to four. Further, several industries were opened to the private sector, accompanied by a dilution of the Monopolies and Restrictive Trade Practices Act (MRTP Act).

At the same time, the government created conditions to attract more private investment in the telecom, automobile and information technology sectors, which would set the foundation for strong economic growth by the end of the eighties. The finance minister V.P. Singh in his first budget speech quoted Rajiv Gandhi by saying, 'We have to change the thinking of the people of India to look ahead and not to keep on dwelling on the past [...] We have to create a dynamic country that is equal to any other country in the world.'[215]

The government followed this promise by unveiling for the first time a 'Long-Term Fiscal Policy' (LTFP) document, which aimed to provide clarity and assurance on India's tax architecture. The document specifically promised no imposition of new taxes and was designed to give a preview of the direction the government wanted fiscal policy to move towards. The move was path-breaking, and even usual government baiters such as Nani Palkhivala praised the tabling of the document.[216] From the Reserve Bank's perspective, the tabling of the LTFP with a focus on fiscal discipline and promised improvement in direct taxes over time meant lower net credit to the government. The document also promised to widen the definition of budgetary deficit to include RBI's support to long-term securities, and gave assurances on setting monetary targets with greater coordination.[217]

Serendipitously, the RBI was pursuing its own reforms, which had been fast-tracked by some of the recommendations of the Chakravarty Committee on the monetary system. However, the impact of some of the reforms did not bear fruit immediately. Rather, when the RBI's decision to give commercial banks some leeway to fix deposit rates while maintaining a relatively flexible exchange rate policy was eventually seen as more of a mistake than a calibrated step.

On 6 April 1985, the Reserve Bank allowed banks to fix their own deposit rates on maturities between fifteen days to one year, with a ceiling of 8 per cent. This was done to mobilize more resources and bring some balance to the time liabilities of banks, which were long-term in nature, given high long-term deposit rates. The Reserve Bank described the step as 'an innovative move' in its press release,[218] but soon found that the Indian Banks' Association imposed its own 'guidelines' to ensure some collusion on 8 April. The overreach by the IBA was promptly criticized, and they eventually withdrew their notice by the end of April 1985.

However, the plan soon ran into trouble with the government, as by mid-May, the Ministry of Finance was worried about the 'considerable erosion' of the profitability of public sector banks, leading to suggestions of more discussion between the Ministry and the Reserve Bank. While Governor Malhotra tried to stand by the bank's decision, soon rumours of foreign banks and small banks denting the deposit bases of big banks began to float around the financial circles. While there was no evidence of this switch being in motion, the Reserve Bank caved in to the pressure from the Ministry of Finance and reversed its decision within six weeks, on 25 May 1985, to bring back short-term deposit rates below forty-five days to 3 per cent, ending a short-lived yet innovative experiment.

In terms of the credit policy, the Reserve Bank continued to maintain a tight grip on both exchange rate and credit availability during the first year of Rajiv Gandhi's government. However, with economic performance improving, balance of payments being under control and slowing money supply growth, some easing was deemed necessary in the next financial year. Along with this, the Reserve Bank began its own economic reforms, reducing interest rates for exporters[219] and allowing the government to fund its fiscal balance, within a certain limit.

Governor Malhotra was especially cautious on the nature and fragility of India's fiscal finances. Under Rajiv Gandhi's government, initial signs of fiscal profligacy started to appear in the second budget. While the Planning Commission was out of favour with the prime minister, the growth and spending targets outlined in the seventh plan were ambitious. The target growth rate was set at 5 per cent, but the government was keen to top that and between 1985 and 1987, despite significant improvement in revenue collection, the government consistently missed its deficit targets, as growth took precedence over fiscal sustainability.

In fact, by the end of 1986, when the real GDP and money supply growth was starting to gain momentum and RBI's net credit to the government was rising rapidly, Governor Malhotra in a moment of forbearance decided to tighten banking sector liquidity, along with pre-emptively asking banks to reduce credit limits for large public-sector borrowers. He sounded a word of caution in his note: 'I have a feeling that stronger steps are needed to curb the growth of money supply.'[220]

On the currency, despite facing an upward trend in US interest rates under a hawkish Federal Reserve led by Paul Volcker and a stronger US dollar, the RBI had been able to maintain the value of the rupee, thanks to the IMF loan and an improving balance of payments position in the initial years of the 1980s. However, by 1984–85, the rupee started sliding against the US dollar at a pace of around 10 per cent per year, which caused some discomfort within the RBI. This coincided with rising debt servicing as the IMF loans were coming due for repayments. This would be a pre-cursor to a crisis down the road. Eventually, stability returned through the 'Plaza Accord', which was signed in September 1985 between the United States, France, Germany, Japan and UK to increase the exchange rate of the Japanese yen and German deutsche mark, and to weaken the US dollar.

RBI cautions government on living beyond its means

The government's ambitions far outstripped its ability to raise resources. The desperation to raise funds at a lower cost started to increase by 1986. During the fiscal year 1986–87, as the budget deficit was running much higher than the government intended, Prime Minister Rajiv Gandhi turned to his new finance secretary S. Venkitaramanan[221] to get more money. Venkitaramanan leaned on the Reserve Bank, asking for a higher dividend and for an increase in SLR, which was a cheap source of funds for the government.[222] Currently, this is a standard practice for the government and the Reserve Bank (in 2017–18, RBI was expected to transfer more than ₹70,000 crore in profits), but it was a radical suggestion back in the eighties, given the lack of foreign reserves and interest incomes.

The Reserve Bank naturally pushed back, with Governor Malhotra arguing in a letter that such a step would have significant consequences for monetary policy as the profits for the Reserve Bank were largely notional, given it was directly monetizing the deficit through its holding of bills and bonds. As such, any move to transfer more money from the Reserve Bank would be detrimental to money supply growth, which was already rising at a rapid pace.[223] The governor further said that RBI's transfer had remained constant at ₹210 crore, since there were other agency fees it was paying to banks on the government's behalf. The RBI was hard-nosed on the SLR as well, refusing to raise it given already high rates.

Such a sharp rebuke from the Reserve Bank took the Ministry of Finance by surprise, and the matter was escalated to Rajiv Gandhi. The prime minister invited Malhotra for a meeting, but it was cancelled, and instead, Malhotra made a representation to Finance Minister V.P. Singh. The finance minister managed to convince the government to stop demanding a higher surplus transfer from the Reserve Bank. While the pressure eased for a while, the discussion was kept alive by the Ministry of Finance over the next two years, and eventually as the economy entered a full-fledged crisis in 1990–1992, the surplus transfer was increased to ₹1,500 crore—a sevenfold jump—to tide over the fiscal fences. This decision to give larger surpluses was taken by S. Venkitaramanan, who was by then the governor of the RBI.

Political troubles and poor economic management

The hand-wringing over a larger profit transfer from the Reserve Bank was a harbinger of things to come. Cornered politically despite having a huge majority in the Parliament, Rajiv Gandhi reshuffled his cabinet for the sixth time in two years in November 1986.[224] However, his political problems were just beginning. In an effort to cut his popular finance minister down to size, Rajiv shifted V.P. Singh to the Ministry of Defence on 24 January and assumed the finance portfolio for himself.

Subsequently, the government decided to turn a bit more populist in the budget for fiscal year 1987–88, with Rajiv himself presenting the budget in February 1987. Rajiv Gandhi outlined a budget that seemed conservative on paper but allocated large subsidies to the farm sector. However, given a widespread drought and marginal flooding in some parts of the country, the fiscal position started getting stretched very quickly. Inflation started climbing, but the overall inflationary impact was dented by buffer stocks of foodgrains.[225]

With inflation rising and the balance of payments position deteriorating, the Reserve Bank sounded a note of caution, but given low deficit projections, it was comfortable in raising the SLR by 50 bps to 37.5 per cent in April 1987. However, with the drought looming large over the kharif sowing season, the RBI quickly became cautious about inflation and raised the CRR to tighten liquidity conditions in October 1987. But even with the drought, the economy was doing well, showing growth rates above 4 per cent, supported by the industrial delicensing from 1985.

Rajiv Gandhi was preoccupied with the political storm clouds gathering over his government. V.P. Singh, who had been made the defence minister, was widely recognized as the second most popular man in the government, given his very public confrontation with large business houses over issues of rent-seeking, corruption and tax evasion. V.P. Singh was keen to maintain his anti-corruption image and started looking into defence deals for the purchase of arms and ammunition by ordering a probe, aimed at Rajiv himself, who had held the defence portfolio before Singh. By April 1987, a full-blown controversy broke out over the Bofors gun deal between India and Sweden after *The Hindu* ran a story led by journalist Chitra Subramaniam on the illegal kickbacks paid to top Indian politicians and key defence officials. Singh had resigned as the defence minister[226] before the story broke.

This was perhaps the last blow, and the momentum to reform the economy was lost once the allegations around the defence scandal started tumbling out of the closet. As Vinay Sitapati notes[227] in his biography of Narasimha Rao, in May 1987, a document prepared by the Planning Commission to allow greater private participation in the industrial sector was circulated, but the government had no appetite for any major economic reforms. From then on, the government started pushing for growth, and the gap between budgeted government borrowing and actual borrowings widened sharply.

The Reserve Bank was apprehensive about the rising pressures on the currency and the widespread fiscal mismanagement, and in October 1987, decided to raise the CRR in its credit policy review. However, the government was not on board with the decision, and on 10 October, the finance secretary asked the Reserve Bank to put the CRR on hold.[228] The Governor in his response sent directly to the finance minister N.D. Tiwari indicated that an understanding had been reached before, and both the SLR and CRR would be raised at an opportune time. In fact, Governor Malhotra reminded the finance minister that he had urged RBI to announce the decision early on, and this impasse between the government and the RBI had forced the Reserve Bank to postpone its decision, thus creating 'some embarrassment to the Reserve Bank'.[229] Eventually, the RBI was *allowed* to go ahead with the 50 bps CRR hike on 24 October 1987 to take it to 10 per cent, and the Reserve Bank raised the SLR to 38 per cent by early January 1988.

Losing control of external finances

As the Rajiv Gandhi government was presenting its final full budget in fiscal year 1988–89, the Reserve Bank was mindful of the fact that the deficit targets might have been projected as lower than what could realistically be achieved. With the government aiming for a GDP growth rate of 7 to 8 per cent,[230] the RBI was under enormous pressure to keep monetary conditions in sync with the government's growth objective, despite latent inflationary pressures. However, there were bigger problems developing on the external front, which had not been a hot spot since the IMF's loan.

India's industrial sector had posted a growth rate of above 8 per cent for four consecutive years under the Rajiv Gandhi government,[231] and a similar improvement was seen in export performance. The government's budget deficit was widening, and the current account deficit shot up to 2.7 per cent of GDP. At the same time, India's debt from the IMF was starting to be repaid, and the country was running a debt service ratio of around 30 per cent despite rising receipts.

Indeed, during the growth spurt years, India's financing of the current account started getting riskier as the IMF's inflows turned into outflows and the country turned to non-concessionary borrowings from the IBRD and non-resident deposits.[232] By the time Rajiv Gandhi's term ended in 1989, India's external debt had exploded from around US$20 billion to over US$60 billion, with the current account deficit looking out of control. Foreign reserves had fallen to barely two and a half months of import cover, leaving the RBI vulnerable in its currency defence in 1989 and bringing the rupee back to levels similar to those in 1979 on a real exchange rate basis.[233]

The elections in 1989 took place in a chilly November, and the results left India poised for a period of political instability. V.P. Singh, the former finance minister who was leading a new political party, the Janata Dal (People's Group), became the prime minister on 2 December 1989. Professor Madhu Dandavate, an old socialist hand and a physicist by training, became the finance minister. However, given the inherent instability in his government, V.P. Singh, despite being widely acknowledged as a capable former finance minister, could not focus on the deteriorating economic situation.

There was significant infighting in Janata Dal from the beginning, and despite the Reserve Bank increasingly voicing its concerns on the impending economic malaise, the government under V.P. Singh could not focus on economic matters. Instead, it chose to turn populist by reviving the old Mandal Commission report from 1979 prepared under the Janata Party government, which had called for greater reservations for other backward classes in government jobs and educational institutions.

The last thing the Reserve Bank needed was a distracted minority government as it struggled to apprise the government of the deteriorating economic situation. By the time V.P. Singh came into power, inflation had started rising in India, and the rupee started rising in real terms, despite weakness against the US dollar. A month ahead of the budget presented by Madhu Dandavate on 19 March 1990, Governor Malhotra wrote to Dandavate alerting him to the falling reserves[234] and rising interest costs. Malhotra also pointed to significant external debt stock and urged the government to reduce the fiscal deficit while liberalizing foreign investment rules to attract investments from Japan, Germany and Eastern Europe.[235]

The Iraq war unravels India's external position

The economy muddled through for a few months, but external shocks, as in the past, unravelled the economic situation faster than the government had expected. And as in the past, the shock came through oil prices, with Iraq's invasion of Kuwait on 2 August 1990 sending oil prices through the roof. However, unlike previous shocks, the war in Kuwait not only had a debilitating impact on India's oil import bill, but also hurt its remittances flow from the Middle East dramatically. It also resulted in a loss of exports to both Kuwait and Iraq.[236] Further, the evacuation of non-resident Indians from Kuwait imposed an additional burden on the exchequer.

The Reserve Bank was stuck between a rock and a hard place. Inflation was already rising and any move to weaken the currency amid an unsustainable fiscal deficit would not have been of much use. There was still time to approach multilateral agencies such as the IMF for emergency concessionary funding, but the government of the day did not have the time or the inclination to take any difficult steps as it lurched from one political crisis to another. As former RBI governor I.G. Patel would recount in a speech at IIM Bangalore in October 1991, 'nothing was done to take corrective action or to buy time'[237] in 1988 or 1989, and the V.P. Singh government added fuel to the fire by announcing loan waivers and reservations by accepting the recommendations of the Mandal Commission.

As foreign reserves continued to decline in the wake of the Iraq war, India had limited choices. As an initial step, the RBI advocated a change in the valuation approach of gold held in its foreign reserves.[238] Under the RBI Act, 1934, RBI's gold was kept at a fixed value, which meant that the gap between RBI's value of gold and the market prices, both international and domestic, diverged. In September 1990, RBI's gold price was about one-fortieth of its domestic price. To correct this anomaly, however, a change in the RBI Act was needed, which, given the acrimonious political scenario, looked improbable. On 4 September 1990, the Ministry of Finance proposed the change in the RBI Act to allow the periodic revaluation of gold assets. The amendment was eventually approved through an ordinance on 15 October 1990.[239]

Yashwant Sinha asks Governor Malhotra to resign

The year-long political infighting in the Janata Dal government ended with the party splitting into factions, and its allies such as the Bharatiya Janata Party (BJP) and the communists pulling their support. On 10 November, Chandra Shekhar Singh, or Chandra Shekhar, as he was widely known, became the prime minister with outside support from the Congress Party. Despite the handicap of running a minority government with just sixty-four members of Parliament, Chandra Shekhar made a far more serious attempt to address the impending balance of payments crisis than his last two predecessors.

In one of his first actions, Chandra Shekhar appointed Yashwant Sinha, a former IAS officer who had spent considerable time in the Ministry of Commerce, as his finance minister. Yashwant Sinha pipped Subramaniam Swamy, who wanted the job as well, to the post.[240] Sinha inherited an economy that had just been downgraded by international credit rating agencies and was being flagged as a likely candidate to default on its existing foreign loans.[241] Around the same time, the RBI governor R.N. Malhotra gave one of his last interviews to *India Today*, ruling out a currency devaluation to tackle the ongoing external challenge,[242] while batting for a closer working relationship between the government and the RBI.

India's gradual experiments with liberalization had brought in more Western-trained economists and practitioners in the government. When Yashwant Sinha took charge, Deepak Nayyar, an Oxford trained economist was his chief economic advisor and S. Venkitaramanan was the finance secretary. S.P. Shukla and K.P. Geethakrishnan would later join the team, all of whom had been career bureaucrats. .

Given that Chandra Shekhar had inherited an economy on the verge of a meltdown, his confidence in RBI's leadership was failing.[243] As such, the government through Yashwant Sinha decided to quietly ask R.N. Malhotra to step aside.[244] This was not just due to his operational style, but also a result of the growing turbulence between the RBI and the Ministry of Finance, particularly over the RBI's isolated decision to oversee the operations of financial institutions as a parallel to running monetary policy. While this was being done in the guise of providing 'comprehensive oversight',[245] the differences continued to grow, and even under the new government of Chandra Shekhar, the Ministry of Finance refused to completely endorse RBI's authority to oversee some financial institutions.

Governor R.N. Malhotra eventually resigned on 22 December 1990. As the official history of the RBI notes, although it was rare for a sitting RBI governor to resign, this incident was certainly less acrimonious than the Sir Benegal Rama Rau episode in 1957.[246] On 24 December 1990, just a month after the new prime minister had assumed power, S. Venkitaramanan, who had partly commandeered the Ministry of Finance during the Rajiv Gandhi years, was appointed as the governor of the RBI.

Once at the RBI, S. Venkitaramanan, a long-time bureaucrat and a hands-on leader, decided to take evasive action, which was to be sequenced with other measures taken simultaneously along with the Ministry of Finance. First, the government decided to immediately raise excise duties on several products and enforce strict rationing of foreign exchange on import of capital goods.[247] The government also initiated some soft conversations with the IMF to see what kind of emergency funding could be obtained before the budget was presented in March 1991.

The choking of imports was not enough and in rising desperation, the State Bank of India sent a memo to the Reserve Bank and the government[248] on 16 January 1991, proposing that the government should use its gold holdings, impounded through smuggling crackdowns and other sources, to raise foreign exchange. At the same time, Yashwant Sinha was working on preparing a reforming budget, which he was eventually not allowed to present in the Parliament.[249]

Chandra Shekhar's government did not last until March 1991, being pulled down by the Congress Party over a trivial reason, despite India's fragile economic health. The issue of two policemen from the Haryana Police Department 'snooping' on Rajiv Gandhi led to a ruckus in the Lok Sabha and after the central government refused to sack Haryana chief minister Om Prakash Chautala, the Congress pulled its support to the Chandra Shekhar government.

This irresponsible act of the Congress Party meant that the finance minister Yashwant Sinha could only present an interim budget on 4 March 1991. Sinha's full budget would have enabled India to approach the IMF for funds. Elections were scheduled for May 1991, and the government was asked to carry on until the election results were declared. In the meantime, India's foreign reserves kept declining, and by the end of March 1991, India barely had over US$2 billion of foreign currency exchange.[250]

On the brink of bankruptcy

By April 1991, India's foreign exchange position was officially in its twilight zone. The Reserve Bank had approved SBI's plan to lease gold on 16 March, and in April, the government was almost forced to exercise the option. Stunted by higher oil prices, falling reserves and risks of default, the government decided to lease 20 metric tonnes of gold through the State Bank of India in April.

For a caretaker government, such a move was significant, but it was needed in the national interest. The Reserve Bank, its 'loan ranger'[251] Governor Venkitaramanan and the SBI arranged for a deal wherein the SBI would lease out 20 tonnes of gold in exchange for US$200 million. The gold was to be pledged against currency in a repurchase agreement, where it served the purpose of a collateral. If prices of gold were to increase, the terms would have allowed the Reserve Bank to withdraw more foreign exchange against the gold.

However, the gold was only moved when the new government took charge. The unexpected death of Rajiv Gandhi in Sriperumbudur during the elections led to a wave of sympathy for the Congress Party. In the meantime, the Reserve Bank was exploring new ways of attracting funds, including allowing accredited brokerages to offer bulk deposit schemes to non-resident Indians, who had been withdrawing their deposits in the wake of the ongoing crisis.

The death of Rajiv Gandhi and the unexpected victory for Congress threw up an open question on the Congress Party's leadership. Three members of the Gandhi family—Indira, Sanjay and Rajiv—had died almost within a decade of each other. Maneka Gandhi, Sanjay's widow, had fallen out with the family, and so the burden fell on Sonia Gandhi, Rajiv's widow. She was not keen on the leadership and focus shifted to finding a suitable replacement. There were three main contenders for the position. P.V. Narasimha Rao, an old hand in national politics and confidante of Indira Gandhi, emerged as the frontrunner, with Arjun Singh and Maharashtra's ambitious chief minister Sharad Pawar tailing him.[252]

After a heated Congress working committee meeting, Sonia Gandhi was invited to take over the party leadership, which she promptly rejected.[253] However, she was keen to ensure that the party did not fall completely beholden to new leadership, which meant she would have to rely on someone innocuous who would not threaten the supremacy of the Gandhi family in the Congress party. P.N. Haskar, Indira Gandhi's former principal secretary, advised Sonia Gandhi to choose Narasimha Rao, first as the party president, and then eventually as the tenth prime minister of India, once election results were declared on 18 June 1991.

Resolving the crisis: P.V. Narasimha Rao takes charge

Pamulaparti Venkata Narasimha Rao, or P.V. Narasimha Rao as he was better known, had neither the appearance nor the charisma of a Gandhi, let alone a national leader. Indeed, according to Congress leader Jairam Ramesh, Rao had the 'charisma of a dead fish.'[254] However, he turned out to be the man of destiny, presiding over the most intense period of economic reforms that India had till then experienced. Born in the small village of Vangara in Karimnagar district of Telangana, Rao, a Brahmin, had risen gradually through the ranks of the Congress to become the chief minister of undivided Andhra Pradesh from 1971 to 1973, before shifting base to New Delhi.

Once anointed as the successor to Rajiv Gandhi, Rao, who a month ago had been quietly asked to retire with dignity, started with the task of government formation. P.C. Alexander, a former IAS officer and confidante of Indira Gandhi, assisted him in making his cabinet selections. To instil confidence in the international community regarding India's economic policymaking, Rao wanted to appoint an apolitical economist with international credibility to head the Ministry of Finance.[255] P.C. Alexander suggested the names of two former governors of the Reserve Bank, I.G. Patel and Manmohan Singh. Both were highly reputed economists. Patel was serving as director of the London School of Economics and Singh was the chairman of the University Grants Commission at the time. Dr Singh had briefly served as an economic advisor to the Chandra Shekhar government as well.

Rao consulted President R. Venkataraman on the two names in June 1991, who was of the opinion that both were competent. However, I.G. Patel declined to take the role, preferring to stay out of the limelight, and hence the choice fell upon Dr Manmohan Singh, who was travelling in Europe and was expected to return to Delhi on 20 June.[256] P.C. Alexander in his memoirs recounted that he had to personally wake up Manmohan Singh on 21 June at 5.00 a.m. to offer him the role of finance minister on behalf of Narasimha Rao. Vinay Satapati in his authoritative book on Narasimha Rao also mentions a phone call between Rao and Singh on the morning of the swearing in, and by the afternoon, Manmohan Singh, a quintessential North Block mandarin and a former RBI governor, had taken over India's financial reins.

The selection of a former RBI governor to lead the Ministry of Finance had a cruel sense of irony. For three years, India had been witnessing a slow crisis unfolding and political leadership was found wanting. However, at the crunch time, political masters across the political spectrum were turning to India's bureaucracy and its institutions for a solution. Indeed, on the evening of 20 June, even before the new government had been sworn in, the cabinet secretary Naresh Chandra, a portly man who cut a commanding figure, walked into Narasimha Rao's residence with an eight-page note summarizing the state of the economy Narasimha Rao was inheriting, and what emergency steps needed to be taken as soon as the government took charge.[257] The document contained references to dismantling of trade barriers, fiscal discipline, removal of licences and overhauling the industrial policy, effectively hinting at a clean break from the past socialist regime.

The eight-page document had been prepared with inputs from various ministries. After reading it, Narasimha Rao asked Chandra, 'Is the economic situation that bad?', to which Chandra replied, 'No sir, it is actually much worse.'[258] The Chandra Shekhar government, during its time as caretaker, had initiated a dialogue with the IMF and the World Bank, and the document was an indicative laundry list of reforms the agencies wanted in exchange for granting India funds. The eight-page document would go on to become the blueprint of economic reforms that would eventually be unleashed by Narasimha Rao,[259] even before Manmohan Singh had entered the picture.

Currency devaluation and gold pledging

The team put together by Narasimha Rao had considerable economic heft. Apart from Naresh Chandra and Amarnath Verma in the Prime Minister's Office, Rao ensured that reform-oriented bureaucrats such as Montek Singh Ahluwalia, Rakesh Mohan, Bimal Jalan and Y.V. Reddy were kept in the finance ministry to assist with the crisis management (the latter two would eventually become governors of the RBI). Jairam Ramesh, who had been working with the Congress party on the election campaign along with Pranab Mukherjee also joined the Prime Minister's Office as an officer on special duty, while Ashok Desai, a more reform minded economist joined the Ministry of Finance on Dr Manmohan Singh's suggestion. Most of these gentlemen had been working on documents outlining a gradual reform process since the mid-eighties, guided by the initial reformist impulse of the Rajiv Gandhi government.

Even at the Reserve Bank, Governor S. Venkitaramanan and his deputies S.S. Tarapore and C. Rangarajan were among the most competent senior officers the bank had seen in a long time. To signal his own personal intent, Rao kept the Ministry of Industry with himself, given that it would require the most significant reforms.

When Rao took charge of India, the foreign reserves position was precariously perched at two weeks of import cover, significantly below the three months of cover recommended by the IMF.[260] The government began the execution of a three-step process to show their intentions. There was to be a systematic dismantling of operational controls, which would be eventually followed by steps to grow the economy.

To begin with, the government informally communicated to the IMF that some significant measures were forthcoming. As per Jairam Ramesh, he informed Gopi Arora, India's executive director at the IMF, of a list of steps that the government was planning to take.[261] The prime minister and his finance minister also briefed the opposition on the economic situation, and the steps needed to salvage India's reputation globally.

The first step was taken on 1 July 1991, when the rupee was devalued by 7 to 9 per cent against major currencies. This was followed by another large devaluation, by 11 per cent, on 3 July. This meant that the rupee had lost roughly a fifth of its value in less than three days. On the day of the second devaluation, Narasimha Rao got cold feet given the criticism from the left-leaning intelligentsia in Delhi. On the morning of 3 July, Rao called Manmohan Singh and asked him not to go through with the second devaluation. However, it was too late, as when Singh called the deputy governor C. Rangarajan at the RBI, Rangarajan replied, 'The horse has already bolted. I have already announced.'[262]

From the Reserve Bank's perspective, the devaluation was both the beginning and the culmination of the resolution of India's balance of payments problems. Since the mid-eighties, the RBI had been proactively using the exchange rate to manage pressures on the current account, but in the previous twelve months, the significant appreciation of the real exchange rate had made it difficult to ensure that a meaningful change took place. However, the prime minister and the finance minister took the decision to devalue the rupee, while the RBI just 'effected' the devaluation.[263]

The devaluation was a political decision, and the Reserve Bank followed through with further tightening of monetary conditions with a package of policy steps announced effective from 4 July. The bank rate was raised to 12 per cent from 11 per cent previously, and special interest rates on advances above a certain amount from banks were also raised. Refinancing costs for all kinds of credit were also aligned with the bank rate hike. Even before this, liquidity tightening measures to rationalize credit disbursement and imports had been introduced in May 1991, with incremental CRR being raised to 100 per cent. This was a significant step, as the Reserve Bank was focused on mobilizing resources and reducing credit growth. Only exporters were excluded from this diktat.[264]

On the same day (July 3) as the devaluation, trucks were being loaded with the RBI's gold in Mumbai, as the bank had arranged for an emergency loan of US$405 million with the Bank of England and the Bank of Japan, in exchange for gold as collateral. This deal had been negotiated under the previous government, but the facility was utilized by the Narasimha Rao government. Since the gold held by the RBI did not meet the purity standards of the Bank of England, it was decided to ship the gold to London to purify it to the required standard. There was considerable secrecy around the operation. Governor Venkitaramanan, Deputy Governor Rangarajan and P.B. Kulkarni, the head of the department of external investments and operation, personally supervised the operation.[265] Four tranches of gold shipments weighing together almost 47 tonnes were airlifted to London on 4, 7, 11 and 18 July.

Given the need for secrecy and to ensure the non-accounting of the transfer in the customs trade, the customs department at Mumbai's Sahar airport was instructed to not record the shipment. However, news of the shipment was leaked to Shankkar Aiyar, a journalist with the *Indian Express*, and he waited patiently at Sahar airport so he could confirm the story, which he was able to do thanks to a van that broke down on its way to the airport, and it had to be surrounded by armed guards while the truck got repaired, which gave away the importance of the operations to Aiyyar.[266] The story appeared on 7 July in all sixteen editions of the *Indian Express*, creating a national scandal[267] and another political headache for the government.

In a rare show of solidarity, Manmohan Singh, speaking in the Parliament on 16 July 1991, defended former finance minister Yashwant

Sinha's decision to pledge gold in order to secure the necessary financing. He said that while it was not a moment India could be proud of, it was the 'best possible decision' taken given the circumstances.[268]

Taking away the punchbowl

While the RBI was airlifting gold in secrecy, on 4 July 1991, a day after the second devaluation, Manmohan Singh decided to unilaterally end all the export subsidies the government had been offering to industry, to offset the impact of an expensive rupee. Commerce Minister P. Chidambaram initially resisted the move, but was convinced by his commerce secretary Montek Singh Ahluwalia about the need to save money.[269] As a compromise, the government decided to announce some relaxation in the import policy to soften the impact. Chidambaram and Manmohan Singh together announced the changes, to show coordination in decision-making.

Having delivered the first round of reforms, the focus shifted to containing the political damage. Narasimha Rao gave multiple interviews to the national media to explain the 'drastic remedies'[270] needed to rectify the economic situation. Rao shifted the blame for the currency devaluation to the RBI, and moved ahead with executing the next set of reforms, which would reshape the industrial policy.

Rakesh Mohan, during his stint at the Ministry of Industry under Minister Ajit Singh (son of former prime minister Charan Singh) had drafted a note on a new industrial policy that envisaged dismantling the licence regime. Similar policy documents had been prepared before, but the presence of Amarnath Varma, who had served as industry secretary in the previous government, in the Prime Minister's Office brought the document to life, as he had played a critical role in the preparation of the industrial policy during his stint with Ajit Singh as the industry secretary. It formed the basis of the new industrial policy, and by 7 July 1991, as Rao was firefighting the opposition and the media, a new industrial policy was in place.

Even before the reforms were initiated, a debate sparked between distinguished economists over the efficacy of economic liberalisation and whether it was the best way forward when four people (I.G. Patel, M. Narasimham, R.N. Malhotra and P.N. Dhar), including three former

Reserve Bank governors, published a joint statement backing the efforts of another former Reserve Bank governor and the current finance minister, Manmohan Singh, to carry out reforms. The statement was laid out in a meeting organized by Observer Research Foundation,[271] an influential think tank in Delhi. This statement was similar to the eight-page document prepared by Naresh Chandra, and it called for fiscal discipline, rationalization of various subsidies, an open industrial policy, lowering of tariffs and freer induction of foreign investment.[272] While the left-leaning economists and politicians prepared an alternative view[273] advocating further tightening of controls and government spending, the government had chosen the path it wanted to take.

Industrial delicensing was the single biggest reform undertaken by the Narasimha Rao government. Between 19 and 23 July, the cabinet met several times to discuss the new industrial policy, and it was tabled simultaneously with the budget on 24 July. In fact, the industrial policy was tabled in an innocuous manner by the junior industry minister around noon, without much fanfare.[274] But in one stroke, the government of India abolished industrial licensing for all industries except eighteen industries on the negative list, regardless of the level of investments. It also scoped out a small set of public sector monopolies in eight sectors, liberalized the foreign investment regime with the scope for a controlling stake in several sectors, and virtually removed import licensing. The government also removed anti-monopolistic laws by easing restrictions under the MRTP Act.

That same afternoon, Finance Minister Manmohan Singh presented the budget, citing Victor Hugo and delivering a heavy dose of medicine required to nurse the economy back to health. Subsidies for food and fertilizers were cut, while LPG prices were increased. Aware of the upcoming industrial policy, IMF provided India with emergency funds of US$220 million on 22 July. The finance minister announced that he would approach the IMF for more funds, which would eventually materialize in a standby facility worth US$2.2 billion in November 1991, for a period of twenty months, subject to economic benchmark conditions being achieved by May 1993.[275] The Indian press hailed the budget as 'truly historic,'[276] while international newspapers such as *The Economist* called it an 'economic revolution.'[277]

The budget and its tough measures were harshly criticized by both the opposition and the Congress Party, but the horse had bolted. To calm down tempers, the government agreed to roll back the increase in urea prices to 30 per cent from 40 per cent, and granted some concessions for small farmers.[278] Although a symbolic step, the move allowed the government to preserve the bulk of the changes it had undertaken, while lowering political discontent.

With the blitzkrieg of reforms over, the government and the Reserve Bank shifted gears. The focus moved to improving the balance of payments position and executing a series of medium-term reforms under the guise of various committees, with former RBI governor M. Narasimham chairing the committee on financial systems (announced on 14 August 1991) and Dr Raja Chelliah, a public finance expert, heading the committee on tax reforms (29 August 1991). Simultaneously, a foreign investment promotion board replaced the foreign investment processing board on 22 August 1991, and the Planning Commission was reconstituted in mid-August, under the leadership of Pranab Mukherjee. These committees along with the Securities and Exchange Board of India would have a profound impact on the Reserve Bank's role in India's growth story, the country's financial infrastructure and the buffering of India's external safeguards in the years to come.

Chapter 10

Unshackling the financial sector

The storm clouds of a possible bankruptcy had passed, but the road ahead was still flooded with water stranded due to the blocked drains of the Indian economy. The sudden monetary tightening along with exchange rate depreciation and removal of several fiscal support measures was hurting both the classes and the masses. However, it was also a time of great opportunity as the government appointed several important committees to ensure reforms were undertaken to safeguard India's balance of payments, financial sector and public finances from another bailout. Some of the changes were dictated by conditionalities imposed by the subsequent IMF programme,[279] but a lot of the reforms, especially within the financial sector, were self-initiated.

Among the reforms torchbearers, the M. Narasimham Committee on financial systems in India (1991) played an instrumental role in reducing financial repression in the country and opening up the banking system to encourage market-based instruments,[280] along with liberalizing the banking sector for private participation. The committee report recommended more competition between existing and new players in the financial system, which would enable India's financial savings to rise. It also favoured greater integration between India's capital and money markets, improving financial intermediation and raising productivity.

The first Narasimham Committee report

From the RBI's perspective, running a tight monetary policy was necessary till foreign exchange reserves came under control. In October 1991, while announcing the credit policy, it raised the bank rate to 12 per cent from 11 per cent, while raising lending rate caps of commercial banks by 150 bps, along with higher deposit rates. Concurrently, the RBI raised interest on export credits, and while it reduced margins on import financing, they remained prohibitively high. Fortunately, the balance of payments improved with several constraints getting resolved, and by February 1992, the Reserve Bank reversed course and started gradually relaxing its tight policy stance, in sync with the budget announcement.

While the measures appeared to be pulling back from an extreme position, the rationale was derived from a more medium-term objective. In its report submitted in November 1991,[281] the Narasimham Committee made several key recommendations, twenty-seven to be precise, which included reducing the SLR from its peak of 38.5 per cent to 25 per cent over five years in a phased manner, reducing CRR from its high level, removing direct credit programmes, market-basing interest rates, improving the capital adequacy ratio of banks to a minimum of 4 per cent relative to risk weighted assets (RWAs) by 1993, allowing for debt restructuring of some debt, creating special tribunals to improve loan recovery, restructuring public sector banks to encourage consolidation into larger entities, abolishing branch licensing and opening up the banking system to both private and foreign banks, and ending the dual control mechanism of government and RBI over public sector banks, while giving primacy to the Reserve Bank.[282]

Along with the recommendations for the banking system, the Narasimham Committee report had a blueprint to convert the Reserve Bank into a more independent, more self-sufficient institution with greater control over the financial system. The report recommended giving the RBI a greater supervisory role in the direction of not just the banking system, but also over the development of financial markets. While not all functions could eventually be placed under the aegis of the central bank, the report had a profound impact on the reforms both in the banking system and within the RBI over the next decade.

The government accepted the report in principle and with the external financing pressures easing, the RBI took an early step in front-running the report, arguing for lower direct monetization of government deficit, as early as January 1992.[283] By the second half of 1992,[284] when the balance of payments crunch was all but over, the government sat down with the

RBI to examine the feasibility of the Narasimham Committee report and agreed to move forward with it, but not before it was hit with a short but significant episode in the equity markets.

The Harshad Mehta affair

Animal spirits in economics is a phrase used by John Maynard Keynes[285] in his seminal study *The General Theory of Employment, Interest, and Money* to describe irrational behaviour on the part of economic agents based on an expected outcome that will take a long time to pan out, but which looks probable. Following the liberalization of industrial policy, India's small but influential capital markets saw a surge, with the Bombay stock exchange's Sensex index doubling within a month, and Harshad Mehta, a portly Gujarati stockbroker, became an overnight sensation.[286]

The bubble burst in less than a year. By April 1992, the news of a scandal[287] involving several stockbrokers and the banking system and the siphoning off of about ₹5,000 crore for market speculation was broken by business journalist Sucheta Dalal. Her report indicated that the SBI had about ₹500 crore due from Harshad Mehta, who had raised the funds by short selling SBI shares. Just months earlier, the Securities and Exchange Board of India, a body founded in 1988, was given statutory powers from 12 April 1992 under the SEBI Act, 1992.[288] SEBI launched enquiries into the unabashed rally in equity markets and discovered that Mehta and his friends were using banking system funds to power their profits.

G.V. Ramakrishna, who was the first chairman of SEBI, dived head first into the investigation, but the taint also fell on the Reserve Bank and the public sector banks. The tight monetary conditions meant that government bonds were heavily discounted, and the fraud continued given government securities were cheaper to purchase in the open market, which helped cover the short positions. Effectively, the traders were shorting the bond market and using the funds to be long equities, thus fuelling the rally.[289] This was not just a case of fraud, but also one of significant regulatory oversight. And despite being labelled as an equity market fraud, it was in effect a banking fraud, involving the theft of funds of common depositors.[290]

By the end of April 1992, the Reserve Bank and the government were aware of multiple banks being hit by Mehta and his group, and on 30 April, the Reserve Bank instituted a committee under deputy governor R. Janakiraman to investigate the banks and their dealings with fund managers in several capital and money market instruments. Given the political urgency, the committee submitted three reports, on 31 May, 5 July and 23 August, along with simultaneous disclosure to the public at large.[291] RBI also got involved in a dispute involving ANZ Grindlays Bank and the National Housing Bank[292] over overdue payments, which eventually led to the exit of Grindlays Bank from India.

As one would expect, serious lapses were found and to contain the political damage, Prime Minister Narasimha Rao ordered the constitution of a thirty-member joint parliamentary committee in August 1992. The committee even asked Reserve Bank governor Venkitaramanan to depose in November 1992, where he averred that RBI's regulatory framework had played a key role in discovering the issue, but admitted to the lapses in supervision around banks and their interaction with capital markets.

The whole episode left a bad taste in the mouth of every financial regulator, and on 21 December, Governor S. Venkitaramanan relinquished[293] his office, just two years after he was appointed, to salvage his and the RBI's reputation after the Harshad Mehta scandal. Venkitaramanan's departure paved the way for former deputy governor C. Rangarajan, a favourite of Dr Manmohan Singh, to be appointed as the next governor of the RBI.

Private banks enter the market

The Harshad Mehta episode and the glaring loopholes in financial regulation had a profound impact on not just the government, but also the Reserve Bank. The Narasimham Committee report had shown the path, but once the scandal broke, there was a renewed urgency to implement those reforms. The government approved them in principle, and by the end of 1992, the Reserve Bank had drawn up the sequencing of the reforms.

Dr Chakravarthi Rangarajan was almost sixty years old when he took charge of the Reserve Bank as governor on 22 December 1992. He already had the distinction of being one of the longest serving deputies at the central bank. He had been intimately involved in the reform processes undertaken by several governments since the 1980s and knew what needed to be done to provide India's financial markets with a solid base of financial savings.

Governor Rangarajan's term began on an exciting note. On 22 January 1993, the Reserve Bank issued the guidelines for the entry of private sector banks. Deliberations on this policy had begun under former governor Venkitaramanan in September 1991,[294] but it was Rangarajan who announced the new policy, which eventually led to the entry of ten new private sector banks from 1994 onwards, including ICICI Bank, HDFC Bank, UTI Bank (which was renamed Axis Bank), IndusInd Bank and the Global Trust Bank.[295] The RBI would also ease up on its branch licensing policies in 1994, not abolishing the regulation, but creating a more autonomous environment to operate branches in urban areas and open automated teller machines (ATMs) as per commercial interests.

The government, while comfortable with the entry of private banks, was keen to manage its political interests. It appeased the labour unions by pushing back on public sector banking reform, which was also a key recommendation of the Narasimham Committee. As such, the recommendation to create three to four large public sector banks through mergers remained dormant, except for the merger of a relatively small PSU bank called New Bank of India with the Punjab National Bank in September 1993.[296] Creating international champions among India's public sector banks remains a challenge till today.

Simultaneously, the Reserve Bank accelerated the gradual monetary easing it had begun in February 1992 by announcing a reduction on 8 October 1992 in the SLR requirements from 38.5 per cent to 37.75 per cent over stages by 6 March 1993. It also reduced incremental CRR requirements by releasing back liquidity into the market over a period of six months. Deposit rate caps were lowered from 13 per cent to 12 per cent, and lending rate restrictions were also eased.[297]

By the time Finance Minister Manmohan Singh presented his budget for fiscal year 1993–94, growth was recovering, fiscal deficit was being gradually tamed, the balance of payments position had improved significantly and reforms appeared well placed. The RBI continued to ease policy and announced a further reduction in the SLR to 34.75 per cent from 37.75 per cent by November 1993, along with a reduction in the CRR to

14 per cent from 15 per cent over two steps by May. It also simplified its lending rate structure and lowered savings deposit rates, given manageable inflation. Despite the consistent and seemingly significant changes, market sentiment remained relatively weak.[298]

The Rangarajan Committee on balance of payments

By the end of 1993, the government was ending its IMF funding programme. As part of its standby arrangement programme, the Fund provided over US$2.2 billion over a period of twenty months, with rigorous benchmarks set on both fiscal consolidation and improvement of foreign reserves relative to its imports.[299] India's external position had improved significantly during that period, supported by several tightening measures and improvement in capital flows. This, combined with the reduction in the deficit, meant that the incremental monetization of the deficit could be capped, and hence the reduction in SLR could continue towards the 25 per cent recommendation by the Narasimham Committee.

Even before the Narasimham Committee report was submitted, the government, with inputs from the Reserve Bank, constituted a high-level committee on balance of payments under the chairmanship of C. Rangarajan, who was at the time the deputy governor of the RBI, in November 1991.[300] The purpose of the committee was to study and recommend changes to the way India managed its balance of payments, and to indicate limits and opportunities to improve the underlying balance of payments in respect to a sustainable rate of economic growth.

The committee submitted two reports, an interim report in February 1992 and a final report in April 1993, when Dr Rangarajan was already governor. The report emphasized the need to maintain a realistic exchange rate to avoid imbalances in the balance of payments and advocated maintaining at least three months of import cover and other payment obligations. It also recommended limiting the current account deficit to 1.6 per cent of GDP. These steps would form the preconditions for the rupee to move towards full current account convertibility.[301]

Simultaneously, based on the interim report recommendations, the government made a key amendment to the notorious Foreign Exchange Regulation Act, or FERA on 8 January 1993 through the promulgation of an ordinance.[302] The last major change to FERA had been made in 1973, when draconian laws were imposed on foreign exchange transactions, leading to foreign exchange rationing.

The amendment opened avenues for foreign investors, both industrial and financial, to return and removed the hurdles faced by resident Indians in accessing foreign exchange for trade, tourism and remittances.[303] The law was cleared in the Parliament in April 1993, but was bitterly fought within the government and the Congress Party itself.[304] The changes also brought more foreign portfolio investments through the introduction of foreign institutional investors or FIIs, giving them small but critical access to capital markets, and providing Indian companies with more sources of capital. Over time, smaller amendments and initiatives by the Reserve Bank brought non-resident Indians into the banking system in local currency deposits and eventually in the real estate market as well.

Given the gradual liberalization of current account transactions and some introduction of foreign capital flows, by the end of fiscal year 1993–94, India's balance of payments health had been restored and foreign exchange reserves rose to US$15 billion excluding gold, and over US$19 billion including gold. This was enough to cover 8.6 months of imports for India, and the balance of payments crisis was all but officially over, with the IMF programme having already ended in 1993.

After the two-step devaluation in July 1991, the rupee had been kept relatively stable, with a new system of exchange rate management called LERMS (Liberalized Exchange Rate Management System) being introduced on 1 March 1992[305] to facilitate currency transactions for exporters and remittances. But it charged different prices for exports and capital account transactions, largely to keep a lid on foreign outflows. This practice was abandoned in 1993; as capital inflows surged, the RBI unified the exchange rate structure, resulting in a slight depreciation towards the market rate. This was also one of the recommendations of the high-level committee on balance of payments under Dr Rangarajan.

Large capital inflows in 1993 brought the dilemma of allowing the currency to appreciate in line with the improving external position, but the RBI held its ground, deeming the benefits of competitiveness to outweigh the possible improvement in inflation. In its 1993–94 annual report, RBI indicated its position of 'activism' in exchange rate management,[306] but in an almost contradictory signal, in August 1994, it accepted IMF's Article VIII[307] and agreed to make the rupee convertible on the current account transactions. This was a big step for India, as it was just fresh out of an IMF programme. The current account convertibility rules were further liberalized in 1995–1996.

Ending the decades-long debt financing

Even before the balance of payments crisis was triggered, the government's large borrowings, funded through automatic debt monetization by the RBI through ad hoc treasury bills and higher SLR requirements, were brewing trouble. Governor Venkitaramanan in one his first steps on 8 January 1991 asked the government to reign in the deficits, and stressed the inability of the central bank to keep supporting the government in its fiscal excesses.[308]

Nonetheless, the crisis came and the government was forced into emergency fiscal consolidation, partially through the pressure from the IMF to adhere to the requirements of its standby arrangement facility. As the Narasimham Committee report was tabled, the focus shifted to a long-term solution for fiscal financing, especially one that would reduce financial repression and allow for more market-based pricing of government's borrowing. In such a scenario, deficit financing through the RBI was limited to ₹7,500 crore for fiscal year 1993–94, which allowed for a significant reduction in both incremental and existing SLR requirements.

Further, a large expansion in its net foreign assets meant that to control the money supply, the RBI need not rely on purchasing domestic assets to create reserve money, and the pressure to reduce SLR further increased, to keep debt financing in check. This was a very new problem for the RBI; it had always faced constraints in funding the fiscal deficit, but now it had to reduce sources of funding given rising foreign assets. As early as February 1993, Governor Rangarajan also gave the government options to fund their deficit through 'market sources', including tapping debt mutual funds to subscribe partly to treasury bonds.[309] To strengthen his argument, Governor Rangarajan also spoke at length[310] on the issue of the independence of a central bank and the burden that debt monetization created. In a speech on 17 September 1993, Governor Rangarajan argued for limits on automatic debt financing to ensure a more appropriate control over money supply.

As the RBI history describes it, the 'epochal' moment in India's banking system and for the RBI came in September 1994, when the government signed an agreement with the Reserve Bank to phase out direct and unlimited monetization of the fiscal deficit, thus giving the RBI greater control over its monetary policy. The signposts were present as early as December 1993, when Governor Rangarajan laid out a sequence of reforms[311] to phase out automatic debt monetization and allow SLR rates to settle at 25 per cent by 1995–96, as envisaged in the Narasimham Committee report.

Instead of ad hoc treasury bills, the RBI agreed to provide the government a 'ways and means advances' limit, which would allow the government to make temporary withdrawals to manage its cash flow, but would be kept close to balance for every year. The agreement also gave the RBI greater flexibility to decide bond purchases to control the money supply, and set limits on the base and ceiling amount of debt financing the RBI could provide the government.

The government to its credit accepted the programme, and in the budget speech for fiscal year 1994–95, Finance Minister Manmohan Singh announced limits on the use of ad hoc treasury bills for funding the fiscal deficit. The agreement was formalized on 9 September 1994, with a stipulation that automatic debt funding would cease by fiscal year 1997–98, after being reduced over the course of three years. The announcement was hailed by the Reserve Bank as a 'landmark development,'[312] and began to unwind a practice that had been innocently introduced by Governor Rama Rau in 1955, but had often been misused by governments to finance their political excesses.

Losing the reformist instinct

The early part of the nineties was a time of great crisis, but unlike previous instances, the political leadership had the courage to turn it into a time of unbound opportunities. As Shankkar Aiyar notes in his book, *Accidental India*, in 'political economy, though, an accident can also be fortuitous. India's ascent has been fuelled by serendipity; change has come about as a consequence of circumstance and crisis, and has always been a result of an exogenous force. Most often, that force has been a crisis.'[313]

Once the crisis of 1991 abated, the reformist zeal in the government, bureaucracy and the political leadership also fizzled out. By the end of 1994, the government was staring at the prospect of fighting the 1996 general elections. The government's reliance on debt financing from the RBI had reduced, but large capital flows meant that money supply had risen sharply, prompting inflation to increase. This led to the Reserve Bank reversing course, and it began tightening monetary conditions by raising the CRR by 1 per cent to 15 per cent in June–August 1994.[314]

However, given the falling deficit and gradual shift to market borrowing, SLR rates continued to decline, falling to 31.5 per cent by the end of 1994; they were thus on track to reach the Narasimham Committee recommendation of 25 per cent. The inflationary impulse subsided quickly, but not before the RBI had taken further tightening measures, impounding liquidity on incremental foreign deposits received through the Foreign Currency Non-Repatriable (FCNR) and Non-Resident External (NRE) channels by banks. The mixed signalling of rising CRR and falling SLR was summed up by deputy governor S.S. Tarapore, who indicated that the Reserve Bank had 'long since crossed the Rubicon'[315] to finance the government's deficit, and hence given its more market-driven nature, SLR rates had decoupled from the borrowing programme.

The Congress government under P.V. Narasimha Rao lost the elections in 1996, and Finance Minister Manmohan Singh also lost the Lok Sabha elections from South Delhi. However, the impact the Narasimha Rao government had on financial sector reforms was far-reaching. Fortuitously, despite political fragmentation, economic reforms continued, and unlike past crises, India was on the verge of negotiating one without stumbling.

Chapter 11

Learning by doing

As 1996 dawned, India had a lot going for it. Inflation was low by historical standards, growth was recovering and the currency was stable. India's foreign reserves had grown by leaps and bounds, and its external cover ratios for both imports and short-term debt were high.

But on the political front, instability returned in May 1996, when a Narasimha Rao-led Congress lost the elections and the Bharatiya Janata Party, an alter ego of the erstwhile Bharatiya Jana Sangh, emerged as the single largest group in the Lok Sabha. After a brief period of thirteen days in power, the BJP led by Atal Bihari Vajpayee gave way to a coalition of regional parties, the United Front, led by H.D. Deve Gowda, the chief minister of Karnataka.

The political instability did not have much of an impact on the underlying economic conditions. The economy was in a better shape, and this economic stability was partly achieved by the continuation of the Reserve Bank's restrictive monetary policy stance through fiscal year 1995–96, due to the double-digit rate of inflation India had experienced in the preceding two years, amid strong growth.[316] While the bank rate was maintained at 12 per cent, the Reserve Bank tried to balance that with a gradual reduction in the CRR through 1995–96 to ensure steady flow of credit to satiate the rising demand for funds from both the government and the corporate sector.[317] This was, however, done in a way that would not trigger inflation. RBI began reducing the CRR from 15 per cent on 11 November 1995 and kept gradually reducing the rate until 18 January 1997, finally stopping at 10 per cent. This period also saw the extension of Governor Rangarajan's term by two years. The pace of easing was something India had not witnessed in the past. This coupled with significant foreign reserves accretion meant that liquidity conditions in the money market were flush[318] and the RBI had to step in and withdraw liquidity through its repo window.

The year also marked the end of ad hoc treasury bills being used in monetization of the fiscal deficit. Finance Minister P. Chidambaram, who had left the Congress and formed the Tamil Maanila Congress, which was part of the United Front government, declared his intention of honouring the agreement to end of the use of ad hoc treasury bills in his first budget speech on 21 July 1996,[319] and in his 28 February 1997 budget speech he honoured the promise by abolishing the ad hoc bills and the budget deficit to introduce the fiscal deficit. This was the culmination of a four decade-long practice and heralded a new era in monetary policy management, while significantly bolstering RBI's autonomy and independence. The monetization practice was replaced by a ways and means advance to help during temporary mismatches, while the government signed a supplemental agreement with the RBI on borrowing support on 26 March 1997, which would eventually be phased out as well.

Several other extensive reforms pertaining to the economy and the RBI were also announced in Chidambaram's 'miracle budget' of 1997–98. Apart from putting an end to ad hoc bills, the finance minister also announced large income tax cuts for both individuals and corporates, raised exemptions for the middle class and lowered withholding taxes for non-resident Indians investing in India.[320] But from the RBI's perspective, a key departure was made with respect to foreign exchange regulations, with the government announcing the scrapping of the Foreign Exchange Regulation Act, 1973, which was to be replaced by a new Foreign Exchange Management Act.[321] This was done as the government believed 'that the time has come for a preparatory work towards capital account convertibility.'[322]

The Tarapore Committee and the Asian crisis

The finance minister also asked the Reserve Bank to set up an expert committee to lay out a road map for full capital account convertibility. The committee was chaired by former deputy governor S.S. Tarapore and included Kirit Parekh, A.V. Rajwade, Dr Surjit Bhalla and M.G. Bhide as members.[323] The Tarapore Committee submitted its report on 30 May 1997. The report outlined the sequence of steps needed to move towards full capital account convertibility, including allowing corporates to borrow in foreign currency with limited restrictions, allowing debt-creating inflows to return in a phased manner, and permitting domestic companies to invest abroad.[324] The report perhaps reflected the optimism created by the foreign reserves accretion following the reforms of 1991, and suggested wide-ranging reforms in the investment rules for both residents and non-residents to and from India. The report also had a shadow of the 'Washington Consensus', a set of standard policy prescriptions that multilateral agencies such as the IMF and World Bank suggested to crisis-stricken countries.[325]

Ironically, as the committee was recommending full capital account convertibility in three years, a balance of payments crisis was brewing in the neighbourhood. Thailand ran into trouble with short-term capital outflows, spending over US$33 billion of reserves to defend its currency peg. On 2 July, Thailand's central bank gave up and announced a managed float of the Thai baht, with speculative attacks spreading to other currencies in the region, such as the Philippine peso, the Korean won and the Indonesian rupiah. The Asian financial crisis was spreading rapidly and almost every country affected by it had to approach the IMF for either financial or technical assistance, amidst political turmoil.[326]

Back home, a political crisis was brewing as the Congress Party insisted on the replacement of Prime Minister H.D. Deve Gowda. Eventually, Inder Kumar Gujral, the external affairs minister in Deve Gowda's cabinet, was appointed as prime minister. Although the government under him was doomed from the beginning, financial management did not suffer as Chidambaram continued as finance minister and Governor Rangarajan remained at the Reserve Bank.

India continued to pursue some basic foreign exchange reforms given its own healthy external position. In fact, a day after Thailand's decision to devalue the baht, the Reserve Bank liberalized the outbound remittances limits, raising them considerably for travel and gifts.[327] However, the mood turned pensive as the negative spillover from the Asian financial crisis on trade and financial markets was increasingly felt and the Indian rupee depreciated against the US dollar in September. Governor Rangarajan made a statement on 10 September, citing hedging as the key reason for the depreciation[328] and followed it with stepping up support to encourage non-resident deposits and lower credit rates for exporters.[329]

This was not before an important signal was sent out by the Reserve Bank through Deputy Governor Y.V. Reddy. Internally, RBI had felt the rupee was too expensive and some depreciation was needed in a timely manner to prevent a sharp selloff. In a speech on 15 August 1997, Dr Reddy spoke on the issue of currency overvaluation, which led to a desired correction in an act of 'Open Mouth Operation', as termed by Dr Reddy.[330] But the speech caused a flutter in Delhi and Prime Minister I.K. Gujral spoke to the *Economic Times* about a possible switch in exchange rate policy, perhaps because of the currency depreciation that was witnessed following Reddy's speech. But the depreciation was needed and desired by the RBI.

Governor Rangarajan, in his last monetary and credit policy statement on 21 October 1997, lowered the CRR by 2 percentage points (pp) and brought down the SLR to a uniform rate of 25 per cent, thus achieving the last bit of key financial sector reform that the Narasimham Committee had recommended. The five years under Governor Rangarajan saw not only a significant change in both the regime and form of the central bank, but also fundamental changes such as the phasing out of ad hoc treasury bills, full current account convertibility and reintroduction of private banks into the banking system. Chakravarthi Rangarajan retired from the governor's chair on 22 November 1997. He was replaced by Dr Bimal Jalan, who had donned several hats in the Ministry of Finance during the past two decades and was serving as member-secretary of the Planning Commission at the time of his appointment.

Bimal Jalan does the currency firefighting

Dr Bimal Jalan was born and raised in Kolkata in a Marwari household. He attended Presidency College and later studied at both Oxford and Cambridge. He played a key role during the seventies and eighties in the Ministry of Finance, culminating with his appointment as the chief economic advisor during the 1980s. His arrival at the RBI was largely seen as a sign of continuity after Dr Rangarajan, but he inherited an economy going through mild doldrums, particularly the rupee.

Just before his departure, Dr Rangarajan had declared that the RBI would continue to intervene in the foreign exchange markets to protect the rupee's value and that there were 'no grounds for a further weakening of the rupee.'[331] Perhaps this placed an undue burden on the incoming governor Dr Jalan, since a shift in the intervention policy had been effectively ruled out by the outgoing governor. Economists were somewhat appalled at the change in rhetoric and Dr Surjit Bhalla, who was a member of the Tarapore Committee on capital account convertibility, estimated that the rupee was 20 per cent overvalued and that India was following the 'worst policy any country could follow [...] to have a stable, managed, overvalued exchange rate.'[332]

Dr Jalan was flown to Mumbai on a military plane for his first press conference, during which he was visibly nervous. However, once he settled down, he quickly took remedial action. On 28 November 1997, just six days after Governor Jalan took over, RBI changed the monetary policy course slightly by postponing the CRR cuts that had been announced in the previous policy decisions and tightening short-term liquidity in the money market through a new instrument of fixed rate repo transactions.[333] RBI also prohibited corporates from rebooking their forward contracts to prevent currency speculation.[334] On 6 December, RBI hiked the CRR by 50 bps to tighten liquidity further, while removing the incremental CRR of 10 per cent on non-resident Indian deposits.[335] The cumulative effect of the steps helped reduce the pressure on the rupee, which had still weakened by over 10 per cent against the US dollar to settle at around ₹39.2 to the dollar by the end of 1997.

Meanwhile, the political uncertainty that had begun after the defeat of the Narasimha Rao government in May 1996 continued. The I.K. Gujral government lost favour with the Congress Party, which was providing outside support. After weeks of speculation, President K.R. Narayanan dissolved the Parliament on 4 December 1997. Elections were scheduled for February 1998 and the country was ready to get its fourth prime minister in less than two years. The RBI, perhaps unshackled by the absence of a government watching over its shoulder, continued to tighten its monetary stance by raising the CRR by 50 bps on 17 January 1998, and also raising the bank rate by 2 per cent to 11 per cent. For his actions,

Dr Jalan won plaudits from economy watchers, and in a way, strengthened RBI's credentials to take decisive action independent of the government.[336]

Further, within two weeks of taking over as governor, Dr Jalan announced the setting up of a working group within the RBI to re-examine the analytical aspects of the monetary survey and monetary data and its changing nature given the financial sector reforms that had been undertaken.[337] While vague in its terms of reference, the working group's objectives included the evaluation of the efficacy of the RBI's monetary targeting approach, which had been adopted on the recommendation of the Sukhamoy Chakravarty Committee report in 1985. RBI's experience with monetary targeting had been mixed at best and despite ending the use of ad hoc bills for debt monetization, the lack of control over inflation was cited as a key failure of the monetary targeting framework.[338] The working group's report would have a significant impact on RBI's monetary policy approach, as we shall see later.

The elections in February 1998 proved to be inconclusive again, but the BJP and their allies had gained significant political ground. They came together to forge the National Democratic Alliance (NDA) and formed a government comfortably under the leadership of Atal Bihari Vajpayee. The RBI had in the interim taken steps to boost foreign exchange inflows, largely from the current account.[339] The Vajpayee government was sworn in on 19 March 1998, and Yashwant Sinha, who had briefly served in the Chandra Shekhar government, returned to the Ministry of Finance. While it is customary for an RBI governor to call on the new finance minister, Dr Jalan surprised Yashwant Sinha with an offer to resign since he had been appointed by the previous government. Sinha was taken aback by the offer and refused to accept it, indicating the government's comfort in Dr Jalan and his leadership at the RBI.

By that time, RBI was generally happy with the level of the rupee and its nascent stabilization, and on 23 March, the bank announced a gradual reduction of the CRR by 50 bps in two tranches over a month.[340] It appeared that things were settling down and India had broadly escaped the crisis that began in Thailand. The government in partnership with the Reserve Bank were now aiming at reviving the 'animal spirits' after the brief lull of 1997–98.

Economic sanctions and mounting economic troubles

On 11 and 13 May 1998, the Vajpayee government initiated nuclear weapons tests, detonating five weapons of various configurations at Pokhran, Rajasthan. While India became the sixth country in the world to have nuclear weapons, the euphoria in the government was short-lived, as major economies such as the United States, China and even the United Nations condemned the nuclear tests. The situation was exacerbated when Pakistan tested seven nuclear weapons on 28 and 30 May, escalating the diplomatic stand-off and raising the risk of an armed conflict.

The markets reacted negatively, and within weeks of the nuclear tests, the Sensex was down approximately 20 per cent from its end-April levels. India also faced economic sanctions from Japan, Australia and the United States, which primarily meant that economic aid was suspended. Multilateral institutions such as the World Bank and the Asian Development Bank (ADB) also stopped the flow of aid, except current commitments.[341]

The RBI and Governor Jalan contemplated issuing a press note outlining the steps it was planning to take to stabilize the market, but did not do so on Dr Reddy's advice to Dr Jalan.[342]

By the end of June 1998, Finance Minister Yashwant Sinha presented his maiden 'swadeshi' budget, a reference to making India strong, but it failed to soothe market sentiment. The rupee continued to slide, and foreign reserves had fallen by US$2.5 billion in two months.[343] While the RBI was trying to keep a lid on volatility, news reports citing moral suasion from the RBI on markets started surfacing by the end of May, which were denied by the RBI.[344]

The RBI announced a new set of measures in June to calm down markets and indicated that the rupee was gyrating to the domestic growth uncertainty and external headwinds. Stuck in a tough situation, Governor Jalan had the difficult task of managing the exchange rate while supporting growth in the face of economic sanctions. As a result, RBI reduced the cost of bank funding by a 1 pp cut to 5 per cent on 15 June 1998,[345] but kept liquidity conditions relatively tight.

Finance Minister Yashwant Sinha, who had felt helpless during his first term in 1991, was determined to avoid an economic crisis. Approaching the IMF was not an option, given the nuclear tests and the economic sanctions that had followed. By July, the government and the RBI recognized that while the Asian crisis had not severely impacted India, it did not mean a crisis could not emerge in India as well.[346] Evasive action was needed, and it had to be taken quickly.

Resurgent India Bonds

As in the past, India looked to its diaspora. Yashwant Sinha recalls in his memoirs being pressed by investment bankers in New York and London to issue foreign currency sovereign bonds to raise funds in April 1998.[347] While it was unlikely the sovereign would engage in direct government borrowing, Yashwant Sinha proposed borrowing from non-resident Indians and Persons of Indian Origin (PIOs) through the State Bank of India. The template was similar to the measures deployed during the 1991–92 crisis, but the intensity and timing were different.

The government and the Reserve Bank advised the State Bank of India on the design of the bond, which was named the 'Resurgent India Bond' on the advice of senior BJP minister L.K. Advani.[348] The bonds offered a significantly higher interest rate than was perhaps warranted, with the government taking the exchange rate risk. The five-year bonds were offering a 7.75 per cent interest rate for US dollars and an 8 per cent interest rate for sterling.[349] The government hoped to raise approximately US$2 billion, but the response from NRIs and PIOs was much more positive. This was perhaps partly driven by India's generally sound economy and the surge in patriotism following the nuclear tests and the resultant economic sanctions.[350] The RBI also agreed to create an arrangement to help both SBI and the government manage the currency risk through a maintenance of value account, announced on 10 October 1998.[351]

The bonds were a roaring success, closing three weeks ahead of their due date on 17 August 1998. The government collected over US$4 billion, more than twice what it had intended to raise. Foreign reserves jumped to over US$29 billion by the end of September 1998. Buoyed by the success of the bonds, Governor Jalan went for the proverbial 'kill' and tightened monetary policy further on 20 August, announcing a hike in CRR by 100 bps to 11 per cent, raising the repo rate to 8 per cent from 5 per cent previously, and withdrawing the facility of rebooking of forward cover for importers. The measures were dramatic and had a significant impact on the market.[352] The two-sided pill of tighter money market conditions and improving inflows worked like a charm, and the rupee continued to remain broadly stable through the rest of 1998, despite currency gyrations continuing globally.

After the issuance of the Resurgent India Bonds, Finance Minister Yashwant Sinha in an op-ed asked for both time and patience from India's policy watchers, chiding them for creating a 'mood of self-fulfilling prophecy' and saying that foreign investors were more optimistic about India than Indians themselves.[353] His instincts turned out to be correct, and India experienced macro stability in the years to come, with the reforms undertaken by the NDA government between 1998 and 2004 building a strong foundation for India's growth to take off without creating significant macro imbalances. The RBI declared its own victory through a small press release on 31 December 1998, announcing India's foreign currency assets (foreign exchange within foreign reserves) had climbed to their highest level of US$26.8 billion.[354]

The second Narasimham Committee report

Even in midst of the Asian financial crisis, the government and the RBI were cognizant of the need to strengthen India's financial system. As such, in mid-1997, former governor M. Narasimham, who had presided over the committee on financial systems constituted in 1991, was invited to do a stocktaking of the reforms initiated based on the recommendations of that committee and chart out the future course of the banking system.

The second committee on banking sector reforms submitted its report on 23 April 1998 to Yashwant Sinha. The recommendations were similar to those given in the first Narasimham Committee report,[355] advocating for greater autonomy for public sector banks and a reduced role for government and RBI in running the banks, along with a gradual reduction in government ownership to 33 per cent. The report also reiterated the suggestion to reduce the number of public sector banks through mergers in order to create institutions that were internationally competitive.

Unlike the previous report, the second Narasimham Committee report laid significant stress on improving the risk management and asset book valuation approach of banks, vouching for a greater marked to market approach (to reflect current value on the commercial bank's balance sheet) for government securities (keeping bonds valued on the balance sheet as per market prices and not their maturity), and implementing risk management based on the risk weighted assets technique to derive minimum capital adequacy requirements. This was done in the backdrop of banking systems across Asia coming under significant pressure due to the financial crisis, and hence a conservative approach was advocated to meet Basel II capital requirements, a set of norms issued by the Bank of International Settlements on capital adequacy and liquidity norms for banking systems across the world. It also advocated stronger provisioning norms (setting aside money for covering any future losses) for non-performing assets.

The Narasimham Committee also made significant suggestions with regard to the RBI, pertaining to both its role as a regulator of banks and its monetary policy operations, albeit in a tongue-in-cheek manner. The committee pointed out that in a modern economic framework, the central bank, i.e., the RBI, should focus on regulating the banks and segregate its role in owning banks. The largest ownership RBI had was in the State Bank of India, which had been on its balance sheet as part of the nationalization of the Imperial Bank of India in April 1955. The committee also asked RBI to stop participating in the bills market to manage liquidity, instead advocating a new approach where the interbank call money market was only for the primary dealers in that market.

The suggestion to get out of the money market meant that the RBI needed new policy tools for intervening in the market. This would eventually culminate in the shelving of the monetary targeting framework the RBI had adopted since the mid-eighties, and brought forward a 'multiple indicator approach', something which the RBI had already been gravitating towards by the introduction of the repo window for banks to manage liquidity.

On 10 September 1998, the Reserve Bank announced the guidelines and framework for a new asset and liability management system banks had to adopt by the next fiscal year.[356] This was followed by a timeline provided by Governor Jalan during his mid-year credit and monetary policy review on 30 October 1998, where the policy stance did not change, but the governor announced that many recommendations, such as capital adequacy of 9 per cent and higher provisioning and risk weights for certain types of transactions would be mostly achieved by the end of fiscal year 1999–2000.[357]

The governor also announced RBI's intention to introduce a 'liquidity adjustment facility' for managing liquidity in money markets, where open market operations through injection or withdrawal of funds through the repo window would be initiated. This was a recommendation of the Narasimham Committee. Concurrently, an interest rate swaps market was introduced, which would allow corporations and banks to hedge their interest rate exposure more effectively.

The actions to manage liquidity rather than the quantity of money were preceded by the steps taken by the RBI to shift the nature of policy targets and the variables used to achieve them. With financial repression reducing in the banking system given the lack of debt monetization and the introduction of private sector banks, Governor Jalan in the April 1998 monetary policy review batted for a 'multiple indicator approach', which would consider not only the money supply, but also policy rates, money market rates, inflation, currency, growth and banking system trends in the formulation of policy. This shift in policy approach was based on the premise that with a more liberalized economy, India's money supply was subject to global gyrations and hence a more sophisticated approach based on multiple variables was needed.[358] The approach was similar to the practices of other central banks and gave the Reserve Bank more freedom in setting its policy.[359]

The Reserve Bank started providing some relief on interest rates, delivering a sharp reduction in the repo rate by 2 pp to 6 per cent and lowering the bank rate by 1 pp to 8 per cent. Simultaneously, the CRR was reduced by 50 bps to 10.5 per cent. By April 1999, the market conditions were ripe for the introduction of the new process, and in its monetary and credit policy review announced on 20 April 1999, the new interim Liquidity adjustment facility (LAF) corridor was introduced to inject or withdraw liquidity from banks, while the CRR was further reduced by 50 bps to 10 per cent.[360] The system broadly operates in a similar manner till today and has stood the test of time as far as its efficacy and transmission is concerned.

Chapter 12

Back to the future

India had remained largely unscathed by the Asian financial crisis. Unlike the past, the government and Reserve Bank took decisive action ahead of a crisis evolving, despite the political uncertainty that had prevailed after the 1996 elections. What was impressive was that India's external position was managed domestically through a series of measures, and the country did not have to approach multilateral agencies such as the World Bank or the IMF, not that the option was available in 1998. The exercise of raising funds through the Resurgent India Bonds scheme and tightening of policy conditions was indicative of the Reserve Bank's long institutional memory and a testament to Finance Minister Yashwant Sinha's commitment to preventing a repeat of 1991 crisis.

An improving economic backdrop

At the beginning of fiscal year 1999-2000, political uncertainty returned when Prime Minister Atal Bihari Vajpayee lost his majority in the Parliament after J. Jayalalithaa, leader of the AIADMK, the southern partner of the NDA, withdrew support.[361] The opposition led by Sonia Gandhi and the Congress Party also failed to cobble together a majority, and as a result, on 26 April 1999, President K.R. Narayanan dissolved the twelfth Lok Sabha.[362] Political uncertainty was back, and India was heading for its fifth national election within the decade. As in the past, Atal Bihari Vajpayee and his team were asked to stay on as caretakers till such time as the elections were held and results declared.

Relative to the political backdrop, the economic backdrop was far more peaceful. By the end of May 1999, India's foreign reserves had climbed to

US$33.5 billion, up from US$30 billion at the end of 1998. The currency was broadly stable at around ₹42.5 to the US dollar and optimism was returning. However, Indian equity markets had largely ignored the news reports about an escalation in firing exchanges at the line of control near Kargil, a military town about 200 kilometres from Srinagar. The matter escalated when two Indian Air Force fighter jets were shot down by Pakistan on 27 May, underscoring the seriousness of the situation.

Financial markets globally reacted negatively, and over the course of the first two weeks of June, the rupee weakened by a percent. The Reserve Bank stayed in the shadows but market intervention had likely taken place to prevent the currency from weakening further. By early July, India's victory in the Kargil battle looked imminent and equity markets zoomed higher on the back of a large funds inflow[363] and falling inflation. The rupee was not allowed to appreciate by the Reserve Bank, but the pace of depreciation somewhat subsided and foreign reserves remained broadly flat. While the Reserve Bank played a minor role, its employees did contribute a day's salary for the army's welfare.[364]

Rising foreign exchange reserves

By the end of the Kargil war, India's foreign policy equations had changed dramatically. This had positive effects on the economy as the foreign sanctions imposed against India were poised to be removed, largely due to the improving relations with the United States post the skirmish. With the end of the Kargil war, the government of India and the Reserve Bank shifted focus to the economic issue at hand, the increase in oil prices.

In the wake of the Asian crisis, oil prices had fallen globally, with demand from energy-intensive Asian tigers falling rapidly. To shore up confidence, OPEC announced significant production cuts, which coincided with one of the strongest El Niño weather cycles in 1998, leading to drought, crop failures and higher oil prices at the same time. As Asian economies recovered after the crisis in 1999, global demand for oil picked up and oil prices tripled from US$10 per barrel to over US$30 per barrel between 1999 and 2000.

For India, the oil price shock was nothing new. However, the policy response once again was more measured and targeted. India had seen elevated food inflation through 1998, and when oil prices started increasing in September 1999, food inflation was also declining given better harvests, thus keeping headline inflation in check. Further, Deputy Governor Y.V. Reddy acknowledged the support received from the government on the fiscal front, adding that money expansion was incrementally being determined by foreign reserves expansion, rather than deficit financing, which further helped keep inflation in check.[365]

Given the relatively weak economic backdrop and the hike in oil prices, the government had no option but to raise fuel prices. India's foreign reserves had started moderating, and on 23 August 1999, the Reserve Bank unveiled a new tool in its arsenal to shore up confidence in the rupee, which had depreciated to ₹43.55 to the US dollar.[366] RBI announced a special window for oil companies to source foreign exchange directly from the central bank at market rates to correct the demand-supply mismatch in the market. The Reserve Bank also announced its intention to intervene in the market, as and when needed, through the State Bank of India.[367]

While the market reaction to the RBI's guidance was small, it certainly helped stem the pace of reserves loss. India's foreign reserves showed modest declines through September 1999 and started rising gradually from October onwards. In the mid-term credit and monetary policy, Governor Jalan reduced the CRR by 1 per cent to 9 per cent, while also removing incremental SLR on FCNR deposits. Along with that, he continued to guide the market to expect lower cost of funding and CRR over the medium term, with flexibility to ease or tighten liquidity given the evolving situation.[368] This was effectively forward guidance even before the term came into vogue, but with sufficient degrees of freedom attached to it.

The policy also announced several key changes to improve the depth of India's call money market and repo mechanisms. The RBI had previously announced a list of primary dealers in August 1999. It also announced the constitution of an informal working group for a valuation of the bank's investment portfolio to better understand risk weights that needed to be assigned.

India Millennium Deposits and currency games

During the late nineties, the 'Y2K' bug generated mass hysteria. A computer accounting flaw, it triggered fear close to the turn of the millennium of computer systems collapsing, given the lack of programming updates to account for the years after 1999.[369] The Reserve Bank also made extensive preparations to ensure India's financial sector, especially banks, were ready to take evasive action and had a game plan ready to tackle the situation. Through 1999, several guidelines were released, and the RBI set up a high-level group to study the readiness of the financial sector under the chairmanship of Deputy Governor S.P. Talwar.[370] The Y2K bug had no impact on the Indian financial system, given RBI's push to commercial banks to prepare them in advance for any problems.

Serendipitously, the government was also working on a new policy for the IT sector and had released a draft policy on the setting up of call centres in India. This involved lowering the cost of international calls and allowing companies to hire and fire liberally in the sector. Also, state governments such as those of Andhra Pradesh and Karnataka were offering sops such as cheap land and tax holidays to help drive the BPO offshoring sector. The central government played its part through the Group on Telecom and IT convergence (GOT-IT), set up in December 1999.[371] Over time, this sector would play an instrumental role in buttressing India's current account position through large service exports and remittances.

By March 2000, RBI had accumulated over US$38 billion in foreign reserves. The improving inflation backdrop allowed the Reserve Bank to front load its monetary easing, and it reduced the CRR, bank rate and repo rate by 1 pp each, to 8 per cent, 7 per cent and 5 per cent respectively on 1 April 2000.[372] A few days later, Governor Jalan was handed a two-year extension on his term as RBI governor, a good seven months ahead of the end of his three-year term.[373] The April credit and monetary policy review did not contain major changes, except a firm commitment to roll out the LAF window for liquidity management to replace the previous interim corridor.

So far, the rupee had remained broadly stable, but after the monetary easing in April 2000, it came under renewed pressure, resulting in a sharp depreciation by almost a rupee in May 2000. The RBI issued a statement clearly flagging that 'it does not, repeat it does not, target a particular value of the rupee in relation to the US dollar. The often-cited round numbers, such as, "Rs.42", "Rs.43", or "Rs.44" simply have no significance for the management of the exchange rate by the RBI. Nor does RBI recognise any level such as "lowest ever reached in the past" or "lowest last year" or any such dividing line.'[374] It also introduced harsh penalties on exporters holding back payments, while imposing a surcharge on interest paid on import financing.

While the statement made clear the RBI and Governor Jalan's intentions to stabilize the rupee, after a brief period of stability, the rupee resumed its depreciation trend in July, leading to a bank rate hike of 1 per cent along with CRR being raised by 0.5 per cent on 21 July 2000[375] as the rupee breached the level of ₹45 to the US dollar. Economists and industry were divided on the move,[376] but it failed provide any significant relief.

As oil prices kept rising through 2000 and equity markets were under pressure from the dot-com bubble bursting, India's foreign reserves position was deteriorating, albeit gradually. RBI emphasized that the rupee's weakness was largely against the US dollar, but it also indicated clearly that intervention in the foreign exchange market would be swift and unpredictable. 'Reserve Bank will also continue to monitor developments in the market very closely, and take such further measures as may be necessary from time to time in order to stabilise expectations, to the extent feasible, and to help reduce the effects of "leads" and "lags".'[377]

However, the rupee remained under pressure and by September 2000 it had depreciated by almost 6 per cent since the beginning of the year. By now the RBI was even hedging crude oil risk for oil companies, and by October, the government decided to tap the non-resident Indian community again for funds, to shore up the falling foreign reserves. As always, the playbook of measures from the government remained the same, but as with the Resurgent India Bonds, the timing was more appropriate. The government once again turned to the State Bank of India, which christened its five-year bond the 'India Millennium Deposits', and expected to raise US$2 billion.[378] However, it ended up raising more than US$5.5 billion and by the end of December 2000, India's foreign reserves had risen above US$40 billion and the rupee had stabilized. RBI promptly started easing policy in early 2001, delivering CRR cuts along with a reduction in the bank rate.[379]

Over the course of the next two years, India continued to pursue a policy of gradual currency depreciation while building up its foreign reserves. The rupee depreciated by about 4 to 5 per cent, but foreign reserves increased to over US$70 billion as India's external position improved significantly due to higher remittances, a fall in crude oil prices and better services exports. By 2002, India's current account appeared firmly in surplus and foreign exchange reserve accretion accelerated. On the rupee, barring an episode of sharp depreciation after the terrorist attacks in New York and Washington on 11 September 2001, the foreign exchange market remained broadly range-bound until mid-2002, when the rupee's depreciation path turned into one of gradual appreciation, settling at below ₹48 to the US dollar at the end of 2002.

Ketan Parekh and the Global Trust Bank debacle

Just after the 2001-02 budget was announced, Ketan Parekh, a stock market broker who had found tremendous success in the last two years, was called in for questioning by SEBI. Ketan Parekh had worked with Harshad Mehta during his early years in the market and had been doing remarkably well, picking a niche set of ten stocks, known as 'K-10'.[380] These stocks saw their valuations jacked up through a series of loans financed through promoters, banks and foreign funds. In return, in order to monetize the inflated share purchases,[381] Parekh offloaded the stocks either as collateral to banks, or to institutions such as the Unit Trust of India (UTI).

SEBI launched an investigation into Parekh's activities after the unusual behaviour in equity markets in February and March after the budget was announced. The sharp declines on 23 February, 2 March and 13 March gave SEBI enough signals to haul Parekh in for questioning.[382] What was revealed over the course of the next few months was an intricate web of funding from the commercial banks, cooperative banks such as Gujarat's Madhavpura Mercantile Cooperative Bank (MMCB), and non-bank financial institutions (NBFCs) such as UTI. Parekh was eventually arrested on 30 March 2001.

For the Reserve Bank, which was the custodian and regulator of private banks, cooperative banks and NBFCs, the revelations came as a major embarrassment. Particularly, the governance of the cooperative banks came in for severe criticism after it was discovered that the MMCB had provided Parekh with a ₹200 crore credit line.[383] Further, the financial media published stories alleging that the RBI was taking a 'casual' approach to investigating the evolving stock market scandal, which was firmly refuted by the Reserve Bank.[384]

RBI even served a legal notice to *The Economic Times*, considering the seriousness of the allegation. A week after serving the notice, RBI and SEBI released a joint technical standing committee report, outlining steps to restrict bank financing of equities and IPOs for individuals and institutions.[385] In the RBI's first half credit and monetary policy review, Governor Jalan outlined more steps to minimize the 'contagion' from equities to the banking system, including strengthening the prudential norms on cooperative banks.

On its own, the Reserve Bank had initiated enquiries into the cooperative banks, and also began enquiries with the Global Trust Bank (GTB), which had announced its intention to merge with UTI Bank in late 2000. Global Trust Bank was among the first private sector banks to be set up in India after liberalization, beginning operations in September 1994. Ramesh Gelli, a former chairman and managing director at Vysya Bank, started GTB and served as its first chairman. GTB had a fierce reputation for being competitive, and with a large depositor base, it had also penetrated the small and medium-sized enterprises (SME) sector. However, during the Ketan Parekh debacle, it was found that GTB had very high exposure to capital markets and that it may have used Parekh as a conduit to shore up its share prices ahead of the proposed merger with UTI Bank.

On 27 April 2001, the government constituted a joint parliamentary committee under the chairmanship of Prakash Mani Tripathi, which submitted its report only on 12 December 2002. This did not deter RBI from taking its own measures, and even before the RBI's deposition to the joint parliamentary committee, the central bank asked Mr Gelli to resign as chairman of GTB in April 2001.[386] He was then asked to step down from the board in June 2001.[387]

Governor Jalan's deposition to the joint parliamentary committee took place in September 2001. The committee report questioned the RBI's annual financial inspection, asking whether it was 'a mere formality', and whether the 'inspection system was effective enough'.[388] The committee also noted 'both external audit and RBI supervision to have been weak and ineffective', and pulled up the RBI by saying that 'a good Regulator would have anticipated the possibility of diversion of funds and taken pre-emptive action to forestall it'.[389]

The government was also facing a significant amount of pressure from the opposition, as the UTI suspended both sale and purchase of its popular Unit scheme, 1964, in July 2001[390] leading to the dismissal of UTI chairman P.S. Subramanyam.[391] Yashwant Sinha suggested M. Damodaran's name as the next chief of SEBI to Prime Minister Vajpayee, on the recommendation of Governor Jalan.[392]

In its inspection of the Global Trust bank records, RBI found that the problems in the Global Trust Bank were larger than previously anticipated. The bank's net worth was negative considering its reckless lending practices, and in its auditor's report submitted on 30 September 2003, despite GTB making operational profits in 2002-03, the Reserve Bank had little option but to recommend looking for a buyer. As always, the government and the Reserve Bank looked at the public sector banks. On the evening of 24 July 2004, under Governor Y.V. Reddy, RBI announced a three-month moratorium on deposits placed with the Global Trust Bank[393] and on 26 July, announced a merger with Oriental Bank of Commerce to bail out depositors.[394] This was the first major bank failure in India since the collapse of the Palai Bank in 1960.

The financial press was critical of the Reserve Bank's lapses in supervision, but once the depositors' interests had been kept supreme, the media turned more sanguine on the regulator, blaming the reckless nature of private sector banks as the key reason behind the bank's failure. As S. Gopalakrishnan, former CMD of Vijaya Bank, noted in his op-ed after the merger, 'Credit should definitely go to the RBI for its pro-active steps, particularly in implementing the Basel Committee norms on banking supervision. The record time in which the merger with Oriental Bank of Commerce was announced should put the legitimate fears of depositors to rest and restore public confidence that the RBI is capable of handling such tricky situations efficiently and expeditiously'.[395]

◆

By 1999, the fiscal and monetary interface had reduced considerably, thanks to the reforms undertaken after the 1991 crisis. Fiscal consolidation had been patchy, but the monetization of debt had effectively stopped, and the focus was shifting to moving government borrowing to the market. As part of the March 1997 agreement on debt financing between the government and the Reserve Bank, RBI remained the custodian of government debt issuance and still bore the responsibility of financing the deficit, but at a market-determined price.

Similarly, with regard to banks, which had been recapitalized with bearer securities issued by the government in exchange of bonds purchased under the SLR requirements, the Reserve Bank allowed them to mark-to-market these securities gradually, to ensure a fair price and adequate risk weights were being attached to them. While the government did not pursue significant fiscal consolidation, efforts were made to reduce and rationalize spending, especially revenue expenditure.

In 1999–2000, the Reserve Bank finally managed to set up a consolidated sinking fund to better manage state debt repayments and prevent them from bunching up. This was a recommendation made by the committee of state finance secretaries[396] and involved state governments paying a small part of their total state borrowings into the consolidated sinking fund in order to manage cash flows.[397] The fund was activated in fiscal year 1999–2000. Initially, the response was slow, but by 2002, eleven states were participating in it, with more looking to join.

Simultaneously, the positive drift on fiscal policy started changing in 2000, as the finance minister tabled the Fiscal Responsibility and Budget Management (FRBM) bill in the winter session of the Parliament in December 2000. The intention was to lower the central fiscal deficit from over 5 per cent of GDP to 2 per cent by 2006, and reduce the revenue deficit to zero, while reducing the overall debt burden to below 50 per cent by 2011.[398]

On 28 February 2000, a day before the 2000-01 budget was going to be presented,[399] the government formed an expenditure commission headed by former finance secretary K.P. Geethakrishnan, with internal and external members such as Kirit Parikh also a part of it. This was a significant step to show the government's intention to manage its expenditure.

Meanwhile, the RBI continued to see lower government borrowing on its balance sheet, with net bank credit to government declining, and focus quickly shifted to longer-term fiscal reforms. The government had also shown its intent to reduce subsidies by gradually raising fuel prices, and was moving ahead with reducing its employment programme by introducing a voluntary retirement scheme.

In the April 2001 credit and monetary policy review, Governor Jalan and his team at RBI outlined several key reforms pertaining to the role of the Reserve Bank as the government's debt manager. As per a working group's recommendations, Governor Jalan listed several preconditions before RBI could give up its role as the government's debt manager, such as development of financial markets, reasonable control over fiscal deficit and necessary legislative changes, of which some had already been met. The Reserve Bank also welcomed the FRBM bill that had been tabled by the finance minister in the winter session of the Parliament, and indicated that once the bill was passed, the bank could move forward with separation of debt management from monetary policy.[400] However, with the escalation of the Tehelka tapes scandal which had the ruling party BJP's president Bangaru Laxman being caught on video accepting a bribe, and the Ketan Parekh stock market fraud, the opposition decided to put the passing of the bill on the backburner and instead sent it to a parliamentary standing committee on finance under Shivraj Patil.[401]

To further improve transparency in the conduct of both fiscal and monetary policy, the government had previously set up two committees, the Advisory Group on Fiscal Transparency (chaired by Montek Singh Ahluwalia) and the Advisory Group on Transparency in Monetary and Financial Policies (chaired by M. Narasimham), which suggested some important changes in the operational conduct of monetary and fiscal policies and highlighted the need for better coordination between them.[402]

The Reserve Bank continued to ease monetary policy, reducing CRR in May 2001, but kept conducting open market operations through the daily repo and reverse repo transactions on the LAF window. Further, in September 2001, Governor Jalan reconstituted the Technical Advisory Committee on Money and Government Securities Markets for another two years to advise the Reserve Bank, on an ongoing basis, on the development of both the money and government securities markets.[403] There was also a sharp reduction in the CRR for banks, from 7.5 per cent to 5.5 per cent, with the bank rate being reduced to 6.5 per cent from 7 per cent, the lowest in almost three decades, in the mid-year monetary and credit policy review.[404]

The new-found macro stability was allowing for an unprecedented easing cycle after India was out of the currency doldrums. RBI also raised the level of interest paid on CRR balances. For financial development, it announced that the newly formed Clearing Corporation of India Limited (CCIL), which was registered on 30 April 2001, would begin a test run from November 2001, while a new uniform price auction format and a negotiated dealing system for facilitating electronic bidding in government auctions and secondary market trading would be rolled out. These changes would bring significant transparency in both pricing and liquidity of government securities markets down the line.[405]

The government, on the other hand, found pushing its fiscal agenda more difficult. In the presentation of his budget for fiscal year 2002-03, Finance Minister Yashwant Sinha defended his fiscal austerity drive, saying that 'putting our fiscal house in order must remain our highest priority',[406] and vouched to table the FRBM bill, which had returned from the standing committee during the budget session of 2002. Yashwant Sinha was not happy with the dilution of some provisions of the bill, but in his memoirs, admitted to being unable to fight the changes, given that the government needed Congress's support in passing the legislation, since the government did not have a full majority in the upper house of the Parliament to get it passed on its own.[407]

However, Yashwant Sinha would not see the bill being passed during his tenure as finance minister. This was despite implementing the right mix of fiscal conservatism and enabling an environment for inflation control, and facilitating the reduction in long-term interest rates. Yashwant Sinha was moved from the Ministry of Finance on 1 July 2002, in a direct swap with Jaswant Singh, who was serving as the external affairs minister.[408] Ironically, around the same time, Dr Jalan's term as governor was extended for another two years, putting him on track to become the second longest serving governor at the Reserve Bank after Sir Benegal Rama Rau. The financial press was impressed by the continuity at the Reserve Bank, even calling Dr Jalan a potential candidate for the Ministry of Finance down the line.[409]

Bimal Jalan leaves early

In September 2000, Rakesh Mohan replaced Dr Y.V. Reddy as the deputy governor in charge of monetary policy under Governor Jalan.[410] The October 2002 monetary and credit policy review continued easing monetary policy cautiously. In February 2003, the cabinet approved the reformed FRBM bill, which had incorporated changes recommended by the standing committee on finance,[411] and by August 2003, it received the president's assent to be signed into law. The bill was diluted somewhat to accommodate the dissenting voices of fiscal conservatism, and the target to finish the revenue deficit was pushed back to 2008, instead of 2006, while the fiscal deficit target was raised to 3 per cent by 2008.

However, the provision of not using RBI to participate in primary auctions from April 2006 and not financing the government deficit was broadly accepted, a major victory for enhancing the Reserve Bank's autonomy, which had flourished under Governor Jalan's term, enabled by Finance Minister Yashwant Sinha. As we shall see in later chapters, the FRBM bill and its impact on RBI's autonomy was evident through the next five years, as India battled with the problems of plenty.

With low inflation, stable growth, a significant balance of payments surplus and falling fiscal deficit, Governor Bimal Jalan presided over one of the longest periods of monetary easing in the Reserve Bank's history and significantly strengthened RBI's balance sheet and the institution's autonomy. His deputies also played their part in adding to the institution's credibility. However, in a turn of events, after seeing several reforms being cleared, Dr Jalan informed the government of his intention to retire ahead of his term's end in 2004.[412] He was nominated to the Rajya Sabha by the government on 27 August 2003.

In his final public address as the governor,[413] Dr Jalan emphasized that 'India should be the strongest in external sector' and that a strong external position 'gave a sense of security and confidence to the entire country'. He also added that it was of vital importance 'to have shared objectives between the central bank and the government though the instrumentalities of achieving those objectives may be different'. He acknowledged the whole-hearted support the Reserve Bank had received from the government on matters of strategy. Dr Jalan handed over the reins of the Reserve Bank to former deputy governor Dr Y.V. Reddy, who was serving as the executive director of the IMF for India at the time, on 6 September 2003. Dr Reddy became the twenty-first governor of the Reserve Bank.

Dr Jalan had completed almost six years as the governor when he stepped down, and in an interview later to *The Hindu*, advocated that his term at the Reserve Bank was spent trying to demystify policymaking as 'demystifying makes for transparency, in turn leading to accountability and responsibility. If more people understand the nuances of, say, exchange rates or interest rate policy, there will be substantial gains to public policy itself.'[414] Former governor S. Venkitaramanan also paid his compliments to Dr Jalan, calling India's approach to currency and reserve management under Dr Jalan's term[415] the best in Asia. Incoming governor Y.V. Reddy pledged to ensure that 'continuity and change will be mixed appropriately depending on the context.'[416] As Dr Reddy had spent almost six years working with Dr Jalan as his deputy governor, RBI had an almost seamless transition from one insider to another.

Chapter 13

Flow of new capital, flight of a hawk

D r Yaga Venugopal Reddy was over sixty-three years old when he took charge of the Reserve Bank. Having spent six years as the deputy governor at the bank (from 1996 to 2002), Dr Reddy was quite familiar with the institution, but also had the distinct advantage of overseeing critical reforms in the banking sector and financial markets, as well as in the fiscal monetary interface that the Reserve Bank had been facing since India's independence.

Dr Reddy, who shared his birth date with outgoing governor Dr Jalan (11 August 1941), was among the older governors to be appointed, but the Vajpayee government felt comfortable enough with his experience to offer him a five-year term instead of the customary three-year term. The last governor who was offered a five-year term was I.G. Patel, who was appointed by the Janata Party government.[417] Recounting the importance of a longer term, Governor Reddy indicated that the stability of tenure boosted his and the Reserve Bank's autonomy.

Market Stabilization Scheme

Dr Reddy's term at the RBI began with unprecedented macroeconomic stability in India. India's growth was recovering after a long period of stagnation, inflation was low, policy and market rates had been declining for some time, and the currency was appreciating almost on a trend basis, given the current account surplus and rising capital inflows. India's foreign reserves had risen multifold under Governor Jalan, and Dr Reddy at the beginning of his term was grappling with an unusual problem. There was too much money sloshing around in India's financial markets, given the lack of appropriate sterilization instruments, especially with the FRBM bill coming into force in 2003.

Initially, in the run-up to the introduction of the landmark fiscal bill, the RBI was absorbing the excess liquidity through the sale of government bonds, giving a positive signal to the domestic markets and international investors. Further, it was a clear sign that the RBI's autonomy, which had been rising since the liberalization of 1991, was accelerating, as net credit to the government was declining.

As Dr Reddy described in his seminal speech on central bank autonomy in 2001 at IIM-Indore, while 'it is difficult to measure the degree of independence [...] the abolition of the ad hoc treasury bills [...] elimination of automatic monetization of government deficits [...]' and the considerable change in the 'operational framework of the RBI [...] with clearer articulation of policy goals' had led to the central bank enjoying a high degree of operational autonomy and instrument independence for attaining monetary policy objectives.[418]

The foreign exchange reserves rose to over US$92 billion by September 2003, and the Resurgent India Bonds issued in 1998 were redeemed without any visible decline in the reserves.[419] The Reserve Bank had also dramatically lowered the deposit rate ceiling on non-resident rupee deposits[420] and was actively looking at ways to manage the foreign reserves accretion it was experiencing. In November 2003, while presenting the mid-year monetary and credit policy review, Governor Reddy noted that both money supply and reserve money growth were in control, despite significant capital inflows, and this had largely been achieved through 'substantial open market operations' by the Reserve Bank.[421] Equity markets continued to rally, with Sensex breaching 5,000 for the first time in forty-two months. Both foreign and domestic investors were bullish on the government's reforms programme, and RBI's net credit to the government was declining rapidly.

Worried over rising capital inflows and the impact on domestic liquidity, the Reserve Bank's working group on instruments of sterilization, led by RBI's executive director Usha Thorat, submitted its summary of recommendations on 2 December 2003.[422] The report outlined the emerging issues around rising capital flows, and the various options India's policymakers had in terms of sterilizing excess capital flows.

The report examined existing instruments such as the LAF, CRR, open market operations (OMOs) and foreign exchange swaps, but found them inadequate to manage liquidity and with the potential to cause negative spillovers in monetary policy. As such, the working group recommended looking at a variety of new instruments, which would enable liquidity management to operate somewhat independently of RBI's own monetary policy stance. These included the introduction of central bank securities, issuance of interest-bearing deposits by banks with the Reserve Bank, and issuance of market stabilization bonds by the government.

The report was comprehensive, and it advocated flexibility on capital account management. However, keeping the Reserve Bank's new-found operational independence in mind, the report stressed the need to explore new instruments such as bond issuance by the government, which would not require an amendment to the RBI Act. The media reacted cautiously to the idea,[423] while foreign reserves crossed US$100 billion for the first time in December 2003.

In Delhi, Finance Minister Jaswant Singh commended RBI for its reserves management and brushed aside rising questions in Parliament over the costs of maintaining such 'high levels of foreign reserves'.[424] The government, in coordination with the Reserve Bank, also prepaid some of its existing high cost foreign currency loans.[425] The Reserve Bank and Governor Reddy continued to emphasize the need to look at new tools. At a speech delivered at the National Institute of Bank Management on 21 January 2004, Governor Reddy stressed the need for fiscal deficit control and his unwillingness to 'take too many risks in financial sector' when it came to capital account convertibility and capital flows management.[426] The RBI's report on currency and finance released a few days later also stressed on 'careful calibration of instruments to moderate market pressures without any distortionary shocks on the performance of the economy'.[427]

February 2004 was a busy month for the government and the Reserve Bank. Buoyed by its success in state elections held in late 2003, the NDA government led by Prime Minister Vajpayee decided to bring forward the national elections, hoping to capture votes on 'the feel-good factor' in the country. While the Lok Sabha was dissolved on 6 February,[428] Finance Minister Jaswant Singh presented his interim budget for fiscal year

2004–05 on 3 February. The budget had plenty of sops for the industry, government employees and agriculture. The government also announced its desire to allow the industrial sector to access foreign currency loans, which are called external commercial borrowings (ECBs), for which revised guidelines had been published on 31 January 2004, just days ahead of the budget. The policy was further boosted by Moody's Investors Service, a reputed global credit rating agency, lifting India's foreign currency credit rating to 'investment grade' on 22 January 2004, which fuelled the feel-good factor for the government.[429]

The new guidelines allowed industries to borrow a maximum of US$500 million for five years through the automatic route, without seeking pre-approval from the Reserve Bank, except for financial institutions. To ensure that the quality of institutions seeking foreign funding was sound, the Reserve Bank put a cap on interest payments that companies could make on their borrowings.[430] The improving credit ratings and better financial health encouraged the Reserve Bank to gradually allow Indian corporates to venture overseas, and later in February 2004, it allowed eligible corporates to raise foreign debt funding to pursue investments or joint ventures overseas.[431]

While the government was waiting for the elections, the finance minister gave the green light for the Market Stabilization Scheme (MSS), which would allow the Reserve Bank to issue special securities to withdraw excess liquidity on behalf of the government. The MSS would be managed by the Reserve Bank, but its ownership would rest with the government, who would service its interest costs, but would not utilize the funds to meet its expenditure.[432]

It was an incredible moment in the history of the Reserve Bank and its interface with fiscal policy. From facilitating direct monetization of budget deficits, the Reserve Bank was now being empowered to issue securities for the government to mop up excess liquidity, without the government being able to use the funds. The RBI was also empowered to decide the amount, tenor, timing and nature of securities to be issued, with a large limit of ₹60,000 crore. This significantly boosted the Reserve Bank's autonomy to conduct its monetary policy, and in its press release, the bank expressed its gratitude to the government.

The market reaction was concerning, as there were fears of liquidity tightening through an additional tool of liquidity management.[433] However, the RBI saw little reason to change its path,[434] and the MSS came into effect from 1 April 2004 and was immediately utilized by the RBI to start calibrating liquidity conditions.

A former RBI governor becomes the prime minister

Despite having favourable ground reports, opinion polls and a strong economic backdrop, the NDA government under Vajpayee lost the 2004 elections to the Congress-led United Progressive Alliance (UPA).[435] With the support of the leftist parties, the Congress managed to cross the required threshold for forming a stable government. However, Sonia Gandhi, who was widely seen as the prime ministerial candidate, refused to become the prime minister and instead anointed Dr Manmohan Singh, the former finance minister and former governor of the Reserve Bank, to serve as the thirteenth prime minister of India.

It was a moment of pride for the Reserve Bank to see a former head take up the top political job; while former governors had served as finance ministers, Dr Singh was the first former governor to become the prime minister. Despite his reformist credentials, the incoming government's tie-up with the communist parties and the noise around the discontinuation of economic reforms and privatization led to a sharp equity sell-off, leading to trading being suspended a few times.[436] While the selection of Manmohan Singh as prime minister did help markets recover, there was still apprehension about the unexpected turn of events, and over the course of May-July 2004, foreign reserves fell while the rupee came under renewed pressure.

The government appointed P. Chidambaram as finance minister. Chidambaram signalled continuity on economic reforms, but promised to give them a 'human face', in line with the UPA's agreed terms under the common minimum programme.[437] In an unusual delay, the Reserve Bank released its annual monetary and credit policy only on 18 May 2004,[438] after the election results were declared. However, the policy itself did not contain any major changes, perhaps as a nod to the political changes that were afoot.

In the government's first budget, Finance Minister Chidambaram vouched to maintain the economy on a path of high growth and fiscal consolidation, while maintaining the new government's promise to increase welfare programmes.[439] With regard to capital markets and the Reserve Bank, the budget was largely silent, except raising the limits on foreign institutional investor (FII) investment in debt markets at the margin.

The Reserve Bank was still busy during this period with the Global Trust Bank's failure in July-August 2004. But it continued to introduce new tools to improve banking efficiency, such as its Real Time Gross Settlement (RTGS) facility for bank customers on 16 August 2004, after introducing it for inter-bank settlements in March 2004.[440]

For the Reserve Bank, there was some noise to be faced on its foreign exchange reserves management, as several proponents of the new government were openly calling for using foreign reserves to promote domestic investment.[441] While the issue may appear trivial to some economists, there were some economists arguing for higher investments to run down reserves,[442] which were deemed to be too high. In fact, in its Article IV discussion (regular dialogue between IMF and member countries) for 2003, even the IMF advocated more flexibility in India's exchange rate management, but in 2004, cautioned against utilizing foreign reserves for domestic infrastructure investment.[443]

The RBI did actually spend some time looking at this proposal and even considered setting up a special investment vehicle in London to bring back the funds for domestic investments in India. In fact, even Larry Summers, a renowned American economist and former Treasury secretary in United States to the Clinton administration between 1999–2000, who had visited India in 2006 to deliver the L.K. Jha memorial lecture backed the idea[444] and wanted the 'excess reserves' of emerging markets to be pooled into an infrastructure fund, which would in turn drive growth and investments across the global economy. The idea kept resurfacing, but never really took off.

However, at the end of the day, the argument of using foreign exchange reserves for infrastructure was a bit whimsical, since foreign reserves were effectively a signage for India's external earnings being high and would be converted into domestic currency, which was effectively being sterilized through the MSS. Beyond that, there was neither a legal nor ethical framework under which the Reserve Bank could transfer its 'foreign reserves' to the government for infrastructure spending, since its rupee equivalent was already placed in the markets.

Speaking before he demitted office, Dr Jalan candidly brushed aside criticism of the policy to not use reserves for investment, since the 'decision to invest, consume or deposit the additional rupee resources lies with recipients, and not with the RBI. By all means, let us [RBI and government] urge them to investment, but there is not much of a case for pointing a finger at additional reserves as a "cause" of lower than desirable level of investment activity in the economy.'[445]

Reddy begins to signal caution on inflation

The UPA government took over at a time when India's growth was improving, while the global recovery in activity and commodity prices was in full swing. China had joined the World Trade Organization in 2001 and had been clocking a stratospheric growth rate since then, driven by investment and trade. This pushed up commodity prices generally, and by mid-2004, Brent crude oil prices had risen by more than 50 per cent.

While inflationary pressures were manageable in India, the Reserve Bank was cautious. For starters, Governor Reddy had resisted easing policy rates further, and given that inflation was starting to trend higher, RBI started turning marginally hawkish in its guidance. When the wholesale price inflation spiked above 7.5 per cent year-on-year in August 2004, Governor Reddy said that inflation was higher than previously expected and that the Reserve Bank was 'monitoring the developments carefully'.[446] Speaking at Institute for Development and Research in Banking Technology (IDBRT) in August 2004, Governor Reddy further outlined the emerging imported price pressures and indicated that supply shocks emanating from rising oil prices were driving up inflation, but emphasized the 'importance of Reserve Bank's credibility in maintaining price stability consistent with the compulsions of the growth dynamics"[447].

As inflation continued to rise amid ample liquidity, the Reserve Bank's monetary policy reversed course, and on 11 September 2004, the Reserve Bank raised the CRR by 50 bps to 5.0 per cent in two tranches of 25 bps each. This was the first hike in CRR since August 1998, when India was grappling with rupee weakness, and was done largely keeping inflation in mind. Further, the RBI also reduced compensation on CRR deposits by banks from 6 per cent (i.e. the bank rate) to 3.5 per cent, justified on basis of substantial reduction in CRR over the recent years, based on recommendations of the Internal Group on Liquidity Adjustment Facility.[448]

The government reacted cautiously, preferring to focus on inflation management by easing import restrictions and reducing duty on petroleum products.[449] The RBI maintained a relatively hawkish stance in its mid-year monetary and credit policy review by cutting its growth projection and raising its inflation forecast. RBI also shelved its long-term repo operations, instead shifting the LAF facility to overnight transactions. The bank raised the repo rate by 25 bps to 4.75 per cent, while cautioning markets to be 'prepared for the uncertainties' even as the RBI would 'pursue stability'.[450]

On 21 September 2004, two new deputy governors began their terms at the Reserve Bank, Vittaldas Leeladhar, a former banker, and Shyamala Gopinath, an executive director of the Reserve Bank. However, the appointments were overshadowed by the selection of Deputy Governor Rakesh Mohan as Secretary, Department of Economic Affairs in the Ministry of Finance, rather than as finance secretary, a post held by his predecessor D.C. Gupta. This raised eyebrows within the government and the media, but nonetheless, Rakesh Mohan left the Reserve Bank on 31 October 2004 to take up his new role.[451] As his replacement, Dr Reddy tried to recruit Dr Raghuram Rajan, an upcoming Indian economist who was then serving as the Chief Economist at IMF, who Dr Reddy saw as a future governor of the Reserve Bank. Unfortunately, Dr Rajan did not accept the position and chose to stay on at the IMF.[452] Rakesh Mohan's stint with the Ministry of Finance was quite short and ended with him returning to the Reserve Bank within eight months to be reinstated as deputy governor for monetary policy.[453] Further, to accommodate greater responsibilities to other deputy governors, the Reserve Bank created a new financial markets department to oversee its monetary operations.

Reddy turns hawkish on inflation

The year 2004 ended on a tragic note with the tsunami on 26 December causing death and devastation across Asia and especially in southern India.

The Reserve Bank instantly swung into action, forming a task force to oversee distribution of relief loans and ensuring enough cash was supplied to the affected states in southern India.[454] But on the economic front, the impact of the tsunami was negligible as the economy's resilience was rising. Growth was strong, and the current account surplus of 2003 was giving way to a current account deficit. However, foreign reserve accretion was robust, and India ended 2004 with reserves having grown to US$131 billion, an increase of over US$28 billion in one year.

The RBI chose monetary policy and its issues in India as the theme for the 2003–2004 edition of the report on currency and finance. The report stated that inflation was likely to moderate but also defended the multiple indicator approach against a precise inflation targeting mandate, saying that 'Given the random nature of the shocks hitting the economy, central banks are increasingly acting as shock absorbers [...] to manage these shocks effectively, a constant innovation is required by central banks in terms of instruments and operating procedures while strengthening their balance sheets.'[455]

The RBI was advising banks to increase lending, especially to the farm sector and the small industries, and reduce holdings of government bonds, which had been categorized as 'lazy banking' by Rakesh Mohan in 2003. At the beginning of 2005, credit growth was picking up. Governor Reddy welcomed the development but also reiterated that sustainable growth was the 'unswerving objective' along with moderate inflation and social justice, to maintain overall stability.[456]

At the beginning of 2005, the government, as part of its election promise, unveiled the National Rural Employment Guarantee Act (NREGA), which was the existing food for work programme redesigned with a much higher central government allocation, which had almost tripled from ₹4,000 crore to ₹11,000 crore.[457] The government also proposed amendments to the Reserve Bank Act so the bank would have more flexibility in fixing both SLR and CRR without any limits. Simultaneously, RBI liberalized its policy on foreign banks to enable them to function more freely in India, while allowing Indian banks to expand their presence overseas.[458]

The RBI was advocating strengthening of the banking system through higher capital adequacy norms at 9 per cent, which was more than the 8 per cent that was the norm globally. Further, exposure norms were raised from a sector perspective. However, a key task ahead of the Reserve Bank was the transfer of ownership of State Bank of India, which had resided on the RBI's balance sheet since its nationalization in 1955. This was a key recommendation of the second Narasimham Committee in 1998, and was under implementation. Speaking at a function in Karachi, Pakistan, Governor Reddy outlined that the share of public sector banks in all banking sector assets had fallen from 90 per cent in 1991 to 75 per cent in 2004[459] while the ownership in public sector banks had to be kept around existing levels, given the capital infusions public sector banks needed.

The annual monetary policy review of 2005 also announced the RBI's intention to conduct a policy review once a quarter, rather than every six months as done previously. The first quarter review was scheduled for July, while a third quarter review was added in January. The RBI also added that the quarterly reviews would be released to the press to facilitate structured communication with markets on a more frequent basis while retaining the flexibility to take measures as warranted by the evolving circumstances.

Even as inflation kept moderating, the RBI maintained a relatively hawkish bias, but throughout 2005, it was grappling with the issue of how best to manage monetary policy in an increasingly globalizing India. Speaking at a BIS working party meeting, Governor Reddy outlined that while 'there is also a great sophistication in the conduct of monetary policy today [...] the challenges facing monetary authorities have become sharper'. Governor Reddy also flagged that mobile capital flows led to merging of financial markets across borders, and that the Reserve Bank's multiple indicator approach was serving it well.[460]

This challenge of managing domestic interest rates, liquidity in banking system and foreign exchange is well documented in economic literature as the 'Impossible Trinity', which states that a country can control only two out of the following three at the same time: its domestic interest rates, exchange rates and an open capital account. However, for a capital-stricken India, which had since Independence grappled with the problem of weaker exchange rates and lack of foreign reserves, the problem was still a relatively happy one. In fact, in mid-2005, the RBI released its draft guidelines to deepen India's foreign exchange markets, extending the trading time to 5.00 p.m. from 4.00 p.m. previously for interbank foreign exchange markets, and giving banks greater freedom to choose products and solutions for their customers for foreign exchange-related transactions.[461]

Before its October 2005 policy review, the Reserve Bank instituted a Technical Advisory Committee for Monetary Policy with a view to further strengthening the consultative process in monetary policy with external experts. The committee was headed by Governor Reddy, and had four external members, including former deputy governor S.S. Tarapore. The committee was supposed to meet at least once a quarter, but the recommendations were not to be binding on the governor.[462]

Just before the RBI's first quarterly review on 25 July 2005, China announced a change in its fixed exchange rate policy on 21 July, with limited implications for India. RBI welcomed the move, indicating that a stronger yuan would make Indian exports more competitive, especially in the textile sector.[463]

In its policy review, the RBI left interest rates unchanged but took macro prudential measures to restrict lending for real estate and capital markets by hiking risk weights for bank lending to the sector. This was despite the improving manufacturing and business performance amid relatively low inflation. The appreciating rupee had helped fight off some imported price pressures, but the central bank remained more focused on domestic credit dynamics.

Setting policy in a globalized world

Growth in India was improving rapidly, even as the RBI was trying to ensure sustainability of growth through pre-emptive policy tightening. This brought expectations of high growth through rising foreign direct investment (FDI) and expectations from the government to continue to boost investments through reforms and fiscal policy. Despite introducing NREGA, the government had managed to curtail its fiscal deficit for two years given strong revenue growth. While initially the government's fiscal management led to inflation remaining range-bound, it started showing signs of increase in the beginning of 2006.

The Reserve Bank could see the inflationary signposts. In its October

2005 policy statement, the bank noted that despite the acceleration in growth to over 8 per cent, inflation had moderated to 3 per cent in end-August, even with oil prices increasing globally. RBI advocated cautiousness on the part of the government to treat the increase in oil prices as a shock rather than a permanent move, highlighting that the lack of pass-through of oil prices to local prices could create risks of 'latent' price pressures. It raised the repo and the reverse repo rate by 25 bps each in October 2005, delivering the first major round of policy tightening since 1998.[464]

Deputy Governor Rakesh Mohan delved into RBI's thought process a week later in a speech in Beijing, calling the lack of global inflation amid ample liquidity the 'greatest puzzle', citing that 'Despite the prolonged period over which monetary policy all over the world has remained accommodative, inflation has been unusually benign, relatively impervious to soaring crude prices and the elevated levels of prices of non-fuel commodities. This phenomenon is unique in recent history.'[465] But the RBI was erring on the side of caution and its accommodative monetary stance was on course to be reversed. Back home, the financial press was broadly in support of the RBI's shift to price stability and Finance Minister Chidambaram called it a 'measured step'.[466]

In between the October 2005 and January 2006 policy review, RBI appointed Usha Thorat as a deputy governor, to take the place of retiring Deputy Governor K.J. Udeshi. It also introduced critical tools such as the National Electronic Funds Transfer (NEFT) on 21 November to dramatically change the payments landscape in India's banking system.[467] The Reserve Bank also successfully oversaw the redemption of the India Millennium Deposits by the end of December and suspended issuance of MSS bills as liquidity conditions continued to tighten going into 2006.

Opening multiple fronts

In its quarterly policy review in January 2006, RBI was looking at resurgence in price pressures and hiked the reverse repo and the repo rate again by 25 bps to 5.5 per cent and 6.5 per cent respectively. RBI also continued to flag upside risks to inflation from lack of price adjustments in LPG and kerosene prices (both administered by the government), and laid out the theoretical argument for beginning the monetary tightening in a pre-emptive manner. 'It is important to respond in a timely and even pre-emptive manner to these developments to ensure that generalised inflation spirals do not develop in an environment of higher than anticipated expansion in money supply and bank credit with large shifts in liquidity.

'A measured policy response at this juncture would stabilise inflation expectations and prevent corrosive effects on growth.'[468] Former governor Venkitaramanan translated this statement as 'tougher actions may be in store depending on developments on the demand front,'[469] but also hoped the RBI would not over-tighten policy to hurt growth. He was to be prescient in his assessment.

The monetary tightening cycle had begun in earnest, and the government was not impressed. Within hours of the policy decision, Finance Minister Chidambaram asked the RBI to reconsider withdrawing the decision. 'The RBI is trying to be ahead of the curve. As soon as the external situation is clearer, this [rate increase] could be reversed', he told journalists after the policy decision,[470] once again stepping into the policy territory as did some of his predecessors. The RBI ignored the comments, and the relation between the finance minister and the RBI governor remained cordial. In fact, they would often meet in Delhi over cups of filter coffee, either at the RBI house or at the finance minister's residence.[471]

Ahead of the first quarter policy review, the government, led by the finance minister, boasted of its inflation management as prices stayed manageable. However, over a short period of time, the RBI was validated in its concerns as WPI inflation rose above 5 per cent by April 2006 from 3.7 per cent in December 2005.

The central bank kept rates on hold in the April 2006 meeting, but strengthened macro prudential measures for credit disbursal and raised interest rate ceilings on non-resident deposits to improve liquidity conditions. Governor Reddy continued to express his cautiousness regarding inflation dynamics, indicating that global developments could have an adverse impact on domestic growth and inflation dynamics. Inflation was pegged to average 5 per cent to 5.5 per cent across fiscal year 2006–07.[472]

Lack of a rate hike came as a pleasant surprise to the markets, but the relief was short-lived. Even with strong economic growth of over 8 per cent year-on-year, monsoons were feared to be much weaker than initially forecast. By mid-May, WPI inflation had started rising rapidly again, and on 5 June, the government announced a large increase in petrol prices, prompting the RBI to unexpectedly hike policy rates mid-cycle on 8 June.[473] Both repo and reverse repo rates were raised by 25 bps each, with the RBI giving little explanation beyond calling the move a step taken considering the evolving macroeconomic situation.

Finance Minister Chidambaram commented later that the move was 'precautionary' and expressed a view that no further moves in the upcoming July policy meeting would be needed.[474] However, as inflation continued to press higher, RBI in the July quarterly review hiked the repo and the reverse repo rate by another 25 bps, raising them to 7 per cent and 6 per cent respectively.

The July rate hike was the fourth rate hike in less than a year, and RBI indicated further concerns, warranting caution on inflation management, rapid credit growth north of 35 per cent on an annual basis and placing its inflation and credit concerns front and centre in terms of policy priority. RBI flagged that the lack of full pass-through of higher oil prices could create inflation pressures in the future, and it would 'consider measures as appropriate to the evolving global and domestic circumstances impinging on inflation expectations and the growth momentum.'[475]

In his statement given after the July policy meeting, Governor Reddy sounded the alarm bells on the widening gap between deposit and lending growth, highlighting the need for more balanced growth between the two variables. Further, the trade deficit was widening rapidly, with both energy prices and strong domestic growth propelling imports higher, even amid relatively strong export growth. With oil, metals and food inflation rising amid rampant credit growth, Governor Reddy summed up RBI's policy stance by saying that 'We consider this is an extraordinary situation.'[476] In August and September 2006, inflation remained sticky and the RBI delivered another hike in the repo rate in October, but chose to leave the reverse repo rate and the CRR unchanged, underpinning its inflation-fighting credentials.

The inflation measures were overshadowed by significant easing in the use of foreign exchange by domestic corporates, which was welcomed by industry bodies. The measures stemmed partly from the recently submitted report by the S.S. Tarapore Committee on capital account liberalization, and among the major decisions, RBI allowed domestic banks and corporates to get more foreign capital through the ECB and other windows, while also making it easier for foreign portfolio investors to invest in Indian government bonds by raising the quotas.

The hike in repo rate had no immediate implications, but the lack of further policy tightening and easing of foreign exchange regulation reignited animal spirits, and over a period of two months in October and November, India's foreign reserves climbed by almost US$10 billion. However, the larger issue was perhaps around the foreign investment regulatory easing's impact on RBI's ability to conduct unsterilized intervention in the foreign exchange market to prevent rupee appreciation, which could create excess liquidity in the money markets, even beyond the MSS issuance.

Creative tensions

The RBI governor was not necessarily worried about the constant utterances made by the finance minister on monetary policy, but he was a bit perturbed about sending conflicting signals to the markets. When Governor Reddy asked the finance minister to be more 'circumspect' in his briefings, Chidambaram professed sympathy for the governor and his concerns, but cited a 'democracy' as being a legitimate cause for the finance minister to opine on monetary matters.[477]

In his book, Dr Reddy labelled the equation that evolved between Chidambaram and himself as 'creative tensions'. There was a lot of respect between the two, but they also had their differences. Chidambaram wanted perhaps to be seen as the first finance minister to preside over consistent double-digit growth, but the persistent rate hikes from the RBI clearly turned into a headwind for growth.

There were several instances in which the finance minister and the RBI governor clashed. Whether it was the issue of policy rates or RBI setting its own internal inflation target of 4 per cent, there were disagreements. These would often manifest themselves as committees that the government would form, which would directly or indirectly look at taking away some form of power from the RBI.

Among them were the Percy Mistry Committee on making Mumbai an international financial centre and the Raghuram Rajan Committee on financial sector reforms, neither of which had representatives of the Reserve Bank on their panels. In the case of the Deepak Parekh Committee on infrastructure financing, Governor Reddy was asked at the last moment by Chidambaram to agree to the suggestion of using foreign reserves for infrastructure funding, even though the RBI had indicated its unwillingness to do so. In other instances, such as the deliberations under the Ashok Lahiri expert group on promissory notes, RBI through its nominee left a dissent note to register its opposition to the significant push for capital account liberalization that was emerging from Delhi.[478]

One incident where Governor Reddy caused significant stress to both the finance minister and the financial markets was when he broached the issue of a 'Tobin tax', i.e., raising the cost of transacting in foreign currency in India in light of the surge in currency inflows. While a theoretical discussion, it caused a significant flutter in currency markets, and even Finance Minister Chidambaram was not comfortable with the RBI governor broaching a subject that would be in the fiscal domain. Chidambaram clarified the matter with Dr Reddy on his intention to raise the issue of the tobin Tax, but in his memoirs, Governor Reddy averred that his reference to the Tobin tax was deliberate, even though he made changes in his published speech later on.[479]

A New Year liquidity shock

After a strong GDP print came out at the end of November, RBI decided to deliver a significant shift in policy on 8 December 2006 when it hiked the cash reserve ratio by 50 bps in two tranches,[480] citing inflation management and excess liquidity as key problems, while reinforcing its commitment to keep growth supported. But markets were surprised by RBI's move to take the wind out of their sails. Money market rates started moving higher, while equity markets started falling. Finance Minister Chidambaram tried to assuage market concerns by siding with the RBI, but also added that growth would remain robust despite RBI's measures.[481]

At one point in December, call money rates moved above 10 per cent, partly due to off-cycle issuance of special bonds for financing oil marketing companies and the food corporation of India in lieu of subsidy payments. The issuance combined with the CRR hike triggered a switch in policy corridor, with the repo rate becoming the operative rate. Suddenly, there was an invisible 125 bps rate hike the banks had not factored in. Average call rates rose above 12 per cent by the end of 2006[482] amid some concerns in the markets around policy intentions. Banks started to pass on the rate hikes more aggressively, with SBI delivering a 50 bps increase in its lending rates and other banks following suit. The tightening cycle, which had thus far been gradual, started to look ominous as the RBI had raised the stakes in its growth-inflation trade-off.

Chapter 14

Ascending, descending

On 30 January 2007, credit rating agency Standard & Poor's (S&P) upgraded India's sovereign credit rating to BBB- (BBB minus) which put India in the category of investment-grade economies. S&P was the only agency out of the three major rating agencies that had been holding out on announcing an investment grade for India,[483] and when the upgrade came, it paid closure to India's humiliating downgrade in 1991 during its balance of payments troubles. While the rating may have appeared to be a mere realignment on the credit metrics, it also announced India's arrival as a major propeller of the world economy, with growth rates being consistently above 9 per cent, a burgeoning consumer class and rapidly rising foreign reserves.

The ratings upgrade was another sign that India was open for business, and between October 2006 and January 2007, India's foreign exchange reserves rose rapidly, with the Reserve Bank accumulating more than US$15 billion. This sudden surge in external liquidity led to the Reserve Bank picking up the cudgels once again against credit growth and inflation risks, with liquidity tightening through CRR hikes.

The banking system was flustered and call money rates spiked over 19 per cent on 2 January, the first trading day of the new year. While the money market situation normalized quickly, RBI continued to tighten monetary policy as inflationary pressures became broad-based at around 6 per cent year-on-year, leading to another repo rate hike of 25 bps on 31 January, just on the heels of S&P's upgrade. The RBI made it clear that it would place liquidity management higher in the 'policy hierarchy' as tighter market liquidity would amplify the impact of monetary policy.[484]

After the Central Statistics Office pegged growth for fiscal year 2006–

07 at 9.2 per cent, RBI came out on 13 February to raise CRR again by 50 bps in two tranches, following through on its warning to maintain appropriate liquidity conditions to keep inflation in check. As the usual seasonality of tax payments came around in March 2007, money markets went completely haywire, with call money rates rising as high as 75 per cent because of liquidity shortages. This garnered little sympathy from the RBI, which delivered another dose of repo rate increase in an unscheduled decision on 30 March 2007, the penultimate day of the fiscal year. It also raised the CRR further, increasing it to 6.5 per cent by the end of April 2007, frontloading policy action for the next policy meeting as well.

An avalanche of foreign capital

A key driver behind RBI's rampant policy tightening led by CRR hikes was the surge in foreign capital inflows. In the first quarter of 2007, India's foreign reserves rose by almost US$22 billion to reach close to US$200 billion. While FDI had increased, a large part of the flow was coming through portfolio inflows into the equity market, along with external commercial borrowings by the corporate sector. While the rupee was being allowed to gradually appreciate against the US dollar since November 2006, the avalanche of capital inflows and monetary tightening precipitated the strengthening in Indian rupee against the US dollar, taking it from ₹44.31 to the US dollar at end of February 2007, to below ₹41 to the US dollar by early May.

The ongoing inflows turned around the banking system liquidity shortages, but the banking system was now in a new fix. On 2 March 2007, while the RBI was tightening liquidity through CRR and repo hikes, it issued a nondescript circular restraining banks from parking more than ₹3,000 crore with the Reserve Bank to maintain a generally tight liquidity stance while forcing banks to go to the interbank money market to trade liquidity.[485] This came to be known in the market as the 'reverse repo ceiling'.

While the circular did not have much of an impact in its initial days, by mid-2007, it started to have a significant impact. As the RBI continued to see foreign inflows as reserves crossed US$213 billion in June, the problem turned to one of plenty as banks were restricted in parking their excess liquidity with the RBI. Money market rates traded close to zero on several days in June as the system's excess liquidity came to over ₹35,000 crore while the RBI's cap remained intact at ₹3,000 crore.[486] Further, RBI had already hit the upwardly revised MSS issuance limit of ₹1 lakh crore, leading to unsterilized intervention and plunging the system into surplus territory.

In a state of thoughtful inaction...

This was the time when RBI kept every market player guessing, with rumours of a CRR hike floating around every Friday evening before the markets closed. The currency continued to appreciate as the rate fell closer to ₹40 to the US dollar on the eve of the first quarter policy review and the call money rates hovered close to zero for almost the entire month. Inflation was also showing signs of moderation as monsoon rainfall was on track. The pressure on the RBI to ease up on the reverse repo ceiling was building. Both from a policy signal and its impact on lending, RBI had reasons to be worried about the frothiness in the money markets.

As such, in its first quarter policy review, not only did the RBI keep policy rates unchanged, it also removed the reverse repo ceiling from 6 August onwards. It did raise the CRR by 50 bps, but its impact on liquidity was marginal. This policy came as a major relief to the banks as the normalization in the policy corridor lowered their cost of holding deposits. RBI emphasized its focus on anchoring inflation within 5 per cent, but the bias remained largely to manage liquidity more than anything else.[487]

The stronger exchange rate had helped reduce price pressures, and by end of the third quarter of 2007, inflation had fallen below 5 per cent, the threshold level that RBI had in mind. Real rates were climbing higher while the rupee remained biased to appreciate. In an interview, Governor Y.V. Reddy welcomed the moderating price pressures but said that the ideal rate of inflation was around 3 per cent.[488] The shifting goalposts led to several market watchers calling on RBI to begin easing policy rates, especially to prevent the rupee from appreciating further. Indeed, it is said that in one of the regular meetings with the IMF staff, Governor Reddy was being goaded by the Fund representatives to cut rates and was asked whether RBI was in 'inertia' after hiking rates for so long. Governor

Reddy, after giving them a patient hearing, said that rather than inertia, perhaps it was just 'thoughtful inaction' on RBI's part that was making them refrain from policy easing for now.

State Bank of India sold back to the government

Ever since the nationalization of the Imperial Bank in 1955, there had been an ongoing tussle between the government, RBI and SBI over who controlled the bank through the ownership, and its policy actions. After years of lethargy, several committees examining India's financial system had pointed to the problem of the central bank 'owning' the biggest commercial bank in the country—the RBI held a 59.7 per cent stake in the SBI.

While several experts wanted SBI to operate more freely, the government decided otherwise, and in 2006, announced its intention to take over the SBI ownership from the Reserve Bank, along with its subsidiaries. This announcement was made after the S.S. Tarapore Committee on capital account convertibility re-advocated the move in its July 2006 report. However, S.S. Tarapore, a former deputy governor of the RBI, himself later advised the government not to follow the recommendation[489] if it was a mere transfer and not a reduction in ownership.

In early February 2007, the cabinet approved the transfer, and by mid-2007, the government of India was handed over the stake that RBI had held in the State Bank of India after the government passed an ordinance promulgating a change in the SBI Act of 1955. The transfer took place on 29 June 2007, with the RBI handing over shares worth about ₹35,531 crore.[490] While the press release indicated that the government had paid cash against the transfer, the move had no impact on government finances as RBI's transfer to the government had jumped sharply in fiscal year 2006–07 to almost ₹46,000 crore from just ₹8,400 crore in the previous year.[491] This included the entire price paid by the government for SBI's stake.

Losing control of inflation amid debt waivers

By the end of 2007, the RBI had raised the CRR once again, but foreign portfolio inflows continued and India's foreign reserves rose to US$275 billion, rising by almost US$98 billion in one year. The RBI remained cautious on inflation, and in its January 2008 policy statement, while all key rates were left unchanged, the bank was unusually cautious on price pressures as globally, commodity prices of both energy and food had been climbing for some time. The government, keeping the upcoming electoral cycle in mind, had not let prices of diesel, LPG and kerosene rise, thus widening the price gap and leading to the drop in headline inflation.[492]

In the press conference that followed, Governor Reddy in his usual witty style said that the decision of the RBI was affected by 'more uncertainty about the duration of uncertainty'[493] globally as India faced a unique situation of rising global commodity prices but a stronger exchange rate pulling inflation in different directions. Even Finance Minister Chidambaram publicly backed the RBI on its standstill approach and reiterated their operational autonomy.[494]

The focus within the Ministry of Finance was shifting to the critical budget being prepared for fiscal year 2008–09, which was the last full year the government led by Dr Manmohan Singh would be in power. The budget prepared by Finance Minister P. Chidambaram opened the fiscal taps to support an already burgeoning economy. Among the key measures announced was a whopping ₹60,000 crore debt waiver for farmers, the largest such waiver granted till then in independent India.[495]

The fact that the government could afford such a hefty waiver while reducing the fiscal deficit indicated the growth in revenues. The RBI had little to counter the loan waiver bonanza, despite its adverse behavioural impact on debt repayments in other sectors. In early 2008, a research paper published by the RBI looked at measures that could help improve farm credit penetration, with waivers also being marked as a possible solution.[496] Even the RBI board congratulated the finance minister on the budget, including the waiver.[497]

The public backing of one another's policies was not necessarily indicative of policy coordination. By early 2008, inflation had once again started rising despite the rupee appreciating further, falling under ₹40 against US dollar. The latest spurt in WPI inflation began in the early weeks of February as the weekly inflation print climbed above 4 per cent (later revised to above 5 per cent), a six-month high. By March, provisional inflation crossed 5 per cent, despite no major change in fuel prices, which had barely moved despite oil prices moving up sharply in the first quarter of 2008.[498]

Governor Reddy was in fact looking for possible means of an exit from the RBI as he felt his relations with the finance minister were not ideal. He made a pitch to become the head of the new finance commission, but Chidambaram refused to let Governor Reddy go.

By mid-April 2008, RBI lost patience as crude oil had stayed above US$100 a barrel for several weeks and the government's fiscal bill was ballooning. A fuel price hike was all but given, and WPI inflation, which had been rising for the previous several weeks, was set to cross 8 per cent. The result was a resumption in policy cycle after the RBI had taken a breather for almost six months. The RBI took another intra-meeting decision, announcing an increase in CRR by 50 bps in two tranches on 17 April, taking the rate to 8 per cent.[499] This was followed by another hike in CRR in the 29 April annual credit and monetary policy review, where RBI raised CRR to 8.25 per cent by the end of May.[500]

In his press conference, Governor Reddy flagged a 'constellation of uncertainties'[501] as a reason for not touching the key policy rates, but indicated that RBI was well placed to achieve price stability while maintaining growth at around 8 per cent for the current fiscal year. But the pause was short-lived as international oil prices rose above US$120 a barrel by the end of May, triggering a fuel price hike in early June amid fears of a burgeoning fuel subsidy burden on oil marketing companies.[502] This hike meant that while the government's subsidy bill was likely to come down, the Reserve Bank's warning on the latest price pressures from fuel came to fruition.

The RBI responded to the fuel price hike after a full week, when protests for a rollback in prices had died down. The central bank raised the repo rate on the night of 11 June 2008 by 25 bps to 8 per cent[503] while strengthening the special market operations to support public sector oil companies by increasing their foreign exchange holdings by repo-ing their oil bonds.

In next two months, the Reserve Bank raised rates twice again, taking policy rates to 9 per cent by the end of July. On the surface, the government continued to back RBI's actions as inflation reached 12 per cent by the end of July, but within government circles, there was significant disagreement among the RBI, Governor Reddy and the Ministry of Finance over the path of interest rates going forward. In fact, in a story that has not been dated, Governor Reddy indicated that the prime minister summoned him on a Sunday to inform him that the finance minister was not happy with the RBI and its governor.[504] Upon hearing this, the governor immediately called up Chidambaram and asked for a meeting but was promptly refused.

Most senior officials in the government, including in the Ministry of Finance, were firmly of the view that inflation was close to peaking and there was little to be gained by hiking rates further. However, the RBI continued to look at the extent of negative real rates and was not averse to raising rates further, if needed. The matter came to such a point that Prime Minister Manmohan Singh had to step in, and on his advice, the RBI agreed to take it a bit slow, leading to a thaw in the relationship between the Reserve Bank and the government.[505]

An unprecedented leadership transition

As the world was transitioning through the global financial crisis from August 2008, the Reserve Bank was also going through a critical leadership change. Governor Reddy had just stepped down, and the baton of leadership at the Reserve Bank had passed on to the ever-gentle Dr Duvvuri Subbarao, an IAS officer from the Andhra Pradesh cadre, who had been serving as the finance secretary to Chidambaram before moving to the Reserve Bank on 5 September 2008.[506]

Governor Subbarao's appointment came under somewhat strenuous circumstances. By mid-2008, the RBI and the Ministry of Finance were firmly on a collision course. Dr Reddy was sounded out for a short extension to see India through the global financial crisis and as late as 28 August, his extension was being considered.[507] However, the government, including the finance minister, also were interviewing other candidates, including Finance Secretary Subbarao, Planning Commission Chair Montek Singh Ahluwalia and Deputy Governor for Monetary Policy Rakesh Mohan, who was an overwhelming favourite to succeed Governor Reddy.[508]

Rakesh Mohan, who had a strong standing within RBI and had worked with the institution for over six years, was a symbol of policy continuity.

While he was invited by the Ministry of Finance for an interview, it was Dr Duvvuri Subbarao, a senior ministry official in line to be cabinet secretary, who was on Finance Minister Chidambaram's mind. In his memoirs, Governor Subbarao recalls that while he was on his way to Brazil for a G20 meeting on 26 August, Chidambaram asked him to confirm whether he would be interested in the RBI leadership.

Subbarao responded positively and was formally interviewed by Chidambaram and former governor Rangarajan (then the chairman of the Prime Minister's Economic Advisory Council), largely on issues around constituting a monetary policy committee (MPC), further liberalization of the bank licensing regime and global monetary conditions.[509] On 1 September, Chidambaram announced that Duvvuri Subbarao would become the twenty-second governor of the Reserve Bank of India.

Governor Subbarao had many firsts linked to his appointment. He was the first governor of the RBI to be born after Independence. While he was not the first Ministry of Finance bureaucrat to occupy the position of governor, he certainly was the first to move from the ministry directly to the Reserve Bank. A similar step had been contemplated five years previously, when both S. Narayan and N.K. Singh were keen on the role, but did not get the support of then governor Bimal Jalan, as he did not wish the RBI governorship to be seen as part of a 'natural progression' for Ministry of Finance mandarins.[510] Governor Subbarao's arrival on Mint Road was viewed with suspicion from all sides as the media speculated whether he was a Ministry of Finance plant or whether he would switch sides to continue with RBI's hawkish rhetoric. However, the pink press quickly changed their focus as within a week of Dr Subbarao taking over the mantle, financial Armageddon struck the world.

Lehman collapses

In July 2007, investment bank Bear Stearns decided it was going to close two of its hedge funds specializing in subprime mortgage loans. It was not a major change, since funds crashed and burned on Wall Street regularly. What seemed to be localized issues in the US housing market came to the world's attention on 16 March as Bear Stearns, a small but aggressive investment bank, went into liquidation, sending global markets haywire.

Indian equities markets reacted cautiously to the global events, falling over 6 per cent in a day, but policymakers in emerging markets, especially India, continued to ride high, flagging the US investment bank crash as an aberration, boldly stating that emerging markets, particularly India, had 'decoupled' from the developed markets,[511] especially when it came to their historical dependency for growth. IMF fuelled this hysteria of 'decoupling' as well through various academic papers, as emerging markets led by China believed double-digit growth was the norm and not the exception going ahead.

From March to August 2008, the decoupling idea seemed sound as the US economy continued to face headwinds while emerging markets showed robust growth, driving up commodity prices. This situation changed in September, when within a week, the global financial markets came to a grinding halt, resulting in significant loss of value and wealth.

Governor Subbarao entered the RBI with crisis at the doorstep, and while India's vital signs were strong, the economy was still burning up with inflation in double digits. In his first week, he saw the United States' two biggest housing lenders, Fannie Mae and Freddie Mac, go into government control. Bank of America bought Merrill Lynch, a large investment bank, and on 15 September[512] Lehman Brothers, among the largest investment banks globally, was declared bankrupt.

Too many cooks...

The entire government machinery, including the RBI, was in crisis management mode. Governor Subbarao put out a statement in his first week, reiterating price stability as a key policy objective, but also advocating a wait and watch approach in slowing inflation momentum, given the several 'known unknowns' the Indian economy faced.[513] The wait and see approach would prove to be temporary as once Lehman Brothers collapsed, the RBI had to pull all its resources together to ensure liquidity in both domestic money markets and foreign exchange markets would not disappear. RBI increased its liquidity injections and ring-fenced Indian assets of Lehman Brothers to preserve a semblance of orderly market conditions.[514]

These actions came in tandem with those of other critical regulators, such as SEBI, which had the challenging task of settling all accounts within Lehman's defunct trading portal, to achieve normalcy. As P. Vaidyanathan Iyer noted in his enlightening article published a couple of years after the crisis, 'SEBI was quick to react. Not only did India's stock market regulators work till midnight and beyond on many days of that crisis period, they asked the stock exchanges, BSE and NSE, to settle all Lehman accounts in India the moment news broke that the investment bank had collapsed in the US. Lehman India managers were asked on Monday morning, September 15, to call up their bosses in the US, where it was night. They were reluctant to call their bosses that late, recall SEBI officials. But the regulator was taking no chances.'[515] The response time from India was rapid, and that was partly due to the political leadership being very sensitive to a slowdown ahead of the 2009 general elections.

Further, after the United States saw major banking collapses, rumours started circulating about problems within India's banking system as well, particularly with respect to ICICI Bank, the second largest private bank in India. The bank was at that point seen as the most exposed bank to the global financial crisis, given its relatively high reliance on wholesale foreign funding[516] and a small exposure to Lehman Brothers. While the loss made from the high exposure to foreign liabilities was relatively high, its impact on the financial position of ICICI Bank was negligible.

Still, as liquidity conditions deteriorated, queues outside ICICI Bank branches became longer and on 30 September, the Reserve Bank stepped in, publishing a brief memo indicating that the commercial bank and its subsidiaries were not only well capitalized, but also had enough funds to meet the needs of their depositors. Even Finance Minister Chidambaram publicly backed ICICI to restore a sense of calm around the embattled bank.[517] However, the markets were not convinced, and the probability of ICICI defaulting on its outstanding bonds rose four times in a matter of days. The situation came to a point where around the second week of October, the finance minister advised ICICI chairman K.V. Kamath to bite the bullet and make a public appearance, assuring the depositors their money was safe. Kamath did so, and Chidambaram helped by adding that 'no Indian depositor need be apprehensive.'[518] The situation gradually normalized, but gave regulators including the RBI a sense of the uneasiness within the public at large around the nature of contagion

India was staring at.

A flood of money released in the markets

Globally, commodity prices were collapsing, and the US dollar was getting stronger. The rupee had sold off more than 7 per cent against the US dollar in September. Inflationary pressures were set to roll over. The Reserve Bank had two challenges to meet as the financial walls collapsed around it. First, it had to shore up confidence by ensuring normal market conditions. Second, it had to provide support to the corporate sector, which had seen its external leverage rise dramatically in recent years, to shield it from the quickly spreading global contagion as foreign currency liquidity and short-term funding dried up.[519]

The RBI started by raising liquidity injections, and on 6 October, it slashed the CRR by 50 bps, to be followed by another 100 bps reduction four days later, to inject a total of ₹60,000 crore into the banking system.[520] This was followed by a further reduction in CRR by 100 bps on 15 October, followed by a 100 bps reduction in the repo rate on 20 October, along with a further reduction of 50 bps in CRR to bring it down to 6 per cent by the end of October, injecting almost ₹1,20,000 crore of liquidity in a month.

The decision to cut the repo rate was internally opposed by the majority within the RBI, as it was being undertaken despite inflation being in double digits. However, Governor Subbarao overruled the majority in order to send a strong signal to the markets about the Reserve Bank's resolve to ensure financial stability and restore market confidence.[521]

Not to be left behind, Finance Minister Chidambaram saw an opportunity to take the lead in managing the liquidity crisis as his key men, Governor Subbarao, Finance Secretary Arun Ramanathan and Economic Affairs Secretary Ashok Chawla had taken up their positions just a month ago. On 10 October, the finance minister suo moto announced the constitution of a committee on liquidity management under Arun Ramanathan, with members including an RBI representative, a few bank heads and the chair of SIDBI, to advise the government on liquidity management.[522]

The statement and the committee undermined Governor Subbarao's authority very early in his term, and he was miffed with the announcement as liquidity management was RBI's turf. In his book, Governor Subbarao recalls raising the issue with the finance minister, calling his actions 'inappropriate'. But Chidambaram defended his call to constitute a committee and Governor Subbarao, who was handpicked by the finance minister himself, ended the discussion by indicating that the Reserve Bank would not be nominating a representative.[523]

But the move by the finance minister to set up his own committee on liquidity management did in hindsight work as a strong inducement for RBI to step up its own game. With the contagion spreading, RBI was also forced to adopt unconventional policies. This included steps to increase liquidity available for mutual funds and other market participants. As the financial crisis hit close to the advance tax payments schedule in September, liquidity was disappearing from the capital markets both on a seasonal and structural basis.

Mutual funds had been facing an avalanche of redemptions in the face of plunging markets, and the tax payments sucked the life out of several funds, including large ones managed by Reliance and HDFC. To prevent a downward spiral, the government instructed SEBI to step in, which was a bit too slow for its own good. With markets crashing, Chidambaram decided to take the matter into his own hands and intervened deftly through the liquidity management committee, much to the RBI's chagrin.[524]

As P. Vaidyanathan Iyer recalls in his article, Chidambaram's most difficult task was to get the RBI on board with proposed actions to help the mutual fund industry. But once the RBI started significantly easing liquidity, the next step was to provide targeted support to the mutual funds themselves, which the RBI announced on 14 October after a meeting with SEBI chairman Chandrashekhar Bhave.[525]

On the same day, Chidambaram released another statement[526] saying that the Ministry of Finance was preparing to take measures to infuse liquidity and make credit intermediation smoother. The following day, the ministry released another statement indicating that Governor Subbarao had met several officials including the prime minister, and he was on his way to Mumbai to announce more steps to ease liquidity conditions.[527]

By the end of October, the financial system appeared somewhat stabilized and normalcy in operations was starting to return. The Reserve Bank had shown a proactive response and was open to taking more steps to reinstate business confidence. The government was also opening the fiscal spigots,[528] and the RBI looked the other way as growth concerns were paramount. The finance minister continued to play up the possibility of further rate reduction, advocating that 'If inflation continues to moderate, we will revisit the [policy] rates. We have to revise policy whenever it is time to do it.'

On 1 November, RBI further reduced the repo rate by 50 bps to 7.5 per cent while retrospectively cutting the CRR by 100 bps to 5.5 per cent, injecting another ₹40,000 crore into the system. It also reduced the SLR to 24 per cent, the first reduction in it since 1997.[529] An emerging cause of worry for the Reserve Bank was the rapid depreciation in the rupee, which had fallen to almost ₹50 against the US dollar by the end of October, undermining the easing process. While some policy easing had taken place with respect to foreign currency deposits and NRE deposits, the central bank still saw roughly US$39 billion of foreign reserves being withdrawn between October and November 2008.

Confidence was further tested when a group of terrorists attacked Mumbai's landmark Taj Mahal Hotel among other sights on 26 November 2008. The Taj Mahal Hotel is within walking distance of the Reserve Bank, and the operational preparedness of India's commercial capital along with its financial markets was put to the test. Chidambaram was insistent on markets reopening as early as possible to signal normalcy to the world, and the RBI, along with SEBI, turned around India's markets to reopen completely by 28 November.[530] Finance Minister Chidambaram was transferred to manage the Ministry of Home Affairs, with Prime Minister Manmohan Singh taking over the Ministry of Finance in the interim.[531]

Still, the Reserve Bank was more worried about domestic conditions and perhaps egged on by a government facing elections, the RBI delivered more repo rate reductions in December, January and March, with the operating policy rate being at 3.25 per cent by the end of April 2009, about 575 bps lower than where it was in July. CRR was also brought down to 5 per cent from 9 per cent. Within the same time period, India's inflation fell to lower than 2 per cent by March 2009, before turning negative for a couple of months.

The Reserve Bank emerged from the crisis looking both orthodox yet flexible in its approach, but only after Finance Minister Chidambaram cajoled it to take significant steps. As Deputy Governor Rakesh Mohan noted in a speech in April 2009, the Reserve Bank had pumped in almost ₹4,90,000 crore in actual/potential liquidity since mid-September 2008 (about 9 per cent of GDP). Such a large injection was enough to prevent RBI's balance sheet, and in turn money supply, from contracting, and was aimed at ensuring non-inflationary growth of money supply in the economy to support the needs of the real economy.[532]

For Governor Subbarao, it was a 'baptism by fire', as he stepped into the biggest financial crisis the world had seen while having the tough task of winning the confidence of the RBI staff, which viewed him with suspicion given his previous allegiances were with the Ministry of Finance. As he notes in his book, his bigger concern was preserving his own credibility with the Reserve Bank senior staff and their perception of his ability to protect RBI's turf.[533] Gradually, both the staff and economic commentators turned more favourable towards RBI's role in helping manage and later diffuse the crisis as the bank helped to prevent India's financial sector from tipping over the precipice.

Chapter 15

The return of the fiscal interface

In May 2009, the United Progressive Alliance led by Prime Minister Manmohan Singh and Congress Party Chairperson Sonia Gandhi won a resounding victory in the fifteenth general elections. Dr Manmohan Singh returned as the prime minister, and his cabinet was largely intact. Pranab Mukherjee, the elder statesman in Manmohan Singh's cabinet, had become finance minister in January 2009 as the prime minister underwent a heart bypass surgery.[534] Pranab Mukherjee carried on in his new role, becoming the full-time finance minister once again in the new cabinet.

Congress's reliance on allies had reduced significantly after the 2009 elections and with the communist parties out of the picture, expectations of economic reforms speeding up led markets to hit their upper circuits as election results trickled in.[535] But the joy of electoral victories apart, the Reserve Bank and the Ministry of Finance had different yardsticks for determining how much stimulus was needed and for how long the stimulus was required. This conflict set the tone for the next four years of Governor Subbarao's term, as India's fiscal policy, led on by an orthodox borrow and spend policy, created significant difficulties for monetary policy, especially both currency and bond market management.

New finance minister, old fiscal tricks

In the UPA government's final budget before the 2009 elections, Finance Minister Pranab Mukherjee, presenting the interim budget on 16 February 2009, had raised the revised estimate of fiscal deficit to 6 per cent of GDP from an initial projection of 2.5 per cent of GDP.[536] This was largely on account of the two massive stimulus packages the government had announced in December[537] and January,[538] along with a much lower revenue path due to indirect tax cuts. The surge in fiscal deficit was seen as an aberration to prevent India's growth from slowing down dramatically, and even though the finance minister had outlined a small drop in deficit to 5.5 per cent in fiscal year 2009–10, markets were wary of a slippage, forcing the Reserve Bank to step in and start buying bonds in the open markets to inject liquidity in February and March, to the tune of ₹26,000 crore.[539]

By the middle of 2009, India's high frequency growth indicators and inflation were starting to bottom out, and RBI began contemplating how to exit the extraordinary monetary stimulus it had put in place between October 2008 and April 2009. As Governor Subbarao recounts in his book, RBI had plans to unwind the stimulus by first withdrawing the excess liquidity pumped into the system and following that up with any interest rate normalization consistent with inflation.[540]

In May, Deputy Governor Rakesh Mohan announced that he was leaving RBI in June to take up the post of a consulting professor at Stanford University.[541] A week after his departure, K.C. Chakrabarty, former chairman of Punjab National Bank, was announced as a new deputy governor, but he was replacing V. Leeladhar, who had retired several months ago. Chakrabarty was the first deputy governor to be chosen by a panel, which included Governor Subbarao and Arun Ramanathan.

Even as activity kept improving, a complication came in the form of a terrible southwest monsoon season in 2009. By August, it was apparent that the monsoons were failing, and inflationary pressure, particularly on food items, was likely to rise significantly. At the end of the season, India was officially in a drought, with rainfall being only 77 per cent of normal levels.[542] This would prove to be the worst drought India had faced since 1972. The shock was largely expected to be felt on both growth and inflation, but the impact never came on growth since farm prices were high in 2008 and along with the debt waiver, helped support rural spending. However, inflation kept rising, and by the end of September, it was clear that inflation was returning as growth recovery was faster than anticipated.

By the end of the monsoon season, the RBI had a policy challenge on their hands. Food inflation had started rising, but the price shock was largely supply-driven in nature, and manufacturing inflation was low for the time being, supported by tax cuts and low fuel costs. But the highly accommodative monetary policy meant that economic growth was recovering nicely, despite the drought conditions. Hence an exit from the significantly easy monetary conditions was necessary, especially given the fact that RBI's inflation projection of 5 per cent was likely to be surpassed by the end of March 2010.[543] In its October monetary and credit policy review, RBI began to 'exit' from its ultra-accommodative policy by normalizing the SLR back to 25 per cent, removing interest subsidies for exporters, and removing liquidity support facilities for mutual funds and term repo facilities for commercial banks.[544] The RBI also raised its end-March inflation forecast to 6.5 per cent.

In November, RBI appointed Dr Subir Gokarn as the deputy governor in charge of monetary policy.[545] Prior to joining the Reserve Bank, Dr Gokarn had been chief economist for Standard & Poor's Asia-Pacific operations. His appointment was unusual in that he was from the private sector, instead of the civil service, as had been the norm in the past. He was also one of the youngest deputy governors to be appointed to the position, at the age of forty-nine.

Deputy Governor Gokarn would go on to have a profound impact on RBI's policy assessment, particularly in the measures of inflation it would track. In his very first speech as deputy governor, Dr Gokarn outlined how capacity constraints, particularly in the agricultural sector, would need to be addressed, without which generalized price pressures were bound to return as growth recovered.[546] This would prove to be prophetic during his three years with the central bank, as the RBI was looking at robust growth, rising inflation and ample liquidity by the end of 2009.

Restoring India's pride

By the middle of 2009 it was becoming apparent that international multilateral funds such as IMF and World Bank were undercapitalized and in need of funding. The emerging market economies such as China and India were approached to provide funding for IMF so it could continue to support countries in economic stress. In return, these emerging economies were promised a greater say in the running of the Fund. The Indian government was keen to display its new-found economic muscle, and the RBI purchased 200 metric tonnes of gold in October worth almost US$7 billion to diversify its foreign exchange reserves, after the sale of over 400 metric tonnes of gold was announced by the IMF to shore up its coffers.[547]

Former governor S. Venkitaramanan, who had overseen the gold pledging in 1991, welcomed the purchase,[548] saying that 'the wheel has now come full circle', and the purchase was a risk mitigation exercise given that India's US$285 billion of reserves were largely in US dollar denominated debt instruments. He added that the execution of such a large deal without creating any problems in the local market displayed the distance India, and indeed the Reserve Bank, had travelled since 1991, when the country had to pledge its gold to stay financially afloat.

RBI begins monetary stimulus withdrawal

Ahead of the RBI's January 2010 policy review, WPI inflation had already risen over 5 per cent, coming in at 5.6 per cent as food inflation continued to rise. RBI began taking more blunt measures in its policy review, raising the CRR by 75 bps to 5.75 per cent as it hoped that the withdrawal of excess liquidity would help anchor inflation expectations. But the bigger change in tone from the central bank came on the government's fiscal position, which it termed as 'a bigger risk to both short-term economic management and medium-term economic prospects', further adding that the 'reversal of monetary accommodation cannot be effective unless there is also a roll back of government borrowings'.[549]

By mid-March, inflation was dangerously close to double digits once again, prompting the Reserve Bank to take the ad hoc policy action of hiking the repo and reverse repo rates on the evening of 19 March 2010, followed by another rate hike and liquidity tightening in its annual credit policy review on 24 April, thus raising the policy rate by 50 bps in just over a month. Speaking at the post-policy press briefing, Governor Subbarao described the inflation situation as worrisome, but said that the RBI was taking 'subtle baby steps' towards policy normalization as the RBI 'must cross the river by feeling the stones'.[550] Indeed, the pace of gradual yet consistent hiking was maintained through 2010 as inflation proved to be sticky, and by the end of 2010, policy rates had climbed to

6.25 per cent, including another ad hoc hike in July, executed outside of the usual meetings. Following the second ad hoc rate action taken in July, RBI instituted a mid-quarter review of monetary policy to bring about more predictability regarding the timing of policy actions.[551]

Fiscal profligacy and a constrained RBI

The consistent rate hikes and the constant references to the large fiscal deficit were a spot of botheration for the government and paved the way for starker differences between the government and the RBI, resulting in some unfortunate incidents. As Governor Subbarao notes in his book, Finance Minister Pranab Mukherjee was 'always miffed about it [making an issue out of the fiscal stance].'[552] The budget presented in February 2010 continued to maintain an expansionary fiscal stance with the deficit pegged at 5.5 per cent of GDP for fiscal year 2010-11, down from approximately 7 per cent in the previous fiscal year.

But the tension between the RBI and the government continued to fester, and in a first show of the dispute, Finance Minister Pranab Mukherjee refused to extend Deputy Governor Usha Thorat's term for another two years, in a break from the convention to reappoint deputy governors till they reached the age of sixty-two. Governor Subbarao speculated that one of her decisions may have irked the finance minister, but he nonetheless asked the government to nominate Usha Thorat for another term, given her stellar track record.[553] The government decided to constitute a selection committee to choose her successor, despite Governor Subbarao's recommendation. The Ministry of Finance and the government refused to budge from their respective positions, resulting in Deputy Governor Usha Thorat retiring in September 2010, despite the governor firmly backing her reappointment.

The turf battle also spilled over to regulatory issues, but Governor Subbarao put up a spirited fight to preserve RBI's domain and autonomy. In April 2010, the various financial regulators in India including SEBI, IRDA and RBI were sparring over the jurisdiction of regulating unit-linked products. The government responded by setting up a Financial Stability Development Council (FSDC), which would resolve issues among the various financial regulators.

The Reserve Bank was not pleased with the development, and Governor Subbarao wrote a letter to the finance minister expressing concern over the government's actions to become the final arbiter in any future disputes.[554] Former governor Jalan also chipped in, asking the government to drop the idea of setting up an FSDC, if needed through a legislative amendment.[555] The government finally relented and made Governor Subbarao the vice-chairman of the committee to allay the Reserve Bank's fears regarding any loss of autonomy.

In the second quarter of 2010, the government had a large fiscal windfall as telecom spectrum usage for 3G and broadband services were auctioned, garnering the government more than ₹1 trillion in licensing fees and royalties.[556] Despite that, the fiscal position remained expansionary, and the RBI continued to flag deficit financing as being a constraining factor for monetary policy and inflation management. In its annual report published in August, RBI highlighted that 'persistence of fiscal imbalances over extended periods tends to increase risks to inflation.'[557]

The Reserve Bank also pointed to structural deficiencies in India's agricultural sector, asserting that the excessive focus on producing cereals and not enough production of pulses, proteins and meat was the root cause behind double-digit food inflation. Deputy Governor Gokarn was a lead propagator of this idea, terming the high pulses inflation as 'entirely consistent with an emerging structural imbalance between demand and supply.'[558] He called on the government to engineer a 'green revolution' equivalent for pulses production, in order to provide enough protein for India's population.

The government, for its part, appeared clueless on inflation management. Several government officials, including chairman of the Planning Commission Montek Singh Ahluwalia and Finance Minister Pranab Mukherjee would periodically affirm that inflation would fall to 5 per cent by the end of the fiscal year,[559] but the evolving fiscal situation resulted in several fuel price hikes, which compromised the inflation forecasts. The inflation-fighting credentials of the government were further compromised by significant increases in minimum support prices for the farm sector, along with a massive increase in buffer stocks of grains, which led to broad shortages in the open market, further pressuring prices. The government, especially officials of the Ministry of Finance, also took the liberty of advising the market on monetary policy, which was a constant source of irritation for the RBI. Eventually, Governor Subbarao raised the issue with the prime minister, who promptly intervened, thus stopping the constant chatter.[560]

The cabinet committee on prices, an existing body within the central cabinet had turned broadly defunct, and at the end of 2010, India went through another major price shock, led by a spike in the prices of vegetables, especially onions. RBI responded by resuming policy tightening in January 2011, raising policy rates by 25 bps, and also flagged the widening current account deficit as a cause for concern, on top of the fiscal and inflationary pressures.[561] In the budget for fiscal year 2011–12, the government partially revealed the extent of fiscal slippage India was looking at, despite the one-off fiscal gains made in the year. Fuel and farm subsidies coupled with significant expenditure excesses meant that the fiscal deficit remained elevated, weighing on national savings.

In an op-ed, Niranjan Rajadhyaksha, a noted journalist and economist pointed out that India's macro indicators had effectively returned to the same level as 1991 except for economic growth, which was racing along at close to 9 per cent. He flagged that 'we are running out of soft options' and advocated for faster fiscal consolidation to correct the increasing imbalances in the economy.[562] In its April policy statement, RBI speeded up the policy tightening as inflationary pressures seemed firmly entrenched, raising the policy rates by 50 bps in the ninth consecutive rate increase. It also firmly established the repo rate as the key benchmark rate, indicating liquidity conditions would be kept tight.

Speaking at the post-meeting press briefing, Governor Subbarao took a very hawkish stance on inflation, dismissing the negative effects of the policy tightening on growth, adding, 'There is no trade-off between growth and inflation. We need to bring down the inflation.'[563] He also questioned the government's fiscal policy, particularly the assumptions set in the budget on subsidy-related spending, and flagged its detrimental impact on inflation management.[564] The stance was perhaps also influenced by the surge in cash management bills that the Reserve Bank was issuing on the government's behalf to meet the latter's short-term funding needs.

In July 2011, the Reserve Bank continued with an accelerated pace of policy tightening, raising the policy rate again by 75 bps over June–July, taking it to 8 per cent. The central bank once again flagged 'significant upside risks to the projected fiscal deficit for 2011–12'[565] as a key source of demand pressures and justified its policy tightening based on inflation remaining stubbornly high. Policy rates in India had reached broadly the same levels that they were at before the RBI started easing back in 2008.

The tussle over the term extension

The finance minister was not happy with RBI's aggressive positioning on monetary policy, and given his past run-ins with the governor over issues of policy and regulation, the renewal of Governor Subbarao's term turned out to be a longer than expected affair. The government was coming under political pressure as several scams were breaking, and as early as April 2011, the media started speculating on Governor Subbarao's term extension,[566] especially since his role as finance secretary came under the scanner in the telecom scam that was breaking at that point.

For Governor Subbarao, a term renewal was welcome, but he did not wish to ask for one. In a meeting with the prime minister on 21 July 2011, Dr Manmohan Singh asked the governor whether the finance minister had discussed his extension, to which the governor replied in the negative. Perturbed by the lack of contact, Dr Singh asked his principal secretary to follow up, but there was still no response from the ministry.[567]

The extension was eventually announced on 9 August and was for two years. When Governor Subbarao called the finance minister to thank him for the term extension, Pranab Mukherjee told Subbarao that he had earned his extension. Still, in his book, Dr Subbarao appears to indicate that it was the push from the prime minister that got him his two-year term extension. The kerfuffle around the term renewal had little impact on RBI's policy stance, as policy tightening continued in September and October 2011, with another 50 bps of hikes delivered. The government had given up as inflation stayed high and the political distractions around the various scandals breaking out were keeping them occupied.

By the end of 2011, inflation started showing the initial signs of tempering, after two years of near double-digit inflation. Further, growth was also starting to slow down, amid ongoing external uncertainty and slowing activity, particularly in the investment sector. Governor Subbarao and the RBI received their fair share of flak, with one op-ed asking whether he was the man 'killing India's growth.'[568]

In early 2012, RBI finally relented and began providing some growth support as signs of a slowdown were becoming apparent. It injected liquidity in January and March through CRR reduction and cut rates aggressively in April by 50 bps at one go, as growth slowed to 6 per cent and inflation moderation appeared to be baked in. The finance minister, however, broke the news first, telling the media on the sidelines of an industry engagement event that 'the governor will shortly give you good news'. Clearly, the government and the finance minister were happy with the RBI's decision, and as Governor Subbarao notes in his book, perhaps the policy paralysis setting into the government made the finance minister anxious to provide some good news.[569]

Chidambaram brought back to revive confidence

Pranab Mukherjee left the Ministry of Finance in June 2012 to become the thirteenth president of India, and for a brief period, Dr Manmohan Singh was back to being the finance minister. But it was a temporary arrangement, and in a move cheered by markets, P. Chidambaram was brought back to the Ministry of Finance to arrest an economy fast spiralling out of control.[570] The reshuffle came on the eve of a major blackout that affected over 300 million people in north India and was symbolic of the governance deficit that was setting in.

In his initial interaction with the media, Chidambaram vowed to reverse fears of retrospective taxation introduced by the former finance minister and restore India's fiscal health.[571] He also brought in Arvind Mayaram, the then chief secretary of Rajasthan as the secretary of economic affairs immediately after joining the ministry. Further, Dr Raghuram Rajan, the noted economist who had worked on several committees with the government, also joined the Ministry of Finance. He was appointed the chief economic advisor, replacing Dr Kaushik Basu.[572] Hence by the end of August, Chidambaram had put together a formidable team of technocrats to manage the economy.

It appeared that Finance Minister Chidambaram was in sync with his predecessor regarding the monetary policy settings. In September's mid-quarter policy review, the RBI injected liquidity through a CRR cut, which Chidambaram called a 'small, but welcome step.'[573] However, he was not happy when Governor Subbarao informed him during the pre-policy consultations in October that the RBI was not ready to cut rates as the government's promise of fiscal consolidation had not come to fruition.

Walking alone but in different directions

The finance minister 'argued strongly for a rate cut' and when Subbarao did not yield, he convened a press conference a day before the RBI's policy meeting on 29 October 2012[574] to outline the government's fiscal roadmap, noting that 'I sincerely hope everybody will read the statement and take note of that.'[575] The RBI chose to reduce the CRR by another 25 bps, prompting a sharp rebuke from Chidambaram in his press interaction post the policy decision. An upset Chidambaram emphasized that 'Growth is as much a challenge as inflation. If the government has to walk alone to face the challenge of growth, then we will walk alone.'[576]

The differences over monetary policy spilled over into the personal equation between the governor and the finance minister, with the latter feeling that it was necessary to bring 'fresh thinking into the Reserve Bank'. Chidambaram declined to waive the selection process for reappointing Subir Gokarn, who Governor Subbarao was actively backing for a term extension. Despite Governor Subbarao's repeated pleas, the finance minister felt that all the lateral entrants were becoming hostage to the technocrats at the RBI and constituted a search committee for the role under Governor Subbarao's chairmanship.[577]

The government was not keen to back Dr Gokarn as the leading candidate out of the three interviewed for the position. His the term was not renewed and Dr Gokarn bid adieu to the central bank at the end of 2012, having made a long-lasting contribution to RBI's inflation analysis and diagnostic tools. The Reserve Bank, on the other hand, continued to pay the price for asserting its autonomy as the government tried its best to censure Governor Subbarao through his deputies.[578]

Losing control of the rupee

In early 2010, as economic growth was rebounding in India and the currency had reached a post-crisis high of around ₹44 against the US dollar, Governor Subbarao gave a speech in Zurich outlining his thoughts on volatility in capital flows and its impact on India. He said, 'Our [India's] exchange rate policy is not guided by a fixed or pre-announced target or band. Our policy has been to intervene in the market to manage excessive volatility and disruptions to the macroeconomic situation. This "volatility centric approach" to exchange rate also stems from the source of volatility which is capital flows.' He further added that 'current account deficits whose reserves are a result of capital inflows in excess of their economy's absorptive capacity' is inherently not sustainable. India falls in the latter category. Our reserves comprise essentially borrowed resources, and we are therefore more vulnerable to sudden stops [...].'[579]

By the end of 2012, India was consistently printing current account deficits north of 4 per cent. In fiscal year 2011–12, India's current account deficit widened to more than 4 per cent of GDP and was set to widen further in fiscal year 2012–13. India's external debt had risen by more than US$100 billion in the last five years, aided by low interest rates globally and tight liquidity conditions domestically. This surge in current account deficit had two primary sources. First, India, being a large importer of commodities, faced high commodity prices between 2010 and 2013. Second, India's gold imports had risen rapidly, climbing to US$56 billion in fiscal year 2012, as speculative demand for the precious metal increased amid persistent negative real rates in India.

In 2011–12, as the European debt crisis flared up, emerging markets, including India, saw capital flows turning around, leading to significant disruption and volatility in the exchange rate markets. Between August and December 2011, the rupee had its first major sell-off from ₹44 to ₹54 to the US dollar, with the Reserve Bank eventually arresting the upward move in the currency with significant liberalization of deposit rate regulations for NRE accounts, bringing them at parity with local currency resident accounts, thus taking another step towards capital account liberalization.[580]

However, the central bank largely adhered to the 'market determines rupee's value' stance, creating some mini crises along the way.[581] The next small blow-up took place in April-May 2012, triggered partly by a widening current account deficit and also by the deteriorating investor confidence in India following the introduction of a retrospective tax. Further, a jolt came from credit rating agency Standard & Poor's in April 2012 as they put India on a negative watch, five years after upgrading the country to an investment grade.[582]

Even before the second currency sell-off began, the government had begun raising import duties on gold and silver as a means of shoring up its revenues and also to try and wrestle down the current account deficit. But it had limited impact, and by the time 2013 dawned, the Reserve Bank was firefighting its large current account deficit with the limited ammunition of external commercial borrowing liberalization and more quota releases for debt investments for FIIs.

In its January 2013 policy statement, RBI noted that the widening current account deficit, which was at 'historically high levels', was the biggest risk for India, exposing it to twin deficit risks. The statement also said that 'financing the CAD with increasingly risky and volatile flows increases the economy's vulnerability to sudden shifts in risk appetite and liquidity preference, potentially threatening macroeconomic and exchange rate stability.'[583] These words would prove to be sage advice as India and the Reserve Bank were about to face their most difficult challenge since 1991.

In the fragile five

In May 2013, a small but impactful speech by US Federal Reserve Chair Ben Bernanke triggered a significant crisis in emerging markets. Between 2008 and 2013, the Federal Reserve had conducted three rounds of asset purchases, with the last one being an open-ended asset purchase programme. In May 2013, as economic growth appeared robust, Bernanke indicated that the Fed was considering 'tapering' the pace of purchases it was making in the open market.[584]

The news of tightening triggered an immediate sell-off in the currency markets across emerging markets, with India, Brazil, Indonesia, Turkey and South Africa being among the worst hit. These five were popularly named the 'fragile five' by analysts at Morgan Stanley,[585] a name that caught the media's attention.

In early June, the rupee followed the other currencies to hit all-time lows, weakening to above ₹58 against the US dollar by mid-June, an almost 8 per cent loss in less than three weeks. Reserve Bank and Ministry of Finance officials went into a huddle, with each giving their own opinion on the reason behind the sharp currency weakness. Raghuram Rajan pegged the weakness down to the large current account deficit, while iterating the weakness could be temporary. The RBI, led by Governor Subbarao, reiterated the central bank's stance of intervening only to iron out any sharp volatility in the rupee's movement and not to protect a level.[586]

By the end of June, it was becoming clear that the Reserve Bank would be 'relatively hands off'. The rupee started consistently testing ₹60 against the US dollar, ending the month at a rate of ₹59.6 to the US dollar. The government's damage control exercise was being led by Raghuram Rajan, who said that the rupee was not 'in shambles',[587] and the weakness could be turned around. However, the RBI's comment on the rupee finding its own level was interpreted by the market as a signal of further weakness, and the currency continued to remain under pressure in the first week of July, selling beyond ₹61 against the US dollar.

As the government was looking for ways to stabilize the currency, foreign currency debt issuance, a new deposit scheme for NRIs and sharp reduction in imports were being considered.[588] The government was certain that a monetary policy response was not needed and that shoring up foreign inflows to manage the capital account would broadly suffice.

In between, the Reserve Bank's guidance was distinctly nonchalant as the governor told the media that it was difficult to estimate when the rupee would stabilize and whether it would make reversals. In his book, Governor Subbarao said that communication between the Reserve Bank and the Ministry of Finance during the rupee crisis of 2013 was fluent, with the governor and his team—Urjit Patel and H.R. Khan—being in constant touch with Raghuram Rajan and Arvind Mayaram. However, the government was quick to blame external factors for the currency weakness while the RBI tried to be objective on domestic mistakes as well, especially the widening fiscal and current account positions.[589]

Bringing out the big guns

On the evening of 15 July 2013, RBI finally relented and used the 'big bazooka' of monetary policy to kick-start its exchange rate defence in earnest. The government on its part raised the import duty on gold, even though fears of smuggled gold were there at the back of their mind. The Reserve Bank tightened monetary conditions and raised the Marginal Standing Facility rate by 200 bps to 10.25 per cent and decided to sell down government securities to further tighten liquidity.[590] Governor Subbarao calls the decision to use monetary policy to manage exchange rate one of the toughest he took at the Reserve Bank, and by July, the excessive one-way bets in the offshore NDF market also needed to be curbed. The Reserve Bank was contemplating taking punitive action but finally refrained.[591]

As it was just weeks before Governor Subbarao was due to retire, it could be speculated that he did not feel completely comfortable taking extreme steps to stabilize the currency, especially since the media was having a field day speculating on who could replace him. Liquidity was further tightened on 23 July, but in its July quarterly policy review, the Reserve Bank surprised the market by not taking any further steps to stabilize the rupee.

The market was also surprised by Governor Subbarao's assertions following the policy review. He said that the Reserve Bank was not targeting any currency levels but was aiming at facilitating an orderly adjustment of the currency to a market-determined level.[592] As Governor Subbarao notes, while this was a benign statement to make in normal conditions, given the circumstances, it was seen as too dovish, and the rupee plunged once again within hours of the policy decision. This was also Governor Subbarao's last policy decision, and he was perturbed by the market reaction. He managed to get the communication in order in the analyst call the next day, asserting that the Reserve Bank retained the flexibility to use all instruments to defend the rupee, helping the rupee gain some ground. The government did its part by raising FDI limits and eventually raised the gold import duty to 10 per cent.[593] However, some bizarre decisions such as restricting passenger imports of large televisions baffled and confused markets[594] as the authorities battled perceptions of a weak currency defence.

The 'rock star' governor comes to the RBI

Positive news came in early August when it was announced that Raghuram Rajan would succeed Governor Subbarao once the latter's term ended on 8 August 2013.[595] Rajan was widely seen as the consensus candidate, and while he was a long-shot choice in 2008, in 2013, his candidature hardly surprised anyone. He was appointed as an officer on special duty to Governor Subbarao in a sign of all hands being on deck to manage the currency crisis.

However, the situation continued to spiral out of control as the currency sell-off intensified in the third week of August. The rupee started weakening rapidly, depreciating by almost a percent a day. This was partly driven by the equity market sell-off and withdrawal of foreign funds as RBI's significantly tight policy was weighing on growth. Further, on 20 August, as the rupee was trading close to ₹65 against the US dollar, RBI announced steps to ease liquidity somewhat. Meanwhile, social media jokes on the rupee's fall were rampant, signalling that the economic stress had spilled over into pop culture.[596]

On 28 August, the rupee hit its worst ever level, weakening to ₹68.4 against the US dollar. The RBI stepped in to introduce crisis measures similar to those adopted in 2008, with a currency swap facility introduced for oil companies in order to fight against persistent currency demand.[597] Amid calls for harsher measures, Governor Subbarao reiterated there was no need for stricter currency controls, especially in the last week of his term. Eventually, the day of 28 August would prove to be the worst, and on 5 September, when Raghuram Rajan took control, RBI unveiled a string of measures to stabilize the currency, improve confidence and increase the flow of foreign capital to boost reserves.

Speaking to the media, Governor Rajan announced that India would allow banks to swap their new foreign currency non-resident deposits for three years and above for a fixed rate of 3.5 per cent, along with significant concessions made on banks raising tier 1 capital to boost inflows. Rajan also announced that under him, RBI's primary objective would remain monetary stability, which would be rooted in low and stable inflation expectations. He also said that the RBI's goal was to maintain the purchasing power of the rupee, and that the policy going ahead would be calibrated as such.[598] The window would be open only until November 30, which would give banks plenty of time to raise funds from non-resident Indians.

The bold measures declared by Rajan in his first press conference as the governor won him many plaudits, but perhaps it was a nice gesture on Governor Subbarao's part to let the new measures be announced by the incoming governor and not by the one leaving the bank. As Governor Subbarao recalls, Rajan had suggested that Governor Subbarao announce them, but the governor thought the measures would be more effective if Rajan announced them as the incoming governor.[599] It was a stellar show of coordination and mutual respect between two governors with a common objective, and the results did bear fruit.

In fact, the policies worked so well that Rajan was hailed even outside the usual financial circles, with gossip columnists such as Shobha De calling Rajan 'the messiah of markets'.[600] Monikers such as 'rock star governor' were being bandied about, but Governor Rajan maintained his focus on stabilizing the rupee.

Over the next three months, a gold rush began in the financial sector for non-residents as banks saw a very strong response to RBI's offering. RBI also reversed course on its policy stance and started normalizing policy operations while raising the benchmark rates in order to provide some stability to the currency and inflation expectations.

By November 30, RBI had normalized currency operations for oil marketing companies and had raised over US$34 billion in the FCNR/bank capital scheme unveiled on 5 September. This was the largest increase in FCNR deposits seen in just three months, and by the end of November, the rupee had strengthened to ₹62 against the US dollar. Governor Rajan was hailed as the saviour of the rupee, even though he downplayed his own role in the measure.

As Governor Rajan notes in his recent book, the key policy objective of these measures was to 'present a façade of confidence to assure the public and investors that the RBI knew what had to be done'. This was complemented by a commitment to lower inflation, the ability to take bold and far-sighted decisions and do so in a transparent manner.[601] With currency markets stabilized, the focus of Governor Rajan shifted toward introducing larger, more systemic changes in the monetary policy formulation. In September, he had asked Deputy Governor Urjit Patel to lead a team of economists and practitioners to suggest improvements in the monetary policy operational regime and the group's report was expected in early 2014. India too was on the cusp of a major change with Narendra Modi, the chief minister of Gujarat, being an overwhelming favourite to become the next prime minister as the UPA II government was largely seen as corrupt and ineffective.

Chapter 16

Conflict, collaboration and catharsis

Raghuram Govind Rajan, born in Indore on 3 February 1963, was already a well-known economist before he arrived at the Reserve Bank. As the recipient of the inaugural Fischer Black prize in 2003 for young academics under forty who have made a significant contribution to the field of finance and having served as the chief economist of the IMF, Rajan's credibility as an academic and a practitioner was well established. He had made a name for himself by calling out the risks associated with financial derivatives,[602] irking the US establishment. Former US Treasury secretary Dr Larry Summers had called him a 'Luddite' for his views, but they were justified in 2008 as the US led the global financial meltdown.

Even within Indian policy circles, Rajan was a well-known face, having been involved with government policymaking through the financial regulation committees in 2007–08, and later as an economic advisor to Prime Minister Manmohan Singh. Hence his presence at the Reserve Bank provided comfort and familiarity, but only for market watchers.

Rajan resets the policy objective and the agenda

In his first speech after taking over as governor, Dr Rajan announced the formation of a committee under Deputy Governor Urjit Patel to examine what needed to be done to revise and strengthen RBI's monetary policy framework. He also asked that the panel be staffed with outside experts. The move to relook at the monetary policy framework was nothing new, as previous governors, including Dr Manmohan Singh and Dr Bimal Jalan, had taken similar steps to ensure that monetary policy's objectives and its operational framework ultimately achieved the primary role of the central bank, that is, to sustain confidence in the value of the rupee.[603]

The committee was announced on 12 September, with eminent economists from academia, the private sector and policymaking invited to give their inputs. Even before the committee had sent in its report, Governor Rajan promised 'action' on the committee's recommendations, underlining the importance of improving the framework by carefully spelling out what it was that the Reserve Bank was trying to achieve and how it should go about doing it.

Just a week ahead of the third quarter policy review, the Urjit Patel Committee submitted its report late on the evening of 21 January.[604] The committee's work was exhaustive, and its primary recommendation was for the Reserve Bank to have a single primary objective of inflation control. It also recommended that the Reserve Bank formally adopt a flexible inflation targeting policy framework, with 4 per cent as the stable consumer price inflation rate for the economy within a period of two years. The committee also recommended transferring the RBI's decision-making process to a monetary policy committee, comprising five members, namely, the governor, the deputy governor for monetary policy, the executive director of the monetary policy division, and two members nominated by the governor of the Reserve Bank.

While other recommendations were made for revamping the liquidity management and policy instruments of the RBI, in the January policy meeting, Governor Rajan's focus was on discussing the Patel Committee recommendations. The governor backed looking more closely at CPI since it had stayed elevated for a longer than usual period, while the bank had not completely moved away from the multiple indicator approached that had survived since 1997 under Dr Jalan's tenure.

While there was a rate hike, the press conference largely focused on the medium-term policy changes that were being proposed. There was broad agreement on inflation being the key policy objective, although several noted economists, including former governor Jalan had in the past indicated that inflation targeting might not be the way to go for India. In fact, T.N. Srinivasan, professor emeritus at Yale University, went to the extent of expressing 'serious reservations and relevance' of inflation targeting in India.[605]

The government reacted cautiously, flagging that for an economy running inflation at close to double digits for the last five years, a 4 per cent inflation target might be too low, and it may not be the right framework for the economy.[606] However, Finance Minister Chidambaram later found common ground with the RBI,[607] agreeing to set an inflation target for the central bank while emphasizing that the RBI's mandate was to implement the target. However, given that the national elections were around the corner and the UPA II government was widely expected to lose, it meant little in terms of policy direction and all eyes were on Narendra Modi, who was widely seen as the frontrunner for the prime minister's job.

India's economic mojo returns

In the September 2013 to January 2014 policy meetings, Governor Rajan gradually raised the policy rates but simultaneously kept moving the RBI's monetary stance to 'normal' settings. He described the pessimism regarding India's long term economic prospects as a 'sign of manic depressive' behaviour on the part of Indian economy watchers[608] and said that while the analyst community was 'prone to mood swings [...] India can do [...] better'.

In the lead-up to the general elections, the mood swing was apparent as Narendra Modi's arrival and the policy pitch of 'minimum government, maximum governance' found a lot of favour with the international investor community. His landslide victory on 16 May 2014 was the largest by a political party in three decades, and it further confirmed that the policy settings were about to change in India and thus perception too was improving.

However, the media was already painting a picture of conflict between the incoming government and the Reserve Bank governor. There had been a few utterances by BJP leaders such as Piyush Goyal, who had questioned RBI's tight monetary policy saying that it was 'aggravating India's problems'. Dr Subramaniam Swamy, who had been a long-time baiter, also said, 'We can make it worthwhile for him to leave.'[609] The media reports and speculation were rubbished by Rajan.[610]

However, after the cabinet formation, the narrative shifted slightly with the government publicly backing Governor Rajan through a series of meetings. Investors hailed the Modi/Rajan combination as the second coming of the Reagan/Volcker duo in the United States back in 1980s, when Federal Reserve chairman Paul Volcker lowered inflation through tight monetary conditions while President Reagan used fiscal policy to create conditions for robust growth. In fact, Rajan's instinct was not to do a 'Volcker',[611] but his focus on inflation still earned him that moniker.

The focus on boosting consumption and use of technology to foster financial inclusion were common threads for the prime minister and the RBI governor, which further created conditions for collaboration between the government and the RBI. The problems in the banking system had long been festering, and the Reserve Bank was increasingly being asked to intervene more heavily in solving the non-performing asset issues of the public sector banks.

Rajan picks a fight...

The Reserve Bank was always an important player in the global central banking forums, but under Governor Rajan, the attention to RBI's utterances was heightened. Having stabilized the rupee and with the macroeconomic backdrop looking much better, Governor Rajan's speeches turned more broad-based, with a focus on competitive monetary easing, an issue he had been writing and speaking on for some time.

In a speech given at Brookings Institution, Washington DC in April 2014, Governor Rajan emphasized that unconventional monetary policies and the reliance of large central banks on balance sheet expansion as a way to influence exchange rates were having negative spillover effects, particularly on emerging market economies. He concluded by saying that the lack of an 'international monetary policy' coordination where large central banks would pay more attention to emerging market economies and their financial conditions was leading to conditions for competitive policy easing, or a 'beggar thy neighbour' approach, which posed substantial risks to sustainable growth and the financial sector.[612]

The speech did not find favour with former Fed chairman Ben Bernanke, who 'told off' Rajan by claiming that Rajan's 'speech just reflects the fact that you are very skeptical of unconventional monetary policies. You say that the rules of the game should prevent policies with "large adverse spillovers and questionable domestic benefits". If you have a different empirical assessment than I do, that in fact, emerging markets would be better off if they hadn't been used, then you would have a different view.' He added that Rajan had to be 'taken to task' for ignoring money. The feud took place in the presence of several other central bank governors such as Alexandre Tombini, governor of the Central Bank of Brazil and Vitor Constancio, vice president of the European Central Bank.[613]

Innovation and miscalculation

During the 2014 election cycle, the Reserve Bank had announced full banking licences for two banks, IDFC and Bandhan. While IDFC was a well-known infrastructure financing NBFC, Bandhan was a microfinance institution elevated to a full banking licence. The fact that the RBI had given licenses to only two institutions when twenty-five applications were received underlined the bank's conservative approach to financial and banking services.[614]

At the same time, the RBI was keen to leverage technology for financial services penetration. In the Nachiket Mor Committee report submitted in January 2014, the concept of a payments bank, which would operate in a relatively narrow payments gateway was envisaged, ultimately facilitating electronic transactions, with a deposit facility enabled to a small extent. This was a path-breaking report; it had inputs from the National Payments Corporation of India and was aimed at leveraging mobile technology along with India's unique identification programme, Aadhaar.[615]

By July 2014, the RBI had issued draft guidelines on the issuance of payments bank licences, along with 'small banks', which would enable non-banking financial institutions to operate in a larger area of financial services, including banking. At the same time, Governor Rajan wanted a full-time deputy governor in the role of a chief operating officer to take over the process of licensing supervision, and he had Nachiket Mor, his batchmate from IIM Ahmedabad, in mind for the position. However, the proposal faced a lot of pushback from both within and outside the Reserve Bank, as the governor, who had previously advocated making lateral hires to reduce 'group think', was seen as bringing in too many outsiders at the highest levels of decision-making. A similar issue arose when RBI hired Prachi Mishra, a Columbia University alumnus who had worked with Governor Rajan before and was hired as Director in its research department to strengthen RBI's internal research standards and data studies.[616]

Rajan's intention to appoint a chief operating officer was perhaps to liberate himself and other deputy governors from the day-to-day management issues of the RBI governorship, but his move to 'appoint' an old friend and batchmate was regarded with suspicion. The fear within the RBI staff was that lateral entries at relatively senior positions would make it difficult for existing staff to get promoted. It was a legitimate concern and Governor Rajan met representatives from the RBI staff unions along with his other deputy governors, who had come from within the RBI's cadre.[617] Further, while Governor Rajan was blamed by unions for proposing an overhaul, Latha Venkatesh, a noted journalist in an article chronicled the background of the move, pitching it to be initiated during Governor Subbarao's tenure.[618]

As an editorial in *The Hindu* summed it up, 'outsiders often bring fresh perspective and serve as change agents [...] Rajan could well have a strong case for a COO of his choice. But in making one, the RBI must present it transparently and in a manner that explains why the RBI Act must be amended to enable the appointment of a fifth Deputy Governor [...] Also, it is important to dispel the misimpression that the RBI is batting for the appointment for a specific person rather than for the creation of a post that will strengthen and improve its functioning.'[619]

The Jan-Dhan Yojana

Narendra Modi is a powerful orator, perhaps the best in India's recent political class. His speeches are forceful and have often broken down complex policy issues into simple viewpoints. However, few of his speeches are as memorable as his first speech on Independence Day, 2014. Speaking from the ramparts of the Red Fort in Delhi, Narendra Modi sought to cajole a nation from inertia to achieve outcomes it thought it was incapable of. Among the policy decisions that impacted economic policymaking was the scrapping of the Planning Commission, and a financial inclusion drive that would enable every unbanked family in the country to open a bank account and thus join the formal economy.

The scheme was called 'Pradhan Mantri Jan-Dhan Yojana' (Prime Minister's People's Money Scheme) and was officially launched two weeks later on 28 August 2014. Under the scheme, the government asked the RBI and especially the public sector banks to reduce their know your customer (KYC) policy checks[620] in order to facilitate account openings, with a backward linkage to Aadhaar and certain insurance benefits in order to provide a social safety net cover. Given Modi's clarion call to open bank accounts on a mission mode, commercial banks opened over fifty-five million bank accounts in the first five weeks and would eventually go on to open almost three hundred million bank accounts under the scheme.

However, banks were not necessarily excited by the prospect of opening low balance accounts, given that they were largely expected to be deposit bearing and would entail little prospect of loans. Even RBI, which broadly acquiesced to the government strategy of opening the accounts, sounded a note of caution with Governor Rajan, speaking to an audience of industrialists and bankers, flagging that while the Jan-Dhan scheme would help financial inclusion, banks should focus on universality of coverage rather than on speed and number of accounts opened.

Rajan further advised banks to avoid duplication of accounts and expressed concerns over whether the bank accounts would actually be used.[621] While the advice was relevant given past experiences of financial inclusion drives, the government perhaps did not appreciate the tone, and just two weeks later, Rajan softened his tone on the financial inclusion drive, batting for its success.[622] The government let this slide, and in early October, gave indications that it was ready to give RBI and Governor Rajan an explicit mandate of inflation targeting, along with a monetary policy committee, but with a slightly different composition than that proposed by the Patel Committee report.[623]

Make for India or Make in India?

Apart from the Jan-Dhan scheme, Modi also launched 'Make in India', a renewed investment push to improve ease of doing business to attract greater FDI and domestic investment and thus bolster India's manufacturing to serve both the domestic and international demand. What followed was a glitzy campaign, but for the Reserve Bank, and especially Governor Rajan, it proved to be another bump along the way as tensions mounted over the Make in India scheme.

In a speech titled 'Make in India, largely for India', given at the Bharat Ram Memorial Lecture in December 2014,[624] Governor Rajan outlined multiple reasons why there was a generally weak supply and demand backdrop in developed economies and how a strategy of export-led growth might not be feasible if financed through fiscal incentives. Governor Rajan raised a pertinent question, whether 'Make in India' was a superior strategy to 'Make for India', given that India had both critical mass and domestic savings to keep growing on the back of its own demand.

Rajan expressed fears that 'There is a danger when we discuss "Make in India" of assuming it means a focus on manufacturing, an attempt to follow the export-led growth path that China followed. I don't think such a specific focus is intended'. He further advocated against export subsidies and instead backed agnostic policies that did not necessarily pick sectors or manufacturing champions, but rather acknowledged that 'India is different, and developing at a different time, and we should be agnostic about what will work'. Thus a 'Make for India' strategy, where cost of doing business for local firms was lower, would be more optimal.

The government was clearly not impressed as the media spun Rajan's measured speech as one panning the government's efforts to increase manufacturing. The matter went on, even drawing a rebuke from Finance Minister Arun Jaitley, who said it did not matter whether goods manufactured were being sold in India or outside, as long as manufacturing was on the rise.[625] Once again, while Governor Rajan's policy advice was prudent, it created friction between the government and the Reserve Bank, which would set the tone for the remainder of his term.

Enjoying the energy windfall

By the middle of 2014, commodity prices were appearing shaky, and between July and September 2014, international oil prices fell from US$110 per barrel to US$80 per barrel. The decline was significant, and with the rupee strengthening, the government announced in October 2014 that it was deregulating diesel prices and abolishing the subsidy mechanism.[626] The move was welcomed by the RBI, which in its December statement noted the improvement in fiscal prospects and indicated that despite challenges, RBI believed that the government appeared determined to maintain fiscal discipline. The RBI left the door open for rate cuts, indicating that if inflation continued to moderate, a change in the monetary policy stance was likely early in the following year, including outside the policy review cycle.

In mid-January, the opportunity presented itself with December inflation, particularly the WPI, coming in very low led by falling commodity prices. Fulfilling its promise, the RBI reduced policy rates the next day, outside the policy review cycle, in a major surprise to the market.[627] This was the first rate cut since May 2013, and had come at a time of some thawing in market sentiment around the new government. Governor Rajan left the door open for further rate cuts in the February policy review, signalling his willingness to cut rates as long as fiscal consolidation was on track.

The budget was broadly benign, and Finance Minister Jaitley adhered to the 'difficult' fiscal deficit target set by his predecessor P. Chidambaram, despite revenue headwinds. The signal to maintain deficit consolidation was perhaps enough, and with the government officially backing RBI's new proposed inflation targeting framework and signing a new monetary policy framework agreement, RBI decided to issue another policy review, reducing rates further, and also acknowledging the fiscal progress.[628] The new monetary policy framework agreement, which was put up on RBI's website just a few days before the rate cut, formalized the inflation targeting mechanism, but the RBI Act still had to be amended before the government could constitute a monetary policy committee. The biggest change was the single target of inflation.

A month later, at a function celebrating RBI's eightieth anniversary, the prime minister praised the Reserve Bank and Governor Raghuram Rajan, complimenting him on his grasp of and clarity on economic issues. He also urged RBI to set intermediate targets, looking ahead at a hundred years of celebrations. However, the near-term challenges were still around financial inclusion, and he urged the Reserve Bank to make financial inclusion a 'habit'.[629]

Over the next six months, as inflation declined, the Reserve Bank continued to maintain a tight liquidity stance, but maintained its easing bias, reducing policy rates by more than 100 bps between January and September 2015. However, markets, governments and, especially, banks were generally unsatisfied as lack of capital inflows in 2015 coupled with RBI firmly establishing the repo rate as its policy tool meant that liquidity, and hence credit growth, remained somewhat sluggish.

RBI's insistence on maintaining a high real interest rate was widely criticized and both banks and analysts were questioning why the Reserve Bank was not easing liquidity in order to facilitate credit growth. Even after April, when the RBI had passed 50 bps of rate cuts, only four banks lowered their benchmark rates. Governor Rajan was clearly not impressed with the anaemic pass-through of rate cuts into lending rates, and despite him asking banks and analysts to wake up and 'smell the coffee',[630] banks continued to be reluctant to pass on the cuts into lending rates. SBI chairman Arundhati Bhattacharya retorted saying that in India, the impact of monetary policy on bank funding costs was marginal, and 'in India, things work differently from international banks'.[631]

Despite RBI beginning the rate-cut cycle, certain cabinet ministers linked to the economy continued to press for more rate cuts. Before the June policy meeting, Piyush Goyal and Nirmala Sitharaman, both ministers in the government, urged the RBI to bring down rates further, saying that the 'whole nation was waiting for the RBI'.[632] Further, the Reserve Bank remained worried over the slow pace of policy transmission. In a discussion with the chairman of the SBI in August 2015, sparks flew as Rajan and Bhattacharya publicly disagreed with each other over transmission, with the Reserve Bank governor disapproving the slow pace of pass-through.

The discussion also came against the backdrop of RBI giving payments bank licences to eleven different entities from diverse backgrounds.[633] This was done to encourage lateral thinking across different industries, but the SBI chief publicly expressed concerns over new payments banks 'sabotaging' existing banks with teaser deposit rates, leading to a possible exodus of funds from traditional banks to these new institutions. Governor Rajan allayed these fears, flagging that payments and small banks were necessary to keep pushing towards greater financial inclusion. As Rajan would explain later in his latest book, most of these new institutions or instruments were meant to withdraw the government from 'occupying the commanding heights of the economy, confining itself to providing public goods and the government framework.[634]

Asset quality review and the NPA mess

By the middle of 2015, even though government policies had changed, oil prices had fallen, the fiscal deficit was in control and interest rates were coming down, there was no significant sense of improvement in economic activity. This was in stark contrast to the new GDP series introduced by the Central Statistics Office in January 2015, which had important changes in the methodology for calculation of GDP, but also pushed up the growth rate, which seemed out of sync with both monetary and sectoral data. RBI too was baffled by the new GDP series, calling it at odds with high frequency indicators. Chief economic advisor Arvind Subramanian also indicated he was puzzled by the new series.[635] And it painted an economic backdrop that was at odd with the anecdotal evidence and state of credit demand in the economy.

Compounding the impression of lack of economic growth was the very tepid pace of credit growth in the banking system. This was largely a reflection of balance sheet concerns and asset quality concerns triggered by rising non-performing assets within Indian commercial banks, especially within the government-owned banks. This was a critical impediment towards increasing credit in the system, and was certainly impacting economic growth, which was not completely reflected in the new GDP figures. The government for its part tried to come up with innovative financing schemes such as UDAY, the bond recasting of power sector debt, which would help deleverage bank balance sheets while lowering the interest servicing costs. However, by and large neither demand, nor supply of credit, improved much, despite interest rate cuts.

For RBI, the banking system urgently needed a clean-up, but it was not to be done at the expense of legitimate borrowers. Listening to the grievances of the banks, RBI in its in April 2015 policy statement indicated that it was looking to introduce a new marginal cost of funds-based lending rates, which would allow banks to pass on rate cuts faster to their borrowers. In September 2015, the RBI proceeded to issue draft guidelines, followed by final guidelines released in December 2015.[636]

The RBI was simultaneously cracking down on the rising NPA issue, as commercial banks were starting to report rising loan delinquencies, due to the several infrastructure projects left stuck or unviable from the previous UPA regime. In its financial stability report released in June 2015, RBI flagged that 'the continued stress on asset quality of PSBs and consequent pressure on capital adequacy is a matter of increasing concern'.[637] The RBI was considering adopting stricter norms for certain corporates that were constantly flagged as at risk by banks, and in December 2015 monetary policy review, Governor Rajan stressed that it was his hope that 'banks recognize more of what needs to be recognized and they deal with the stressed assets'.[638] Later that month, senior leadership of RBI met the chairmen of various commercial banks to ask them to speed up NPA recognition, and in its December financial stability report, RBI warned that more than one-fifth of corporates had excessive leverage, which could pose systemic risks to the banking system.[639]

Rajan's strict line on recognition of banking NPAs and his push to reorient the monetary policy framework won him international plaudits, and in early 2016 he won the Central Banker of the Year award, a prestigious honour.[640] RBI's confidence being sky high, it began to lay down diktats for banks to start recognizing more loans as non-performing. This created concerns around profitability within the banking system, leading to protests from both bank employees and banking heads.[641]

RBI also asked banks to set aside more provisions, which followed two months of intense scrutiny of commercial banks' balance sheets.[642] In fact, more than the action, it was the rhetoric adopted by the Reserve Bank and Governor Rajan that was especially caustic, as he brushed aside the clamouring for rate cuts as the 'wrong solution' and asked banks to be 'more firm' when dealing with borrowers. He also flagged that 'if you flaunt your wealth' while owing the system a lot of money, it seems to suggest that those borrowers do not care. Hence it was imperative for the government and the Reserve Bank to make those corporates toe the line.[643]

As Rajan outlined later,[644] the reluctance of public sector banks to take on truant promoters coupled with their perpetual fear of investigative agencies played a significant role in creating the debt distress. Taking on such 'icons of society' was not an easy task for some public sector bank CEOs, and hence they chose to evergreen the loans rather than write them down, as they did not wish to incur the wrath of their customers or evoke the curiosity of various government agencies. This further deferred bad debt recognition, which ultimately grew into the situation we see in India today.

To its credit, the government in its budget announced more capital for well performing banks and also the formation of a Bank Boards Bureau, headed by former Comptroller and Auditor General (CAG) Vinod Rai, to improve governance practices as recommended by the P.J. Nayak Committee on banking governance reforms. It also seemed that the government and Reserve Bank were finally working together to tackle the NPA issues in a collaborative manner.

The impact of the asset quality review started showing up in bank results from mid-2016. State Bank of India announced a large loss in the first quarter of 2016 as it set aside more than double provisions to recognize more NPAs. However, it also announced that it was on track to merge all the remaining subsidiaries into one unit, bringing to closure a debate that had been raging since 1956. Similarly, other PSU banks were also not in good shape, and cumulatively, PSU bank losses were over ₹15,000 crore in the fourth quarter of fiscal year 2015–16.[645]

Forcing governance and disrupting traditional banking practices did not win Governor Rajan much praise in India, and in fact, he was widely seen as an outsider who was trying to enforce 'Western rules' in a 'unique' system. This along with the more frequent run-ins with the government over his speeches and utterances led to a rather rocky relationship as his term extension, which was due in September 2016, began to be debated.

The frequent utterances and the run-ins

In October 2015, Governor Rajan gave a speech at the Indian Institute of Technology, Delhi, his alma mater.[646] The speech focused on the ideas of tolerance and respect for economic progress, but it came at a time when the government was under attack from certain sections of the media and left-leaning intellectuals on the rising 'intolerance' in society. The speech thus provoked a backlash from Dr Subramaniam Swamy, who wrote to the prime minister asking him to sack Dr Rajan.[647] Despite the government appearing uncomfortable with his frequent utterances on issues beyond monetary policy, Governor Rajan defended his speech, saying that it would be crazy for India to give up its longstanding culture of tolerance and respect for opposing viewpoints. [648]

While the controversy around Governor Rajan's term renewal refused to die down, the government in its fiscal year 2016–17 budget announced that the monetary policy committee would be set up later that year and proceeded to amend the RBI Act. In April, Governor Rajan gave an interview to *Marketwatch*, where, when asked about his thoughts on India being the 'only bright spot' in a gloomy world economy, he described India as 'andhon mein kana raja, or the one-eyed king in the world of blind', hinting that while India was more stable, it was far away from fulfilling its potential.[649]

The media and some ministers in the government instantly took umbrage at this comment, with Nirmala Sitharaman, the minister of commerce, criticizing Governor Rajan for his poor choice of words. She said that 'his choice of words, the metaphors that have been used, are unnecessarily giving a handle to [the opposition] to give quirky interpretations like "who is this one-eyed king that Raghuram Rajan is referring to?" I would like people like Raghuram Rajan, who know the truths behind the economy and the dynamics of the economy, to be able to speak with better choice of words'.[650] These constant run-ins were starting to take their toll, and those familiar with the governor remember him being privately flustered by the government's acerbic response.

In public, Governor Rajan responded to the media outrage eloquently. While speaking at the convocation of the National Institute of Bank Management at Pune, Governor Rajan dwelled on why words mattered, but so did intent. He said that, 'As a central banker who has to be pragmatic, I cannot get euphoric if India is the fastest growing large economy [and] we must remember that our international reputation is of a country with great promise, which has under-delivered in the past'. He went on to add that 'when words are hung to dry out of context, as in a newspaper headline, it then becomes fair game for anyone who wants to fill in meaning to create mischief. If we are to have a reasonable public dialogue, everyone should read words in their context, not stripped of it. That may be a forlorn hope!' As he would later recall, the press attention on him was 'intense' and misinterpreted comments made headlines, which created 'unnecessary frictions.'[651]

Dr Swamy makes it a personality conflict

Meanwhile, Dr Subramaniam Swamy, now a nominated member of Parliament in the upper house, continued to voice significant reservations against Governor Rajan, questioning his role in an ongoing investigation against former finance minister P. Chidambaram.[652] Further, he criticized Governor Rajan and RBI policies as misguided, adding that his policies 'led to collapse of industry and rise of unemployment in the economy', and 'the sooner he is sent back to Chicago, the better it would be.'[653] He even went to the extent of saying that Rajan was 'mentally not fully Indian', and hence could not be trusted with the overseeing of the Indian economy.

Further, the government announced that it wanted to have more independent members on the proposed monetary policy committee, rather than give the governor more control. This led to an uproar about the government wresting policy control through nominated members, and a debate ensued on the right balance in the committee.[654] The amendments suggested by the government proposed taking away the governor's veto, which ironically was the purpose of the committee. However, the media criticism was largely centred on Governor's Rajan reappointment, and the monetary policy committee debate was timed unfortunately.

The debate became so loud that in an interview with *The Wall Street Journal*, Prime Minister Modi sought an end to the noise, suggesting that 'the issue of reappointment of RBI governor Raghuram Rajan is an administrative subject and it should not be an issue of interest of the media', and that a decision was only due in September.[655] This was seen by many as a signal that Rajan's appointment was all but guaranteed.[656]

Rajan announces his resignation

However, two weeks later, in a shocking decision, Governor Raghuram Rajan wrote to the Reserve Bank staff announcing that after much deliberation and consultation with the government, he had decided to return to academia at the end of his three-year term. He said that he is 'an academic and I have always made it clear that my ultimate home is in the realm of ideas. The approaching end of my three-year term, and of my leave at the University of Chicago, was therefore a good time to reflect on how much we had accomplished.' He added that while he was open to continuing in his role, 'on due reflection, and after consultation with the government, I want to share with you that I will be returning to academia when my term as Governor ends on September 4, 2016'.[657]

The resignation came just before the crucial referendum in the United Kingdom on its Eurozone membership. While some criticized him for picking a rather awkward time to announce his departure, both international and national media was generally critical of the government for failing to retain Raghuram Rajan. While the BJP stepped back from the brawl calling it Governor Rajan's personal decision, Dr Swamy continued to make personal attacks on Governor Rajan.

This came to an end when Prime Minister Modi announced in an interview that the entire episode was unfortunate and that it was 'not appropriate' on the part of certain individuals to mount an attack on bureaucrats, since they cannot respond. Prime Minister Modi further added that, 'My experience with him has been good and I appreciate the work he has done. It is wrong to say that Mr Rajan is less patriotic than us. It will also be unfair to say that he will not work for India's interests. He is no less patriotic. He loves India. Wherever he will work, he will work for India and he is patriotic.'[658]

A safe pick to replace Rajan

With the governorship of Raghuram Rajan coming to an unexpected end, the government had to look forward to appointing not only a new governor, but also a monetary policy committee. Initially, the names for the governorship included former deputy governors Rakesh Mohan and Subir Gokarn, along with serving deputy governor Urjit Patel and SBI chairman Arundhati Bhattacharya.[659] Even names of former deputy governors Usha Thorat and Shyamala Gopinath, Revenue Secretary Shaktikanta Das and Chief Economic Advisor Arvind Subramanian made the rounds, but the government refused to give any indication as to who would be favoured for the job.

Even though Finance Minister Arun Jaitley initially indicated that a replacement for Governor Rajan would be announced shortly, the government ended up focusing on the monetary policy committee first. The government notified the committee a week after Governor Rajan's resignation, and speculation began on who would be selected to sit on it.[660] The final structure of the committee was to have three internal members from the RBI as the Urjit Patel Committee report had suggested, but the government decided to nominate three external members to hold the position for four years.

As time passed, the government neither announced a replacement for Governor Rajan, nor did it announce the members of the newly formed monetary policy committee. The last monetary policy meeting under Governor Rajan was uneventful, with no changes made in policy rates. However, he did congratulate the government on completing an important institutional reform by way of forming the committee, which 'modernizes India's monetary policy framework'.[661] In his last speech as governor at St Stephens College in Delhi, Dr Rajan emphasized the importance of having an independent central bank and reiterated that its ability to say 'no' to the government needed to be preserved for macroeconomic stability.[662]

Finally, on 20 August 2016, the government announced Dr Urjit Patel,[663] the sitting deputy governor, as the twenty-fourth governor of the Reserve Bank of India. Not a man of many words, Urjit Patel had spent more than three years within the RBI already, and his appointment was seen as an indication of the government's desire for continuity at the Reserve Bank in terms of policy, but not necessarily in terms of speaking 'out of turn'.[664] It was also the first time since Governor Deshmukh was appointed the governor in 1943 that a sitting deputy governor had been offered the governorship for a full term.

Later in September, the government announced the external members of the monetary policy committee, nominating three academics rather than seasoned market commentators. The choice of candidates suggested orthodoxy and commitment to keeping the RBI away from the influence of market commentators, which was largely welcomed. The government nominated Dr Chetan Ghate, associate professor at the Indian Statistical Institute and former member of the Technical Advisory Committee; Pami Dua, Director of the Delhi School of Economics; and Ravindra H. Dholakia, professor of economics at the Indian Institute of Management (IIM), Ahmedabad, as independent members of the MPC, apart from the three internal members, including new governor Urjit Patel, who had a casting vote.

In its first meeting, the MPC unanimously decided to reduce policy rates by 25 bps, triggering fears of the RBI turning more 'growth supportive' and 'in line with government's thinking' than it was under Governor Rajan. However, for Governor Patel and the Reserve Bank, its most difficult task lay ahead of it.

Chapter 17

The demonetization episode

When the Narendra Modi government took charge, one of the first decisions it took was to create a special investigation team to probe the issue of black money. The committee was under the chairmanship of retired justice M.B. Shah. Multiple tax amnesty schemes followed this, run by the Ministry of Finance. The last major scheme was announced in the fiscal year 2016–17 budget and was marginally more successful than the other schemes. The government also amended its tax treaties with Singapore and Mauritius in an effort to curb round-tripping of money and tax evasion.

Speaking on the tax amnesty, Prime Minister Modi in his *Mann ki Baat* address on 26 June 2016 warned tax evaders that the amnesty ending on 30 September 2016 was 'their last chance'.[665] Soon after, in July, he cautioned tax evaders to pay their dues on time, warning them of severe action if they failed to come clean.[666]

However, there was a general sense within the public that the government's efforts to take on illegal wealth were hamstrung, and the measures taken were not making enough of an impact. As such, roughly mid-way through his five-year term, Prime Minister Modi was starting to appear ineffectual on his promise to reduce the role of black money, and his 'promise' of depositing fifteen lakh rupees in everyone's bank accounts was being joked about by his political opposition.

8.00 p.m., 8 November 2016

As the world focused on a mercurial election for the American presidency between Donald Trump and Hillary Clinton, India's prime minister's office announced that the prime minister would address the nation at 8.00 p.m. local time on the evening of 8 November 2016. The address began a little bit late, and unlike his usual speeches, Narendra Modi took his time listing the various government schemes he had launched to provide social security and necessary items to the poor and marginalized. He then proceeded to criticize the persistence of corruption in India, despite its economic progress. He outlined the steps his government had taken to stifle black money generation, including agreements with foreign governments, amnesty schemes and a new law to curb 'benami' (nameless) property transactions.[667]

Then came the bombshell. Roughly fifteen minutes into his speech, Modi announced that the government had decided to render the 1,000- and 500-rupee notes as illegal tender. At the time of his speech, roughly 86 per cent of total currency in circulation was in these notes. He asked Indian citizens to deposit their 1,000- and 500-rupee notes in bank accounts, giving them until 30 December 2016 to do so, roughly fifty days from the date of announcement.

India had gone through two rounds of demonetization previously, once in 1946 and then again in 1978. However, the magnitude of the 2016 demonetization was significantly larger, and its impact on India's economy was expected to be debilitating. In a country with a large informal sector and a general lack of access to banking services, such a significant demonetization was expected to give a body blow to several sectors, including agriculture. The political reaction was one of disbelief, as the popular opinion swung significantly in favour of Narendra Modi initially, despite the negative impact on both businesses and individuals. The moniker 'demonetization' was never used by the government or the Reserve Bank in any of its press releases. However, the term caught on, with its Hindi equivalent 'notebandi' too becoming part of the popular lexicon.

The Reserve Bank closed down banks and ATMs on 9 November to become battle ready, and from 10 November onwards, the queues began to build outside India's banks and ATMs. On the first day of banks opening their doors, RBI reported that over ten crore exchange transactions were reported. Most ATMs were out of cash, and the government had put in place restrictions on the withdrawal of cash directly from the banks and even ATMs, with a promise to raise the limits in two weeks, once the ATMs had been recalibrated to accept the new 2,000-rupee notes that were being introduced to replace the demonetized 1,000- and 500-rupee notes. India is the largest producer and consumer of currency notes, next only to China, hence the entire administrative exercise turned out to be much trickier than initially anticipated.

The government had exempted a few services, such as fuel pumps, hospitals and toll expressways from not transacting in the demonetized currency notes. However, for a few days, several businesses, such as electronics stores, departmental stores and even jewellers did significant business, transacting mostly in cash, according to anecdotal evidence. There were also long-distance tickets being booked through the railways, which were later made non-refundable to prevent money laundering through this loophole. The government swiftly moved to crack down on any conversion of 'illegal wealth' into gold, putting jewellers on the spot.[668]

A willing participant or a mute spectator?

The Reserve Bank found itself in a tight spot post demonetization. While on the one hand it had the arduous task of managing the huge disruption in India's cash flow, on the other, it was the subject of significant criticism, especially from the media and several policy watchers. Former governor Rangarajan called the move a 'standard prescription',[669] while former governor Subbarao welcomed the move, but cautioned the government against using the exercise to derive windfall gains from the Reserve Bank, through extinguished notes. Former governor Jalan was cautious on the implications of the move, but welcomed the spirit of reducing illicit money in which it was undertaken.

Internationally, the move attracted a lot of attention, and some derision. Kaushik Basu, who had previously served as chief economic advisor under Dr Manmohan Singh, termed the exercise as 'poorly designed and likely to fail', adding further that 'demonetisation will only make a minor dent in corruption. It is, however, likely to rock the entire economy'.[670] However, Kenneth Rogoff, former chief economist of IMF, called the move 'bold and audacious', indicating that the long-term gains would significantly outweigh the short-term pains of the exercise.[671]

Even as academics discussed the pros and cons of the move, the remonetization exercise was much slower than expected. The government deployed the Indian Air Force to airlift new currency notes to various remote locations to replenish currency chests.[672] The RBI even waived ATM charges for bank customers to increase the incentive to use machines rather than queue outside branches. The Reserve Bank was posting regular updates on its website, but the lack of direct communication from the bank was criticized by the media.[673]

Governor Patel finally spoke at length on 27 November, reaffirming RBI's commitment to remonetize the economy as rapidly as possible and advocated the use of cashless transactions to ease the temporary pain.[674] Even Finance Minister Arun Jaitley came to RBI's defence, arguing that those who cannot discuss everything in front of the camera should be left to focus on their work. Nonetheless, with the cash crunch remaining high, criticism was mounting, and the long queues outside ATMs and banks continued. Even the government reneged on its promise of raising the cash withdrawal limits two weeks after the demonetization.

In the meantime, the rules around who could or could not use old demonetized notes began to be changed rapidly as the government was getting feedback on various activities, right from the sowing for the rabi crop season to marriages getting disrupted due to demonetization. The government and the RBI responded favourably with some relief measures, but the solutions provided were impractical in design and too bureaucratic to be implementable.

The RBI also had the headache of excess banking system liquidity coming back through the reverse repo corridor. Government bond yields had fallen sharply as banks used the excess deposits to park them into government securities. However, the party ended for banks when on 26 November, the Reserve Bank unexpectedly raised the cash reserve ratio on an incremental basis from 16 September to 11 November to 100 per cent,[675] thus taking back all the extra funds that had been deposited just before the demonetization announcement.

Later, on 7 December, the Reserve Bank met for its first MPC meeting after the demonetization announcement, where it shocked market participants and economists by keeping rates on hold, but it withdrew the incremental CRR measures as the government raised the MSS limits to absorb the excess liquidity in the system. The lack of monetary support was justified on rather flimsy reasons. The committee felt that the impact of demonetization on economic growth was still 'clouded', and hence it would be prudent to wait for more data before assessing the short-term impact of the note ban.[676] In the press conference, Governor Patel justified the decision, saying, 'it is appropriate to look through the transitory but unclear effects of the withdrawal of specified bank notes [...] therefore, it is prudent to wait and watch how these factors play out and impinge upon the outlook'.[677]

Leaping before looking

The government, a few weeks into the exercise, was starting to get flak for not 'thinking through' the process of replacement of currency notes and was losing popular support due to implementation bottlenecks. Further, the demonetized currency notes were coming back thick and fast into the banking system, giving the impression that the entire exercise to extinguish black money was failing, and the targeted sections had managed to 'beat the system' to return the worthless currency notes through several channels, including the recently opened Jan-Dhan bank accounts. Indeed, in its first MPC meeting on 8 December, Deputy Governor R. Gandhi reported that over ₹11.55 lakh crore of demonetized money had been returned to the system, which was almost 75 per cent of total currency notes affected.[678]

The government was also firmly put on the mat in the Parliament, where several opposition leaders, including former prime minister and RBI governor Dr Manmohan Singh who criticised the government on the decision to demonetize such a large sum of currency notes. In a short but powerful speech given in the Rajya Sabha, Dr Manmohan Singh called the demonetization exercise a 'case of organized loot, legalized plunder of the common people', and called the process of demonetization a 'monumental mismanagement' by the government. Dr Singh was acerbic in his criticism of the government and pointed out that GDP was to decline 2 per cent because of the demonetization exercise.[679] While the GDP did not decline by 2 per cent, growth rate indeed fell by 2 percentage points a year down the line.

In such a situation, there was clearly a desire to shift the narrative, and the government came out with the idea of promoting 'cashless transactions' and the digital economy. The real motivation behind this sudden change of narrative remains unclear. Digitization was not mentioned in the early speeches around demonetization, but as it became clear that it would take a while to rebuild the currency in circulation, the government and the RBI actively started to promote cashless payments and mobile wallets. The government even formed a committee of chief ministers led by Andhra Pradesh Chief Minister N. Chandrababu Naidu to promote cashless transactions.

The Reserve Bank was having its own problems, facing criticism for being completely beholden to the government, while losing its own credentials. In a scathing editorial, *The Economist* magazine chided the government for doing considerable damage to institutions, particularly the RBI. The magazine questioned Governor Patel's silence and said that RBI's reputation for 'probity, competence and independence' was in tatters. Similarly, in a conference call with the media, Standard & Poor's questioned the predictability of policymaking in India, with Kyran Curry, the analyst covering India, saying that 'demonetization has cast a shadow over the RBI's competence and independence'.

Former governors and employee unions raised similar concerns as well. Sometime after the exercise concluded, former governor Y.V. Reddy said that he would have advised the government against demonetization had he been the governor. He further added, 'If overruled, I would have admitted myself in hospital and resigned after some time.'[680] Governor Patel was grilled in a deposition to the standing committee on finance, during which he reportedly failed to provide any clarity on when the situation would normalize and when RBI would be able to provide data on how much currency had come back. In fact, it was Dr Manmohan Singh who came to Governor Patel's rescue, asking him not to respond to some questions raised by his fellow party members.[681]

Employee unions at the RBI and other banks had been protesting for a while against the leadership. A banking union even called for Governor Patel's resignation for causing 'havoc' to the economy.[682] The protests stepped up in January, when the RBI employees' union wrote a letter to Governor Patel saying that there was a feeling of 'humiliation' over the 'blatant encroachment' by the Ministry of Finance on currency management. The letter further stated that 'An image of efficiency and independence that the RBI assiduously built up over decades by the strenuous efforts of its staff and judicious policymaking has gone into smithereens in no time. We feel extremely pained.'[683] There was a threat of a strike in February by bank employees, who demanded complete removal of cash withdrawal restrictions.

The protests did not stop within the banking system and the RBI. Given the lack of communication, opposition political parties launched protests against the RBI, which at times created a sense of conflict. In Kolkata, Governor Patel was manhandled by workers of the Congress Party at the Netaji Subash Chandra Bose airport, amid black flags.[684] A similar incident took place in Gandhinagar, Gujarat, when Governor Patel was reported to have run away from a group of journalists. They were waiting for him after a speech he gave at the Vibrant Gujarat Summit on 11 January.[685]

A success or a failure?

By the end of December 2016, the fifty days that Prime Minister Narendra Modi had asked for the currency situation to normalise had expired. While the RBI did not give out any official figures of how much cash had come back, its own currency in circulation figures suggested that over ₹15 lakh crore, or more than 95 per cent of the funds demonetized had returned.[686]

The secrecy over the total currency that came back continued, even as RBI conducted its final monetary policy meeting for fiscal year 2016–17. On 7 February 2017, RBI announced it would be increasing the withdrawal limits for individual depositors to ₹50,000 from 20 February and would completely remove the limits from 13 March.[687] Simultaneously, the RBI's monetary stance turned much more hawkish, with the policy stance changed to neutral, and the bank indicated that the next policy move from it was likely to be a rate hike, despite growth downgrades. This was perhaps a reflection of the government having passed the Goods and Services Tax, to be implemented from July 2017. But the RBI was also facing a weakening currency and rising oil prices. A month after the last MPC meeting for the year, the RBI released a study prepared by the monetary policy department, which catalogued the impact of demonetization across various macroeconomic parameters, including growth, inflation and the banking system.

On growth, RBI noted that the primary channel of negative impact was likely to be through a decline in liquidity, as currency in circulation declined. As such, while there was likely to be a negative shock to discretionary spending, there would also be considerable amount of activity lost through daily wage earners in the informal sector, many of whom were likely to be rendered unemployed due to paucity of cash. The unorganized sector accounts for 45 per cent of total GDP, but over 80 per cent of total employment.[688] This was especially true of the construction sector, but was also the case in labour-intensive industries such as textiles, leather and jewellery.

This sudden loss in income was likely to prove to be a permanent loss, unlike discretionary spending, which could normalize or compensate later for the losses made in the months just after the demonetization. Similarly, any negative shocks to wealth were also likely to be transitory in nature. Still, the Reserve Bank estimated that only 33 bps of downward revisions to headline growth had come about because of demonetization, which felt minor compared to the magnitude of shock the economy was experiencing.

Given the negative aggregate demand shock, coupled with relatively strong farm sector performance, inflation, especially for perishable items, was forecast to drop significantly. But underlying inflation had remained broadly stable and was expected to recover in line with aggregate demand. The impact on bank balance sheets was more meaningful, with almost ₹7 lakh crores in deposits making its way into the banking system on a net basis.

However, the impact of this sudden jump in financial savings was not necessarily very positive for the economy. Banks largely used the money to invest in government securities and barely used this additional liquidity to create credit in the system. As the Reserve Bank report noted, the incremental credit deposit ratio stood at only 18 per cent. For some banks, there was certainly a reduction in cost of funds, but the net impact on banking system profitability was small at ₹45,000 crores (US$700 million).

However, despite putting out a comprehensive study, the number that remained elusive was the total amount of money that had come back through the demonetization exercise. In fact, almost nine months into the exercise in July 2017, Governor Patel informed the standing committee on finance in Parliament that the Reserve Bank was still counting the demonetized currency notes and that it was taking longer than previously anticipated. Further, Deputy Governor B.P. Kanungo informed the standing committee that the Reserve Bank was experiencing a shortage of note counting machines, and it had ordered more to expedite the counting process. However, the standing committee members were not satisfied with the response and pushed back on the RBI top brass over the slow process. In fact, Congress leader Digvijaya Singh quipped that he wondered whether the RBI would be able to provide the figures by 'May 2019', when the next elections were due,[689] which left the parliamentary panel and RBI's team, including Governor Patel, in splits of laughter.

Two weeks after the testimony, the Reserve Bank announced its dividend payments to the government at ₹33,700 crores, which was much lower than the previously anticipated figure of approximately ₹70,000 crores billion. This significant decline was largely attributed to the high printing costs of new currency notes, the rise in liquidity operation costs due to higher liquidity withdrawal, and also possibly the high amount of currency notes coming back through the demonetization exercise.[690]

The irony of this sharp decline in profits was not lost on many policy watchers. From the discussion around whether the government could actually be the beneficiary from windfall gains, the much lower dividend from the RBI was now being seen as an impediment to fiscal consolidation, which the government remained committed to. Former finance minister P. Chidambaram questioned the profits, asking whether the profit amount had incorporated fully the cost of currency note exchange, and indicated that another ₹500 billion should be considered for costs.[691]

Ultimately, the Reserve Bank announced on 30 August 2017 that almost 99 per cent of the total demonetized currency notes had come back into the system. This meant that more than 15 lakh crores worth of currency notes were returned[692] and the total amount of fake currency notes extinguished was very marginal. This naturally evoked criticism against the government, as on the surface, the demonetization exercise looked like a failure. But the government asked for patience as almost ₹3 lakh crore of deposits remained under scrutiny, the results of which could ultimately lead to some gains in the fight against black money.

Cost-benefit analysis of demonetization is unclear

The demonetization exercise remains a conundrum for most people. While there is a sharp division in opinion over the efficacy of extinguishing currency notes to fight black money, the relatively mild economic impact relative to anecdotal evidence of a sharp reduction in consumer and business demand show the divide between data and experience with regard to the entire episode. The government has encouraged markets to look beyond the short-term negative impact and focus instead on the long-term positive effects, but the jury is still out on the overall impact of the exercise.

There was a noticeable increase in electronic payments during the period of demonetization, and the powerful combination of Jan-Dhan bank accounts, direct benefit transfers, the Goods and Services Tax and less cash may lead to greater formalization in the economy, thus helping bring millions of informal sector businesses and workers into the formal sector. Recent growth data has shown signs of a slowdown, and the flip side for businesses and employees can be loss of competitiveness as the formal sector brings with it higher taxes, more social security requirements and regulation, which may render several businesses unviable, given slim business margins.

A year after the demonetization, former governor Rajan shed some light on the exercise, noting that demonetization was being informally deliberated upon in policy corridors in Delhi, and that in February 2016, he had given an oral briefing on his and the RBI's view on it, indicating that 'although there might be long-term benefits, I [feel] that the likely short-term economic costs would outweigh them.'[693] The RBI was then asked to prepare a briefing note, which it did, also suggesting alternative measures. There has been no indication as to what these alternative measures were, however. Rajan did indicate that he was not asked to make a decision on demonetization, but it is plausible that the government chose to wait for Rajan to depart before making a final decision.

From the RBI's point of view, the exercise has been both stressful and laborious, and it has not necessarily added to the institution's credibility in the short term. Nonetheless, the role of the RBI and India's banking system in ensuring a relatively smooth exchange and remonetization exercise should be applauded, especially given India's large hinterland and relatively low banking system penetration.

If the final figure of notes returned and extinguished is published soon, the reputation of the Reserve Bank as a non-political institution working across states and governments can be preserved. This may be at risk, however, if the currency returned is larger than the officially published figure of total currency in circulation of 500- and 1000-rupee notes. As such, it is better that the Reserve Bank takes its time in counting the notes, rather than risk publishing a number that might jeopardize its credibility with the Indian public and international financial community at large.

Chapter 18

Looking forward

The Reserve Bank stands out as a leading institution in the country which has miraculously managed to stay away from the ills that other government institutions face in India. The credit for this development of India's financial sector should also be shared with its recent political leadership, which has had the foresight to leave institutions such as the Reserve Bank of India and its leadership alone when it comes to technical and regulatory matters. After the liberalization of 1991, India has also done well to create new institutions, such as the Securities and Exchange Board of India, to complement the Reserve Bank in regulating financial markets as India's economy grew at a record pace.

But the primacy of the Reserve Bank in India's financial sector is unlikely to be challenged, and hence the institution needs to be further strengthened, both in internal and external matters. In its over eighty years of existence, the Reserve Bank has been an active participant in most areas of economic development, but the policies have often yielded mixed results. As a regulator, RBI has not only had to intervene at times in areas that are perhaps beyond its jurisdiction, but it has also been a key driver of introducing 'best' practices into India's financial markets, especially around bank regulation, minority investor protection and bond market regulation. But there is more that needs to be done, and there are areas of work that the RBI can focus on more, while allocating less time to other functions.

A stronger, more confident institution

In the last two decades, the Reserve Bank has had several victories, both legislative and operational, that have strengthened its autonomy within the government apparatus. The abolishment of ad hoc treasury bills, strengthening of foreign reserves, the introduction of a fiscal responsibility act (FRBM) and the introduction of the market stabilization scheme for capital flows management are major milestones and have allowed the Reserve Bank to carry out its functions in a more independent manner.

Similarly, within the Reserve Bank, several steps have been taken to bolster its decision-making credibility, particularly by introducing transparency and communication with the government, financial markets and policy watchers. The establishment of various technical committees, introduction of more frequent monetary policy reviews, and enhancement of communication methods through regular data releases, media interactions and policy briefings have improved market guidance. On top of that, the establishment of a monetary policy committee in 2016 should be considered a watershed moment as the RBI now shares the setting of monetary policy with three external members, an activity that was widely recognized as an internal best practice.

Nonetheless, there remain areas in which more work can be undertaken. In the research conducted during the writing of this book, several commentators and former employees raised pertinent points regarding areas in which further efforts are required. Addressing these will no doubt help in improving Reserve Bank's credibility with the public at large.

As a conservative institution that has spent several decades in India's political economy, RBI is often pulled up for forming conservative, non-negotiable viewpoints, which are often described as instances of 'group think'. To its credit, several policy formulations or amendments have come through discussions and deliberations with various stakeholders. But given the fact that the Reserve Bank sits in Mumbai, away from the government of India, and maintains its own cadre through a self-designed employment method, the underlying design may eventually encourage group think to protect RBI's turf, especially if unreasonable demands come from the political leadership and its financial institutions.

This issue can, to an extent, be tackled by bringing in more people from outside the Reserve Bank cadre to work with the prestigious institution, even if it is for short-term assignments of three to five years. While that might be a short period in which to make a significant impact, communication and deliberations with these appointees might help the Reserve Bank understand the many viewpoints that exist outside its purview, and at the same time will help those in financial markets understand RBI's viewpoints better. To its credit, the RBI has been systematically bringing in academics and economists from Western universities and India's private sector, but the process can be made more structured and institutionalized.

The second issue that perhaps needs more attention is that of regulatory matters, especially the supervision of the banking system. India is currently undergoing a significant upheaval in its banking sector, largely due to rising non-performing loans, which have been largely due to regulatory problems in the infrastructure sector. The Reserve Bank, which oversaw the banks as they made these large advances to projects with asset liability mismatches, needs to make a decision on whether banks, which are typically funded by short-term deposits, should be financing projects that may only turn profitable over a couple of decades.

Again, the problem is not new, but the lack of adequate depth in India's domestic corporate bond markets both in terms of funds and participants could be a problem that needs urgent redressal. One also needs to acknowledge that from the Reserve Bank's perspective, protecting the depositor's interest reigns supreme, but the low credit demand in recent years amid rising non-performing assets have hollowed out the capital base of India's public sector banks. Even the government, which embarked on an ambitious recapitalization programme, has made only some progress in providing stability.

In fact, the focus of the government has been on improving bankruptcy laws, which is a welcome step. But at the same time, involving the Reserve Bank and giving it more powers to initiate debt recovery proceedings might bring in more work, both in terms of manpower and expertise, than what is desired. In this sense, while the initial steps such as filing twelve key bankruptcy proceedings and formation of the National Company Law Tribunal (NCLT) for distressed debt resolution are important, one needs to ensure this does not become par for the course as far as the Reserve Bank's role in debt resolution is concerned. Further, over the medium term, the RBI needs to continue to audit bank loan books in the same spirit as the asset quality review that was undertaken under Governor

Rajan, and ensure that the disclosure and reporting standards for India's banking system are made more robust and rigorous.

Raising RBI's internal research capabilities

Several key initiatives to improve the quality of research have been introduced in recent years. In 2013, after Governor Rajan's arrival at the RBI, a decision was taken to improve the quality of research output and the internal research models of the Reserve Bank, as well as retrain staff. Currently, the Reserve Bank runs several institutions across India for training and research purposes. Over time, these institutions, such as the College of Agricultural Banking in Pune, CAFRAL in Mumbai, and the RBI's training college in Chennai, will be brought under the auspices of the RBI academy, a new state-of-the-art institution that will be based in Mumbai for retraining existing employees and facilitating the lateral entry of young Indian researchers currently training all over the world.

Changes will likely also take place in the Reserve Bank's own internal modelling exercises as there is an emphasis on hiring doctoral students directly from the most prestigious universities globally, which will help bring in best practices and more recent research ideas in the modelling domain. In fact, one understands that the Reserve Bank has been designing its own dynamic general stochastic equilibrium model, which will eventually help in improving the quality of forecasts and aid the monetary policy process in guiding inflation expectations over time.

To facilitate the improvement in forecasting, the Reserve Bank also needs to continuously collect more exhaustive macroeconomic data, something that it has been prioritizing for several decades now. In fact, the Reserve Bank is currently running more than five regular quarterly surveys on various macroeconomic issues, which to an extent have helped bridge the gap between economic statistics published by the Central Statistics Office in Delhi, and the information provided by private surveys. This is on top of its regular data releases on monetary indicators, along with a monthly bulletin of data. Over time, the Reserve Bank also needs to encourage the government to collect more information about employment figures, since that will most likely be the biggest policy challenge for India in the next two decades.

From a communication point of view, the Reserve Bank should continue to educate the market and the public on the efficacy of the flexible inflation targeting regime, and how it has helped to improve the expectations setting process. This is a challenging task, given that India's inflation basket is largely moved by food and fuel prices, but even then, in coordination with the government, there is scope for communicating the nature of price changes expected in the economy, which may help in stabilizing inflation expectations closer to the desired target of 4 per cent over the medium term.

Finally, it might be worthwhile for the Reserve Bank to set a series of longer-term objectives, which it should look to achieve as we get closer to the centenary of the Reserve Bank's inauguration in 2035. The Reserve Bank of India has a lot of achievements to its credit, but undertaking a perspective planning study based on a longer-term perspective may help derive a path of objectives that need to be achieved as India aims to transition from a low middle-income country to a high middle-income country in next two decades. This would not only reinvigorate a sense of opportunity, but will also help prepare various financial institutions, markets and people associated with India's financial sector to envisage and understand what India's objectives are relative to financial market development and financial inclusion.

Acknowledgements

The idea of this book germinated while reading four humongous and fairly dry volumes documenting the history of the RBI between 1935 and 1997.

It took two years of research to make up my mind on the kind of book I wanted to write, since there have been several far more illustrious individuals who have written about the institution. The considerable encouragement I received from Dr Bimal Jalan, former RBI governor, and Dr Mukul Asher made me take the project more seriously, for which I am grateful.

In particular, Dr Duvvuri Subbarao, former RBI governor, who had been fortuitously been living in Singapore, provided a lot of suggestions, while all along helping me reach out to other senior people connected with the RBI.

Being based outside India, it was a constant challenge to find the necessary material related to the institution, but in my research trips to India, I was lucky to interact with several eminent RBI policymakers, both past and the present. I would particularly like to thank Shyamala Gopinath, Dr Asuri Vasudevan, Dr Chetan Ghate, K. Kanagasabapathy, Dr Partha Ray and Bazil Sheikh for their valuable time and sharing their experiences in the central bank. In particular, I would like to thank Dr R.L. Sahoo and his team at the RBI archives in Pune for graciously hosting me and assisting in the primary research. Former board member of the RBI, Dr Indira Rajaraman, was also very generous in terms of her time and in sharing her knowledge of the institution. Her insights were very useful in shaping my thoughts. T.C.A. Srinivasa Raghavan, who is an authority on RBI 's history, was extremely supportive and his inputs helped immensely.

Further, I am also indebted to Dr Jehangir Aziz, Dr P.J. Nayak, Dr Sajjid Chinoy, Dr Arvind Virmani, Sumita Kale, Vasan Shridharan, Peter Redward, Anuj Gupta, Shankkar Aiyar, Dr Ashima Goyal, Dr Jairam

Ramesh and Dr V. Anantha Nageswaran for their critical inputs and advice.

Niranjan Rajadhyaksha was very supportive of the project right from the beginning, helping me map out several interactions and contacts, for which I am very grateful. Also, Tamal Bandhopadhay, who has followed the RBI closely for over three decades, was immensely generous in his sharing stories, experiences and views on the Reserve Bank.

I am very grateful to my colleagues Sudeep Sarma, Ajay Rajadhyaksha, Jon Scoffin, Marvin Barth, David Fernandez and Siddhartha Sanyal for supporting and encouraging me to complete the book. Friends such as Azad Singh Bali, Amit Paranjape, Aashish Chandorkar, Pari Sarma, Dasharath Upadhya, Ankit Mital, Harsh Gupta and Ankur Gupta, who read the various drafts of the book, had a great impact on shaping my writing.

I am especially indebted to renowned journalist Andy Mukherjee, who gave strong inputs in the design of the book, and also introduced me to Dibakar Ghosh of Rupa Publications. Dibakar, without whom the book would not have happened, helped me navigate the writing, designing and execution of the book, for which I will be forever grateful. Kaniskha Gupta of Writer's Side came on board the project a bit late, but his contribution and suggestions have been immense. I am also thankful to Nidhi Dugar Kundalia for the introducing me to Kanishka.

Lastly, I am also very grateful to my wife Neha and my daughter Reva, who put up with my mood swings and anti-social behaviour during the writing of the book. They have been a constant source of support, and have done more than necessary to ensure I finished the work I had undertaken. Forgive me if I have missed naming anyone.

Endnotes

1 Thomas A. Timberg. *The Marwaris: from Jagat Seth to the Birlas*. Allen Lane, an Imprint of Penguin Books, 2014, p. XXIII–XXIV

2 S. L. N. Simha and Chintaman Dwarkanath Deshmukh. *History of the Reserve Bank of India, 1935–51*. Reserve Bank of India, 2005, p.6

3 Ibid., pp.6–8

4 Ibid., pp.6–10

5 Ibid., pp.12–13

6 Soumitra Das. *The Telegraph*. http://www.telegraphindia.com/1090811/jsp/calcutta/story_11343895.jsp., accessed on 24 October 2017

7 S. L. N. Simha and Chintaman Dwarkanath Deshmukh. *History of the Reserve Bank of India, 1935–51*. Reserve Bank of India, 2005, p.16

8 Ibid., pp.18–19

9 Austen Chamberlain was then the Secretary of State for India in the British Cabinet.

10 John Maynard Keynes. *Indian Currency and Finance*. Original printed by Macmillan, 1913. Reprinted by Cambridge University Press, 2013.

11 S. L. N. Simha and Chintaman Dwarkanath Deshmukh. *History of the Reserve Bank of India, 1935–51*. Reserve Bank of India, 2005, p.23

12 Ibid., pp.26–28

13 Ibid., pp.27–28

14 Ibid., p.28

15 S. L. N. Simha and Chintaman Dwarkanath Deshmukh. *History of the Reserve Bank of India, 1935–51*. Reserve Bank of India, 2005

16 Ibid., pp.33–34

17 Anand Ranganathan. Interview with T.C.A. Srinivasa Raghavan. *Newslaundry*. https://www.youtube.com/watch?v=5wtpSKjs_Gg

18 B.K. Dadabhoy. *Barons of Banking—Glimpses of Indian Banking History*. Random House India, 2015 ed. pp.154–155

19 B. K. Dadabhoy. *Barons of Banking—Glimpses of Indian Banking History*. Random House India, 2015 ed., pp.195–197

20 C.D. Deshmukh. *Course of My Life*. Orient Longman, 1974, p.51

21 Ibid., p.127

22 C.D. Deshmukh. *Course of My Life*. Orient Longman, 1974, p.153

23 S. L. N. Simha,and Chintaman Dwarkanath Deshmukh. *History of the Reserve Bank of India, 1935–51*. Reserve Bank of India, 2005, pp.706–708

24 S. L. N. Simha,and Chintaman Dwarkanath Deshmukh. *History of the Reserve Bank of India, 1935–51*. Reserve Bank of India, 2005, p.706–708

25 Ibid., p.709

26 C.D. Deshmukh. *Economic developments in India 1946–1956—A personal retrospect*. Asia Publishing House, 1957, p.38

27 Ibid., p.39

28 Direct Action Day was a day of large communal riots between Hindus and Muslims in

Kolkata on 16 August 1946, on the call of the Muslim League.

29   S. L. N. Simha and Chintaman Dwarkanath Deshmukh. *History of the Reserve Bank of India, 1935–51*. Reserve Bank of India, 2005, pp.539–540

30   C.D. Deshmukh. *Course of My Life*. Orient Longman, 1974, p.146

31   C.D. Deshmukh. *Economic developments in India 1946–1956—A personal retrospect*. Asia Publishing House, 1957, p.60

32   Ibid., p.61

33   B.K. Dadabhoy. *Barons of Banking—Glimpses of Indian Banking History*. Random House India, 2015 ed., pp.136–144

34   S. L. N. Simha and Chintaman Dwarkanath Deshmukh. *History of the Reserve Bank of India, 1935–51*. Reserve Bank of India, 2005, p.506

35   Ibid., p.524

36   Ibid., p.719

37   Ibid., p.446–447

38   G. Balachandran. *Reserve Bank of India*. Reserve Bank of India, 1998, p.338

39   Ibid., p.322

40   Ibid., p.323

41   Ibid., p.234

42   B.K. Dadabhoy. *Barons of Banking—Glimpses of Indian Banking History*. Random House India, 2015 ed., p.290

43   G. Balachandran. *Reserve Bank of India*. Reserve Bank of India, 1998, p.332

44   Ibid., p.333

45   Ibid., p.364–366

46   Ibid., p.364–366

47   Ibid., p.371

48   The Bombay agitations was organized by the Samyukt Maharashtra movement, which wanted Mumbai to remain in the Marathi speaking state, while the State reorganization committee had recommended linguistic reorganization. Over 105 people were killed in police firing in January 1956

49   C.D. Deshmukh. *Economic developments in India 1946–1956—A personal retrospect*. Asia Publishing House, 1957, p.66–82

50   Amal Sanyal. 'The Curious Case of the Bombay Plan, Contemporary Issues and Ideas in Social Sciences.' 2010. http://journal.ciiss.in/index.php/ciiss/article/view/78/75, accessed on 27 October 2017

51   I.G. Patel. *Glimpses of Indian Economic Policy: An Insider's View*. Oxford University Press, 2002, p.32–33

52   G. Balachandran. *Reserve Bank of India*. Reserve Bank of India, 1998, p.51

53   Ibid., p.51

54   Pranab Mukherjee. 'Congress and the Making of the Indian Nation.' http://inc.in/about-congress/history/literature/6-Congress-and-the-Making-of--the-Indian-Nation/26-The-Nehru-Era, accessed on 27 October 2017

55   G. Balachandran. *Reserve Bank of India*. Reserve Bank of India, 1998, p.29–31

56   Niranjan Rajyadhaksha. 'The Anxiety that lingers.' *Livemint*, 7 December 2012. http://www.livemint.com/Leisure/vSENKsR3LEwbCgaG4zMw8K/The-anxiety-that-lingers.html, accessed on 27 October 2017

57   G. Balachandran. *Reserve Bank of India*. Reserve Bank of India, 1998, p.715

58   M. Narasimham. *From Reserve Bank to Finance Ministry and Beyond: Some Reminiscences*. UBS Publishers' Distributors, 2002, p.17

59   G. Balachandran. *Reserve Bank of India*. Reserve Bank of India, 1998, p.715

60   Ibid., p.716

61   B.K. Nehru. *Nice Guys Finish Second*. Viking, 1997 (republished by Penguin, 2012), p.305

62   G. Balachandran. *Reserve Bank of India*. Reserve Bank of India, 1998, p.1163
63   Shashi Tharoor. *Nehru: The Invention of India*. Penguin, 2012, p.168
64   M. Narasimham. *From Reserve Bank to Finance Ministry and Beyond: Some Reminiscences*. UBS Publishers' Distributors, 2002, p.21–25
65   G. Balachandran. *Reserve Bank of India*. Reserve Bank of India, 1998, p.800–803
66   I.G. Patel. *Glimpses of Indian Economic Policy: An Insider's View*. Oxford University Press, 2002, p.58
67   G. Balachandran. *Reserve Bank of India*. Reserve Bank of India, 1998, p.627
68   Ibid., p.639
69   Ibid., p.654
70   Ibid., p.667
71   I.G. Patel. *Glimpses of Indian Economic Policy: An Insider's View*. Oxford University Press, 2002, p.104
72   Ibid., p.105
73   David B. H. Denoon. 'Cycles in Indian Economic Liberalization, 1966–1996.' *Comparative Politics*, vol. 31, no. 1, 1998, p.43–60. JSTOR, www.jstor.org/stable/422105
74   Ankit Mital. 'India and liberalization: There was a 1966 before 1991.' *Livemint*, 24 June 2016. http://www.livemint.com/Sundayapp/h4nQPwoxX2j8HnftPQt2BI/India-and-liberalization-There-was-a-1966-before-1991.html, accessed on 28 October 2017
75   I.G. Patel. *Glimpses of Indian Economic Policy: An Insider's View*. Oxford University Press, 2002, p.107
76   Vijay Joshi and Ian Malcolm David Little. *India: Macroeconomics and Political Economy, 1964–1991*. Oxford University Press, 1998, p.47
77   Katherine Frank. *Indira: The Life of Indira Nehru Gandhi*. HarperCollins, 2005, p.289
78   Ibid., p.297
79   G. Balachandran. *Reserve Bank of India*. Reserve Bank of India, 1998, p.682
80   B.K. Nehru. *Nice Guys Finish Second*. Viking, 1997 (reprinted by Penguin, 2012), p.499–500
81   G. Balachandran. *Reserve Bank of India*. Reserve Bank of India, 1998, p.683
82   Jagdish N. Bhagwati and T. N. Srinivasan. 'Foreign Trade Regimes and Economic Development: India.' National Bureau of Economic Research, 1976, p.152
83   G. Balachandran. *Reserve Bank of India*. Reserve Bank of India, 1998, p.686
84   Katherine Frank. *Indira: The Life of Indira Nehru Gandhi*. HarperCollins, 2005, p.298
85   G. Balachandran. *Reserve Bank of India*. Reserve Bank of India, 1998, p.687
86   Ibid., p.453
87   Ibid., p.468
88   Ibid., p.473
89   Ibid., p.492
90   Ibid., p.496
91   Ibid., p.499
92   Once upon a Poll: Fourth Lok Sabha election (1967). *Indian Express*, 11 March 2014. http://indianexpress.com/article/india/politics/once-upon-a-poll-fourth-lok-sabha-election-1967/, accessed on 28 October 2017
93   B.K. Nehru. *Nice Guys Finish Second*. Viking, 1997 (republished by Penguin, 2012), p.503
94   T.C.A. Srinivasa Raghavan, ed. *The Reserve Bank of India—1968–1981*. Vol 3. Reserve Bank of India, 2005, p.17
95   D.N. Ghosh. *No Regrets*. India, Rupa Publications, 2015, p.40
96   Ibid., p.41
97   T.C.A. Srinivasa Raghavan, ed. *The Reserve Bank of India—1968–1981*. Vol 3. Reserve Bank of India, 2005, p.29
98   Inder Malhotra. , 'Prelude to a Split.' *The Indian Express*, 9 December 2013. http://indianexpress.com/article/opinion/columns/prelude-to-a-split/, accessed on 28 October 2017

99   T.C.A. Srinivasa Raghavan, ed. *The Reserve Bank of India—1968–1981*. Vol 3. Reserve Bank of India, 2005, p.33

100   B.K. Dadabhoy. *Barons of Banking—Glimpses of Indian Banking History*. Random House India, 2015 ed., p.305

101   I.G. Patel. *Glimpses of Indian Economic Policy: An Insider's View*. Oxford University Press, 2002, p.135–138

102   D.N. Ghosh. *No Regrets*. Rupa Publications, 2015, p.4

103   Ibid., p.7

104   T.C.A. Srinivasa Raghavan, ed. *The Reserve Bank of India—1968–1981*. Vol 3. Reserve Bank of India, 2005, p.38

105   D.N. Ghosh. *No Regrets*. Rupa Publications, 2015, p.21

106   I.G. Patel. *Glimpses of Indian Economic Policy: An Insider's View*. Oxford University Press, 2002, p.136

107   D.N. Ghosh. *No Regrets*. Rupa Publications, 2015, Chapter 3, 'In the Courtroom'

108   B.K. Dadabhoy. *Barons of Banking—Glimpses of Indian Banking History*. Random House India, 2015 ed., p.307

109   Pranab Mukherjee. 'Congress and the Making of the Nation.'http://inc.in/about-congress/history/literature/6-Congress-and-the-Making-of--the-Indian-Nation/27-Indira-Gandhi, accessed on 28 October 2017

110   T.C.A. Srinivasa Raghavan, ed. *The Reserve Bank of India—1968–1981*. Vol 3. Reserve Bank of India, 2005, p.67

111   Vijay Joshi and Ian Malcolm David Little. *India: Macroeconomics and Political Economy, 1964–1991*. Oxford University Press, 1998, p.51

112   Ibid., p.109

113   T.C.A. Srinivasa Raghavan, ed. *The Reserve Bank of India—1968–1981*. Vol 3. Reserve Bank of India, 2005, p.529

114   Ibid., p.530

115   M.G. De Vries, ed. *IMF History (1972–78)*. Volumes 1, 2 and 3. International Monetary Fund, 2007, p.263

116   T.C.A. Srinivasa Raghavan, ed. *The Reserve Bank of India—1968–1981*. Vol 3. Reserve Bank of India, 2005, p.546

117   Ibid., p.546

118   T.C.A. Srinivasa Raghavan. *A Crown of Thorns—The Governors of RBI*. Westland, 2016

119   Vijay Joshi and Ian Malcolm David Little. *India: Macroeconomics and Political Economy, 1964–1991*. Oxford University Press, 1998, p.106

120   Ibid., p.112

121   Ibid., p.117, Table 5.7

122   The fiscal year for India runs from April to March.

123   T.C.A. Srinivasa Raghavan, ed. *The Reserve Bank of India—1968–1981*. Vol 3. Reserve Bank of India, 2005, p.351

124   Ibid., p.368

125   Ibid., p.369

126   Dawn E. Jones and Rodney W. Jones. 'Urban Upheaval in India: The 1974 Nav Nirman Riots in Gujarat.' *Asian Survey*, vol. 16, no. 11, 1976, p.1012–1033, doi:10.1525/as.1976.16.11.01p0235q.

127   T.C.A. Srinivasa Raghavan, ed. *The Reserve Bank of India—1968–1981*. Vol 3. Reserve Bank of India, 2005, p.376

128   Vijay Joshi and Ian Malcolm David Little. *India: Macroeconomics and Political Economy, 1964–1991*. Oxford University Press, 1998, p.115–116

129   T.C.A. Srinivasa Raghavan, ed. *The Reserve Bank of India—1968–1981*. Vol 3. Reserve Bank of India, 2005, p.376

130 M. Narasimham. *From Reserve Bank to Finance Ministry and Beyond: Some Reminiscences.* UBS Publishers' Distributors, 2002, p.54

131 Vinod Mehta. *The Sanjay Story.* HarperCollins Publishers, 2012, p.65

132 Ibid., p.76

133 T.C.A. Srinivasa Raghavan. *A Crown of Thorns—The Governors of RBI.* Westland, 2016

134 T.C.A. Srinivasa Raghavan, ed. *The Reserve Bank of India—1968–1981.* Vol 3. Reserve Bank of India, 2005, p.383

135 Ibid., p.383

136 Ibid., p.129

137 Vinod Mehta. *The Sanjay Story.* HarperCollins Publishers, 2012, p.80

138 Ibid., p.80

139 B.K. Dadabhoy. *Barons of Banking—Glimpses of Indian Banking History.* Random House India, 2015 ed., p.256

140 Ibid., p.331

141 Ibid., p.333

142 T.C.A. Srinivasa Raghavan. *A Crown of Thorns—The Governors of RBI.* Westland, 2016

143 T.C.A. Srinivasa Raghavan, ed. *The Reserve Bank of India—1968–1981.* Reserve Bank of India, 2005, p.384

144 The Twenty point programme was introduced by Indira Gandhi in the Emergency period to work towards eradicating poverty and improving social justice.

145 Vijay Joshi and Ian Malcolm David Little. *India: Macroeconomics and Political Economy, 1964–1991.* Oxford University Press, 1998, p.123

146 Vinod Mehta. *The Sanjay Story.* HarperCollins Publishers, 2012, p.204

147 T.C.A. Srinivasa Raghavan, ed. *The Reserve Bank of India—1968–1981.* Reserve Bank of India, 2005, p.395

148 M. Narasimham. *From Reserve Bank to Finance Ministry and Beyond: Some Reminiscences.* UBS Publishers' Distributors, 2002, p.93–94

149 Sanjaya Baru. 'The Mint Road Blues.' *The Week,* 19 June 2016. http://www.theweek.in/columns/Sanjaya-Baru/the-mint-road-blues.html, accessed on 28 October 2017

150 Jairam Ramesh. *To the Brink and Back: India's 1991 Story.* Rupa Publications, 2016, p.52

151 I.G. Patel. *Glimpses of Indian Economic Policy: An Insider's View.* Oxford University Press, 2002, p.159

152 Bibek Debroy. 'Demonetisation demystified.' *The Open Magazine,* 25 November 2016. http://www.openthemagazine.com/article/essay/demonetisation-demythified, accessed on 28 October 2017

153 Madhav Godbole. *Unfinished Innings: Recollections and Reflections of a Civil Servant.* Sangam, 1996

154 T.C.A. Srinivasa Raghavan, ed. *The Reserve Bank of India—1968–1981.* Vol 3. Reserve Bank of India, 2005, p.451

155 Ibid., p.452

156 I.G. Patel. *Glimpses of Indian Economic Policy: An Insider's View.* Oxford University Press, 2002, p.159–160

157 Hirubhai Patel. Budget speech, 1978–79. http://indiabudget.nic.in/bspeech/bs197879.pdf

158 I.G. Patel. *Glimpses of Indian Economic Policy: An Insider's View.* Oxford University Press, 2002, p.159

159 T.C.A. Srinivasa Raghavan, ed. *The Reserve Bank of India—1968–1981.* Reserve Bank of India, 2005, p.420

160 Ibid., p.421

161 Ibid., p.422

162 T.C.A. Srinivasa Raghavan. *A Crown of Thorns—The Governors of RBI.* Westland, 2016

163 M. Ramakrishnayya. *Two Administrators: Interaction between ICS and IAS.* Booklinks Corp., 1992, p.105

164 I.G. Patel. *Glimpses of Indian Economic Policy: An Insider's View*. Oxford University Press, 2002, p.160
165 T.C.A. Srinivasa Raghavan, ed. *The Reserve Bank of India—1968–1981*. Reserve Bank of India, 2005, p.646
166 'Economic Policy Debate'. *Economic and Political Weekly*, Vol XII No 41, Sameeksha Trust, 8 October 1977, p.1727
167 Rakesh Mohan and Vandana Aggarwal. 'Commands and controls: Planning for Indian industrial development, 1951–1990'. *Journal of Comparative Economics*, 14.4, 1990, p.694
168 T.C.A. Srinivasa Raghavan, ed. *The Reserve Bank of India—1968–1981*. Vol 3. Reserve Bank of India, 2005, p.403
169 Vijay Joshi and Ian Malcolm David Little. *India: Macroeconomics and Political Economy, 1964–1991*. Oxford University Press, 1998, p.146
170 Laurel Graefe. 'Oil Shock of 1978–79'. Federal Reserve Bank of Atlanta, 22 November 2013. http://www.federalreservehistory.org/Events/DetailView/40, accessed on 28 October 2017
171 T.C.A. Srinivasa Raghavan, ed. *The Reserve Bank of India—1968–1981*. Vol 3. Reserve Bank of India, 2005, p.406
172 I.G. Patel. *Glimpses of Indian Economic Policy: An Insider's View*. Oxford University Press, 2002, p.165–167
173 T.C.A. Srinivasa Raghavan, ed. *The Reserve Bank of India—1968–1981*. Vol 3. Reserve Bank of India, 2005, p.51
174 Ibid., p.408
175 Vijay Joshi and Ian Malcolm David Little. *India: Macroeconomics and Political Economy, 1964–1991*. Oxford University Press, 1998, p.150
176 Ibid., p.58–62
177 I.G. Patel. *Glimpses of Indian Economic Policy: An Insider's View*. Oxford University Press, 2002, p.168
178 Ibid., p.168
179 T.C.A. Srinivasa Raghavan, ed. *The Reserve Bank of India—1968–1981*. Vol 3. Reserve Bank of India, 2005, p.660
180 Ibid., p.661
181 S.L.N. Simha and Chintaman Dwarkanath Deshmukh. *History of the Reserve Bank of India, 1935–51*. Reserve Bank of India, 2005, p.205
182 G. Balachandran. *Reserve Bank of India*. Reserve Bank of India, 1998, p.251
183 Ibid., p.259
184 T.C.A. Srinivasa Raghavan, ed. *The Reserve Bank of India—1968–1981*. Vol 3. Reserve Bank of India, 2005, p.270
185 Ibid., p.267
186 Ibid., p.285
187 Ibid., p.302
188 M. Ramakrishnayya. *Two Administrators: Interaction between ICS and IAS*. Booklinks Corp., 1992, p.143
189 T.C.A. Srinivasa Raghavan, ed. *The Reserve Bank of India—1968–1981*. Vol 3. Reserve Bank of India, 2005, p.76
190 Ibid., p.76
191 M. Ramakrishnayya. *Two Administrators: Interaction between ICS and IAS*. Booklinks Corp., 1992, p.145
192 T.C.A. Srinivasa Raghavan, ed. *The Reserve Bank of India—1968–1981*. Vol 3. Reserve Bank of India, 2005, p.80
193 Ibid., p.303
194 Ibid., p.304

195   M. Ramakrishnayya. *Two Administrators: Interaction between ICS and IAS.* Booklinks Corp., 1992, p.107

196   Ibid., p.107

197   T.C.A. Srinivasa Raghavan, ed. *The Reserve Bank of India—1968–1981.* Vol 3. Reserve Bank of India, 2005, p.305

198   Ibid., p.306

199   M. Ramakrishnayya. *Two Administrators: Interaction between ICS and IAS.* Booklinks Corp., 1992, p.108

200   Ibid., p.108

201   T.C.A. Srinivasa Raghavan, ed. *The Reserve Bank of India—1968–1981.* Vol 3. Reserve Bank of India, 2005, p.306

202   NABARD website. https://www.nabard.org/English/Home.aspx, accessed on 28 October 2017

203   M. Ramakrishnayya. *Two Administrators: Interaction between ICS and IAS.* Booklinks Corp., 1992, p.109

204   Ibid., p.115

205   T.C.A. Srinivasa Raghavan. *A Crown of Thorns—The Governors of RBI.* Westland, 2016

206   M. Ramakrishnayya. *Two Administrators: Interaction between ICS and IAS.* Booklinks Corp., 1992, p.116

207   I.G. Patel. *Glimpses of Indian Economic Policy: An Insider's View.* Oxford University Press, 2002, p.176

208   Bimal Jalan, ed. *The Reserve Bank of India.* Vol 4, 1981–1997. Academic Foundation in association with Reserve Bank of India, 2013, Appendix, p.1087

209   Ibid., p.1089

210   Ibid., p.1089

211   Ibid., p.1092

212   Tavleen Singh. *Durbar.* Hachette India, 2012, p.230

213   Vivek Kaul. 'Why Manmohan didn't quit even after Rajiv called him a Joker.' *First Post,* 19 July 2012. http://www.firstpost.com/india/why-manmohan-didnt-quit-even-after-rajiv-called-him-a-joker-382960.html, accessed on 28 October 2017

214   Vijay Joshi and Ian Malcolm David Little. *India: Macroeconomics and Political Economy, 1964–1991.* Oxford University Press, 1998, p.62

215   V.P. Singh. India budget speech, FY1985–86. p.5. http://indiabudget.nic.in/bspeech/bs198586.pdf

216   Suman Dubey and G.p. Mathai. 'Fiscal policy: Easing the burden.' *India Today,* 15 January 1986. http://indiatoday.intoday.in/story/v.p.-singhs-new-fiscal-policy-lays-down-direction-of-governments-fiscal-thinking/1/348051.html, accessed on 28 October 2017

217   Bimal Jalan, ed. *The Reserve Bank of India.* Vol 4, 1981–1997. Academic Foundation in association with Reserve Bank of India, 2013, p.57

218   Ibid., p.122

219   Ibid., p.131

220   Ibid., p.138

221   T.C.A. Srinivasa Raghavan. *A Crown of Thorns—The Governors of RBI.* Westland, 2016

222   Bimal Jalan, ed. *The Reserve Bank of India.* Vol 4, 1981–1997. Academic Foundation in association with Reserve Bank of India, 2013, p.167

223   Ibid., p.167

224   Prabhu Chawla. 'Cabinet reshuffle: Shock treatment.' *India Today,* 15 November 1986. http://indiatoday.intoday.in/story/cabinet-reshuffle-rajiv-gandhi-cuts-to-size-powerful-men-like-arjun-singh-arun-nehru/1/349022.html, accessed on 28 October 2017

225   Bimal Jalan, ed. *The Reserve Bank of India.* Vol 4, 1981–1997. Academic Foundation in

association with Reserve Bank of India, 2013, p.139

226 Prabhu Chawla. 'The Taming of V.p. Singh.' *India Today*, 30 April 1987. http://indiatoday.intoday.in/story/defence-minister-v.p.-singh-quits-office-with-his-image-in-disarray/1/337008.html, accessed on 28 October 2017

227 Vinay Sitapati. *Half Lion: How p.V. Narasimha Rao Transformed India*. Penguin Viking, 2016, p.74

228 Bimal Jalan, ed. *The Reserve Bank of India*. Vol 4, 1981–1997. Academic Foundation in association with Reserve Bank of India, 2013, p.172

229 Ibid., p.173

230 Ibid., p.61

231 Indiabudget, 1988–89. http://indiabudget.nic.in/bspeech/bs198889.pdf

232 Vijay Joshi and Ian Malcolm David Little. *India: Macroeconomics and Political Economy, 1964–1991*. Oxford University Press, 1998, p.186

233 Bimal Jalan, ed. *The Reserve Bank of India*. Vol 4, 1981–1997. Academic Foundation in association with Reserve Bank of India, 2013, p.220

234 Ibid., p.434

235 Ibid., p.436

236 Ibid., p.426–429

237 Yashwant Sinha. *Confessions of a Swadeshi Reformer: My Years as Finance Minister*. Penguin, 2007, p.6

238 Bimal Jalan, ed. *The Reserve Bank of India*. Vol 4, 1981–1997. Academic Foundation in association with Reserve Bank of India, 2013, p.467

239 Ibid., p.469

240 Yashwant Sinha. *Confessions of a Swadeshi Reformer: My Years as Finance Minister*. Penguin, 2007, p.4

241 Shiv Taneja and p.G. Thakurta. 'Moody Blues.' *India Today*, 31 October 1990.http://indiatoday.intoday.in/story/international-credit-rating-agencies-downgrade-india-country-rating/1/315749.html, accessed on 28 October 2017

242 Shiv Taneja. 'We don't want to interfere.' *India Today*, 15 November 1990. http://indiatoday.intoday.in/story/rbi-has-had-very-good-relations-with-north-block-r-n-malhotra/1/315845.html, accessed on 28 October 2017

243 T.C.A. Srinivasa Raghavan. *A Crown of Thorns—The Governors of RBI*. Westland, 2016

244 T.C.A. Srinivasa Raghavan. 'RBI governors and their bittersweet relationship with the govt.' Rediff.com, 2 April 2015. http://www.rediff.com/money/column/column-rbi-governors-and-their-bittersweet-relationship-with-the-govt/20150402.htm, accessed on 28 October 2017

245 Bimal Jalan, ed. *The Reserve Bank of India*. Vol 4, 1981–1997. Academic Foundation in association with Reserve Bank of India, 2013, p.613

246 Ibid., p.613–615

247 P.G. Thakurta. 'The Economy: Hitting rock bottom.' *India Today*, 15 January 1991. http://indiatoday.intoday.in/story/hard-decisions-needed-to-face-the-worst-fiscal-crisis/1/317693.html, accessed on 28 October 2017

248 Bimal Jalan, ed. *The Reserve Bank of India*. Vol 4, 1981–1997. Academic Foundation in association with Reserve Bank of India, 2013, p.469

249 Yashwant Sinha. *Confessions of a Swadeshi Reformer: My Years as Finance Minister*. Penguin, 2007, p.7

250 Bimal Jalan, ed. *The Reserve Bank of India*. Vol 4, 1981–1997. Academic Foundation in association with Reserve Bank of India, 2013, p.452

251 C. Rangarajan. '1991's golden transaction.' *The Indian Express*, 28 March 2016. http://indianexpress.com/article/opinion/columns/1991s-golden-transaction/, accessed on 28 October 2017

252   Vinay Sitapati. *Half Lion: How P.V. Narasimha Rao Transformed India*. Penguin Viking, 2016, p.90–92

253   Ibid., p.93

254   Ibid., p.98

255   Ibid., p.102

256   P.C. Alexander. *Through the Corridors of Power—An Insider's Story*. HarperCollins Publishers, 2004

257   Shankkar Aiyar. *Accidental India: A History of the Nation's Passage through Crisis and Change*. Aleph, 2013

258   Vinay Sitapati. *Half Lion: How P.V. Narasimha Rao Transformed India*. Penguin Viking, 2016, p.102

259   Vinay Sitapati. *Half Lion: How P.V. Narasimha Rao Transformed India*. Penguin Viking, 2016, p.102

260   Ibid., p.108

261   Jairam Ramesh. *To the Brink and Back: India's 1991 Story*. Rupa Publications, 2016, p.32

262   Vinay Sitapati. *Half Lion: How P.V. Narasimha Rao Transformed India*. Penguin Viking, 2016, p.120

263   Bimal Jalan, ed. *The Reserve Bank of India*. Vol 4, 1981–1997. Academic Foundation in association with Reserve Bank of India, 2013, p.480

264   Ibid., p.556–562

265   Ibid., p.470

266   Meghnad Desai. 'I think a stimulus package is necessary, yes. Bailouts, no.' Rediff.com, 25 May 2009. http://business.rediff.com/slide-show/2009/may/25/slide-show-5-lord-desai-on-recession-and-indian-politics.htm, accessed on October 2017

267   Shankkar Aiyar. *Accidental India: A History of the Nation's Passage through Crisis and Change*. Aleph, 2013

268   Jairam Ramesh. *To the Brink and Back: India's 1991 Story*. Rupa Publications, 2016, p.47

269   Vinay Sitapati. *Half Lion: How P.V. Narasimha Rao Transformed India*. Penguin Viking, 2016, p.121

270   P.V. Narasimha Rao. *Selected Speeches*. Publications Division, Ministry of Information and Broadcasting, Government of India, 1993, p.155

271   Jairam Ramesh. *To the Brink and Back: India's 1991 Story*. Rupa Publications, 2016, p.53

272   Statement issued by P.N. Dhar, I.G. Patel, R.N. Malhotra and M. Narasimham. 'Agenda for Economic Reforms.' 1 July 1991

273   'Leading Economists' Alternative View.' Mainstream, 8 July 1991

274   Vinay Sitapati. *Half Lion: How P.V. Narasimha Rao Transformed India*. Penguin Viking, 2016, p.129

275   Bimal Jalan, ed. *The Reserve Bank of India*. Vol 4, 1981–1997. Academic Foundation in association with Reserve Bank of India, 2013, p.458

276   Editorial. *The Times of India*, 25 July 1991

277   *The Economist*, 27 July 1991, p.52

278   Jairam Ramesh. *To the Brink and Back: India's 1991 Story*. Rupa Publications, 2016, p.110–111

279   Subhomoy Bhattacharjee.'How WB, IMF got India to adopt reforms in 1991.' *The Indian Express*, 17 September 2010. http://archive.indianexpress.com/news/how-wb-imf-got-india-to-adopt-reforms-in-1991/682649/, accessed on 28 October 2017

280   Bimal Jalan, ed. *The Reserve Bank of India*. Vol 4, 1981–1997. Academic Foundation in association with Reserve Bank of India, 2013, p.816

281   Ibid., p.1209

282   Ibid., p.816–817

283   Ibid., p.657

284 Ibid., p.817
285 John Maynard Keynes. *The General Theory of Employment, Interest and Money*. Kalpaz, 2017
286 Vinay Sitapati. *Half Lion: How P.V. Narasimha Rao Transformed India*. Penguin Viking, 2016, p.137
287 *The Times of India*, 23 April 1992
288 SEBI website. http://www.sebi.gov.in/sebiweb/stpages/about_sebi.jsp
289 Bimal Jalan, ed. *The Reserve Bank of India*. Vol 4, 1981–1997. Academic Foundation in association with Reserve Bank of India, 2013, p.829
290 Vinay Sitapati. *Half Lion: How P.V. Narasimha Rao Transformed India*. Penguin Viking, 2016, p.145
291 Bimal Jalan, ed. *The Reserve Bank of India*. Vol 4, 1981–1997. Academic Foundation in association with Reserve Bank of India, 2013, p.829
292 'Australian Bank Admits Violating Indian Banking Regulations.' UPI, 29 October 1992. www.upi.com/Archives/1992/10/29/Australian-bank-admits-violating-Indian-banking-regulations/4378720334800/, accessed on 28 October 2017
293 Bimal Jalan, ed. *The Reserve Bank of India*. Vol 4, 1981–1997. Academic Foundation in association with Reserve Bank of India, 2013, p.1211
294 Ibid., p.822
295 Vinay Sitapati. *Half Lion: How P.V. Narasimha Rao Transformed India*. Penguin Viking, 2016, p.150
296 Bimal Jalan, ed. *The Reserve Bank of India*. Vol 4, 1981–1997. Academic Foundation in association with Reserve Bank of India, 2013, p.824
297 Ibid., p.580
298 Daksesh Parikh. 'RBIs New Credit Policy Announcement Fails to Cheer.' *India Today*, 30 April 1993. indiatoday.intoday.in/story/rbi-new-credit-policy-announcement-fails-to-cheer/1/302082.html, accessed on 28 October 2017
299 IMF Annual Report, 1992. IMF, 30 April 1992. https://www.imf.org/external/pubs/ft/ar/archive/pdf/ar1992.pdf, accessed on 28 October 2017
300 Bimal Jalan, ed. *The Reserve Bank of India*. Vol 4, 1981–1997. Academic Foundation in association with Reserve Bank of India, 2013, p.481
301 Ibid., p.487
302 Baidyanath Prasad Singh, ed. *Economic Liberalisation in India*. Ashish Publishing House, 1995, p.89
303 Bimal Jalan, ed. *The Reserve Bank of India*. Vol 4, 1981–1997. Academic Foundation in association with Reserve Bank of India, 2013, p.1161
304 Vinay Sitapati. *Half Lion: How P.V. Narasimha Rao Transformed India*. Penguin Viking, 2016
305 Bimal Jalan, ed. *The Reserve Bank of India*. Vol 4, 1981–1997. Academic Foundation in association with Reserve Bank of India, 2013, p.526
306 Reserve Bank of India Annual Report, 1993–94. Reserve Bank of India, 1994
307 Article VIII of the IMF agreement prohibits member countries from imposing restrictions on foreign exchange transactions for payments and transfers, i.e. making the currency non-convertible for current account transactions.
308 Bimal Jalan, ed. *The Reserve Bank of India*. Vol 4, 1981–1997. Academic Foundation in association with Reserve Bank of India, 2013, p.655
309 Ibid., p.659
310 Ibid., p.674
311 Ibid., p.670–673
312 Reserve Bank of India Annual Report, 1994–95. Reserve Bank of India, 1995
313 Shankkar Aiyar. *Accidental India: A History of the Nation's Passage through Crisis and Change*. Aleph, 2013

314 Bimal Jalan, ed. *The Reserve Bank of India*. Vol 4, 1981–1997. Academic Foundation in association with Reserve Bank of India, 2013, p.595
315 Ibid., p.596
316 Bimal Jalan, ed. *The Reserve Bank of India*. Vol 4, 1981–1997. Academic Foundation in association with Reserve Bank of India, 2013, p.599–600
317 Ibid., p.601
318 Ibid., p.605
319 P. Chidambaram. Budget 1996–97 Speech. 27 July 1996. indiabudget.nic.in/bspeech/bs199697.pdf, accessed on 28 October 2017
320 A.S. Panneerselvan, Sandipan Deb, Arindam Mukherjee and Nikhil Mookerjee. 'Miracle Budget?' Outlookindia.com, 11 Mar. 1997. www.outlookindia.com/magazine/story/miracle-budget/203163, accessed on 28 October 2017
321 P. Chidambaram. Budget 1997–98 Speech. 28 February 1997. http://indiabudget.nic.in/bspeech/bs199798.pdf, accessed on 28 October 2017, point 38
322 Ibid., point 40 and 41
323 Reserve Bank of India. 'Committee on Capital Account Convertibility.' 28 February 1997.https://rbi.org.in/scripts/BS_PressReleaseDisplay.aspx?prid=18545, accessed on 28 October 2017
324 Reserve Bank of India. 'Report of the Committee on Capital Account Convertibility.' 26 June 2000. https://rbi.org.in/scripts/PublicationReportDetails.aspx?ID=169, accessed on 28 October 2016
325 Ajit Ranade. 'A Banker and a Gentleman.' *Times of India*, 6 February 2016. http://epaperbeta.timesofindia.com/Article.aspx?eid=31821&articlexml=A-Banker-and-a-Gentleman-06022016026018, accessed on 28 October 2017
326 Michael Carson and John Clark. 'Asian financial crisis.' Federal Reserve Bank of New York. http://www.federalreservehistory.org/Events/DetailView/51
327 Reserve Bank of India. 'Foreign Exchange Rules Relaxed.' 3 July 1997. https://rbi.org.in/scripts/BS_PressReleaseDisplay.aspx?prid=18540, accessed on 28 October 2017
328 Statement by Dr C. Rangarajan, Governor, Reserve Bank of India, on developments in the foreign exchange market. 10 September 1997. https://rbi.org.in/scripts/BS_PressReleaseDisplay.aspx?prid=18725, accessed on 28 October 2017
329 Reserve Bank of India. 'RBI Announces Measures Relating to Foreign Exchange Inflows.' 12 September 1997. https://rbi.org.in/scripts/BS_PressReleaseDisplay.aspx?prid=18724, accessed on 28 October 2017
330 Y.V. Reddy. *Advice and Dissent: My Life in Public Service*. Harper Business, 2017, P.186–190
331 Statement by Dr C. Rangarajan, Governor, Reserve Bank of India, on developments in forex market. 18 November 1997. https://rbi.org.in/Scripts/BS_PressReleaseDisplay.aspx?prid=18714, accessed on 28 October 2017
332 Shekhar Ghosh and Gautam Chikermane. 'This Snake Is A Ladder.' Outlookindia.com, 30 November 1997. www.outlookindia.com/magazine/story/this-snake-is-a-ladder/204652, accessed on 28 October 2017
333 Reserve Bank of India. 'Recent Developments in Financial Markets: RBI Announces Package of Measures.' 28 November 1997. https://rbi.org.in/Scripts/BS_PressReleaseDisplay.aspx?prid=18706, accessed on 28 October 2017
334 Reserve Bank of India. 'No Rebooking for Contracts Cancelled for Non-trade-related Transactions. RBI Tells Corporates.' 1 December 1997. https://rbi.org.in/Scripts/BS_PressReleaseDisplay.aspx?prid=18705, accessed on 28 October 2017
335 Reserve Bank of India. 'Recent Developments in Foreign Exchange Markets—Package of Measures.' 2 December 1997. https://rbi.org.in/Scripts/BS_PressReleaseDisplay.aspx?prid=18704, accessed on 28 October 2017
336 Robin Abreau. 'RBI Governor Bimal Jalan Reintroduces Controls on His Own to

Check Further Fall of Rupee.' *India Today*, 2 February 1998. indiatoday.intoday.in/story/rbi-governor-bimal-jalan-reintroduces-controls-on-his-own-to-check-further-fall-of-rupee/1/263251.html, accessed on 28 October 2017

337 Reserve Bank of India. 'RBI's Working Group on Money Supply.' 10 December 1997.https://rbi.org.in/Scripts/BS_PressReleaseDisplay.aspx?prid=18569, accessed on 28 October 2017

338 Partha Ray. 'Monetary Policy.' Oxford India short introductions, 2013, p.150–151

339 Reserve Bank of India. 'Reserve Bank Further Liberalises Current Account Transactions.' 18 February 1998. https://rbi.org.in/Scripts/BS_PressReleaseDisplay.aspx?prid=18569, accessed on 28 October 2017

340 Reserve Bank of India. 'RBI Reduces CRR.' 23 March 1998. https://rbi.org.in/Scripts/BS_PressReleaseDisplay.aspx?prid=18670, accessed on 28 October 2017

341 Yashwant Sinha. *Confessions of a Swadeshi Reformer: My Years as Finance Minister*. Penguin, 2007, p.54

342 Y.V. Reddy. *Advice and Dissent: My Life in Public Service*. Harper Business, 2017, p.199–202

343 Reserve Bank of India. Database on Indian economy. dbie.rbi.org.in

344 Reserve Bank of India. 'Statement issued by RBI on 29-5-1998.' 29 May 1998. https://rbi.org.in/Scripts/BS_PressReleaseDisplay.aspx?prid=18779, accessed on 28 October 2017

345 Reserve Bank of India. 'RBI Announces Repo Rate Cut.' 16 June 1998. https://rbi.org.in/Scripts/BS_PressReleaseDisplay.aspx?prid=18617, accessed on 28 October 2017

346 V. Shankkar Aiyar with Shefali Rekhi. 'Rupee Slide Makes Borrowings More Expensive as Interest Rates Rise.' *India Today*, 22 June 1998. indiatoday.intoday.in/story/rupee-slide-makes-borrowings-more-expensive-as-interest-rates-rise/1/262958.html, accessed on 28 October 2017

347 Yashwant Sinha. *Confessions of a Swadeshi Reformer: My Years as Finance Minister*. Penguin, 2007, p.65

348 Ibid., p.65

349 Shefali Rekhi. 'Resurgent India Bonds for NRIs Expected to Rake in $2 Billion.' *India Today*, 3 August 1998. indiatoday.intoday.in/story/resurgent-india-bonds-for-nris-expected-to-rake-in-$2-billion/1/264664.html, accessed on 28 October 2017

350 Shefali Rekhi. 'Vajpayee Government Woos NRIs with Resurgent India Bonds, Makes Impressive Gains.' *India Today*, 24 June 1998. indiatoday.intoday.in/story/vajpayee-government-woos-nris-with-resurgent-india-bonds-makes-impressive-gains/1/264858.html, accessed on 28 October 2017

351 Reserve Bank of India. 'Maintenance of Value Account: RBI-Government of India Arrangement to Cover Exchange Risk for RIBs.' 10 October 1998. https://rbi.org.in/Scripts/BS_PressReleaseDisplay.aspx?prid=89, accessed on 28 October 2017

352 Reserve Bank of India. 'RBI Announces Package of Measures.' 20 August 1998. https://rbi.org.in/Scripts/BS_PressReleaseDisplay.aspx?prid=18570, accessed on 28 October 2017

353 Yashwant Sinha. 'Key Numbers Are Looking up, a Policy Push Is to Follow: Yashwant Sinha.' *India Today*, 7 September 1998. indiatoday.intoday.in/story/key-numbers-are-looking-up-a-policy-push-is-to-follow-yashwant-sinha/1/264888.html, accessed on 28 October 2017

354 Reserve Bank of India. 'India's Foreign Currency Assets Increase to a Record Level at the end of December 1998.' 31 December 1998. https://rbi.org.in/Scripts/BS_PressReleaseDisplay.aspx?prid=527, accessed on 28 October 2017

355 K. Kanagasabapathy. 'Budget and Banking Reforms.' *The Hindu Business Line*, 5 March 2010. www.thehindubusinessline.com/todays-paper/tp-opinion/article985600.ece, accessed on 28 October 2017

356 Reserve Bank of India. 'Asset—Liability Management (ALM) System (Part 1 of 4).' 10 September 1998. https://rbi.org.in/Scripts/BS_PressReleaseDisplay.aspx?prid=41, accessed on 28 October 2017

357 Reserve Bank of India. 'Mid-Term Review of Monetary and Credit Policy for 1998–99.'

30 October 1998. https://rbi.org.in/Scripts/BS_PressReleaseDisplay.aspx?prid=209, accessed on 28 October 2017

358 Statement by Dr Bimal Jalan, Governor, Reserve Bank of India, on Monetary and Credit Policy for the First Half of 1998–99. 29 April 1998. https://rbi.org.in/Scripts/BS_PressReleaseDisplay.aspx?prid=18789, accessed on 28 October 2017

359 Partha Ray. 'Monetary Policy.' Oxford India short introductions, 2013, p.157–159

360 Reserve Bank of India. 'RBI Governor Announces Monetary and Credit Policy for the Year 1999–2000.' 20 April 1999. https://rbi.org.in/Scripts/BS_PressReleaseDisplay.aspx?prid=976, accessed on 28 October 2017

361 Swapan Dasgupta, Sumit Mitra, Harinder Baweja and Javed M. Ansari. 'The inside Story: Is India Heading for a Two-Party System?' *India Today*, 10 May 1999. indiatoday.intoday.in/story/the-inside-story-is-india-heading-for-a-two-party-system/1/253937.html, accessed on 28 October 2017

362 'President dissolves 12th Lok Sabha.' Rediff.com, 26 April 1999. http://m.rediff.com/news/1999/apr/26diss.htm, accessed on 28 October 2017

363 V. Shankkar Aiyar. 'End of Kargil Conflict, Improving Economic Outlook Send Stock Markets into a Tizzy.' *India Today*, 26 July 1999. indiatoday.intoday.in/story/end-of-kargil-conflict-improving-economic-outlook-send-stock-markets-into-a-tizzy/1/255783.html, accessed on 28 October 2017

364 Reserve Bank of India. 'RBI Employees' Contribution to Armed Forces.' 25 June 1999. https://rbi.org.in/Scripts/BS_PressReleaseDisplay.aspx?prid=1286, accessed on 28 October 2017

365 Y.V. Reddy. 'Is inflation dead—some comments.' Speech, Reserve Bank of India, 17 December 1999. https://rbi.org.in/scripts/BS_SpeechesView.aspx?Id=42, accessed on 28 October 2017

366 'RBI steps in to defend rupee.' *Indian Express*, 24 August 1999. http://archive.indianexpress.com/Storyold/117258/, accessed on 28 October 2017

367 Reserve Bank of India. 'Reserve Bank of India's Statement on Forex Markets.' 23 August 1999. https://rbi.org.in/Scripts/BS_PressReleaseDisplay.aspx?prid=1586, accessed on 28 October 2017

368 Reserve Bank of India. 'Mid-Term Review of Monetary and Credit Policy.' 29 October 1999. https://rbi.org.in/Scripts/BS_PressReleaseDisplay.aspx?prid= 1908, accessed on 28 October 2017

369 'Y2K Bug.' National Geographic Society, 9 October 2012. www.nationalgeographic.org/encyclopedia/Y2K-bug/, accessed on 28 October 2017

370 Reserve Bank of India. 'Meeting of the High Level Working Group on Y2K Related Issues.' 31 August 1999. https://rbi.org.in/Scripts/BS_PressReleaseDisplay.aspx? prid=1641, accessed on 28 October 2017

371 Yashwant Sinha. *Confessions of a Swadeshi Reformer: My Years as Finance Minister*. Penguin, 2007, p.168

372 Reserve Bank of India. 'Reserve Bank of India Announces Monetary Easing Measures to Lower Interest Rates.' 1 April 2000. https://rbi.org.in/Scripts/BS_PressReleaseDisplay.aspx?prid=2733, accessed on 28 October 2017

373 Reserve Bank of India. 'Dr. Bimal Jalan Re-appointed RBI Governor.' 26 April 2000. https://rbi.org.in/Scripts/BS_PressReleaseDisplay.aspx?prid=2853, accessed on 28 October 2017

374 Reserve Bank of India. 'Reserve Bank of India's Statement on Forex Markets.' 25 May 2000. https://rbi.org.in/Scripts/BS_PressReleaseDisplay.aspx?prid=3018, accessed on 28 October 2017

375 Reserve Bank of India. 'Reserve Bank of India Announces a Package of Monetary Measures.' 21 July 2000. https://rbi.org.in/Scripts/BS_PressReleaseDisplay.aspx?prid=3354, accessed on 28 October 2017

376   Press Trust of India. 'Chambers Flay Bank Rate Hike, Economists See Stable Rupee.' *The Hindu*, 22 July 2000. www.thehindu.com/thehindu/2000/07/22/stories/06220006.htm, accessed on 28 October 2017

377   Reserve Bank of India. 'Statement by the Reserve Bank of India on Recent Developments in the Foreign Exchange Markets.' 3 August 2000. https://rbi.org.in/Scripts/BS_PressReleaseDisplay.aspx?prid=3445, accessed on 28 October 2017

378   'SBI to Raise $2 b in Millennium Deposits.' *The Hindu*, 10 October 2000. www.thehindu.com/2000/10/10/stories/06100004.htm., accessed on 28 October 2017

379   Reserve Bank of India. 'Reserve Bank of India Reduces the Bank Rate and Cash Reserve Ratio.' 16 February 2001. https://rbi.org.in/Scripts/BS_PressReleaseDisplay.aspx?prid=4594, accessed on 28 October 2017

380   'K-10 Stocks: How Bad Are They?' *Business-Standard*, 18 March 2002. www.businessstandard.com/article/markets/k-10-stocks-how-bad-are-they-102031801034_1.html, accessed on 28 October 2017

381   Prabhu Chawla and Rohit Saran. 'Stock Scam: SEBI Reveals the Men Responsible for Rigging the Market.' *India Today*, 30 April 2001. indiatoday.intoday.in/story/stock-scam-sebi-reveals-the-men-responsible-for-rigging-the-market/1/232357.html, accessed on 28 October 2017

382   'SEBI's First Take on Market Manipulation.' *The Hindu Businessline*, 3 June 2001. www.thehindubusinessline.com/iw/2001/06/03/stories/0703g055.htm, accessed on 28 October 2017

383   Vivek Law. 'Cooperative Banks into Sitting Targets for Scamsters and Freeloaders.' *India Today*, 10 June 2002. indiatoday.intoday.in/story/cooperative-banks-into-sitting-targets-for-scamsters-and-freeloaders/1/219611.html, accessed on 28 October 2017

384   Reserve Bank of India. 'Facts on GTB Investigation.' 5 April 2001. https://rbi.org.in/Scripts/BS_PressReleaseDisplay.aspx?prid=4844, accessed on 28 October 2017

385   Reserve Bank of India. 'Report of the Standing Technical Committee of RBI and SEBI on Review of the RBI Guidelines on Bank Financing of Equities.' 12 April 2001. https://rbi.org.in/Scripts/PublicationReportDetails.aspx?FromDate=04/12/01&SECID=21&SUBSECID=0, accessed on 28 October 2017

386   'Gelli steps down, Hugar appointed CMD of Global Trust Bank.' Rediff.com, 12 April 2001. http://www.rediff.com/money/2001/apr/12gelli.htm, accessed on 28 October 2017

387   Rajalakshmi Menon. 'RBI asks Gelli to step down from GTB Board.' *The Hindu Businessline*, 8 June 2001. http://www.thehindubusinessline.com/2001/06/08/stories/14080801.htm, accessed on 28 October 2017

388   Joint Committee on Stock Market Scam and Matters Relating Thereto, 13th Lok Sabha. 'JPC Report on Stock Market Scam.' 12 December 2002. http://www.prsindia.org/administrator/uploads/general/1292845141_JPC_REPORT%20on%20stock%20market%20scam.pdf.pdf, 224, accessed on 28 October 2017

389   Joint Committee on Stock Market Scam and Matters Relating Thereto, 13th Lok Sabha. 'JPC Report on Stock Market Scam. 12 December 2002. http://www.prsindia.org/administrator/uploads/general/1292845141_JPC_REPORT%20on%20stock%20market%20scam.pdf.pdf, 232, accessed on 28 October 2017

390   'Starred Question No.23, Answered On 24.07.2001 UTI's Suspension of US Scheme.' Rajya Sabha website, 24 July 2001

391   'UTI chairman resigns.' Rediff.com, 4 July 2001. http://www.rediff.com/money/2001/jul/04uti.htm, accessed on 28 October 2017

392   Yashwant Sinha. *Confessions of a Swadeshi Reformer: My Years as Finance Minister*. Penguin, 2007, p.214–215

393   Reserve Bank of India. 'Global Trust Bank Ltd. Under Moratorium.' 24 July 2004. https://rbi.org.in/Scripts/BS_PressReleaseDisplay.aspx?prid=10394, accessed on 28 October 2017

394 Reserve Bank of India. 'Draft Scheme of GTB—OBC Amalgamation.' 26 July 2004. https://rbi.org.in/Scripts/BS_PressReleaseDisplay.aspx?prid=10428, accessed on 28 October 2017

395 S. Gopalakrishnan. 'Global Trust Bank: best possible RBI action.' *The Hindu*, 24 August 2004. http://www.thehindu.com/biz/2004/08/23/stories/ 2004082300351500.htm, accessed on 28 October 2017

396 Pratibha Rathore. 'RBI Plans Sinking Fund for States Debt Repayment.' *Financial Express*, 18 January 1999. expressindia.indianexpress.com/fe/daily/ 19990119/01955715.html, accessed on 29 October 2017

397 'A Consolidated Sinking Fund.' *Business Standard*, 17 April 1998. http://www.business-standard.com/article/specials/a-consolidated-sinking-fund-198041701118_1.html, accessed on 29 October 2017

398 Jairam Ramesh. 'Legislation to Introduce Fiscal Responsibility at the Centre Is Tabled.' *India Today*, 8 January 2001. indiatoday.intoday.in/story/legislation-to-introduce-fiscal-responsibility-at-the-centre-is-tabled/1/233361.html, accessed on 29 October 2017

399 S. Ambirajan. *The Hindu*, 1 May 2000. http://www.thehindu.com/2000/05/01/stories/05012523.htm, accessed on 29 October 2017

400 Reserve Bank of India. 'RBI Governor Announces Monetary and Credit Policy for the Year 2001–2002.' 19 April 2001. https://rbi.org.in/Scripts/BS_PressReleaseDisplay.aspx?prid=4909, accessed on 29 October 2017

401 Yashwant Sinha. *Confessions of a Swadeshi Reformer: My Years as Finance Minister*. Penguin, 2007, p.150

402 Y.V. Reddy. 'Autonomy of the Central Bank: Changing Contours in India.' Speech, Reserve Bank of India, 3 October 2001. https://rbi.org.in/Scripts/BS_SpeechesView.aspx?Id=88, accessed on 29 October 2017

403 Reserve Bank of India. 'RBI Reconstitutes Technical Advisory Committee on Money and Government Securities Markets.' 22 September 2001. https://rbi.org.in/Scripts/BS_PressReleaseDisplay.aspx?prid=5740, accessed on 29 October 2017

404 Reserve Bank of India. 'RBI Governor Announces Mid-term Review of Monetary and Credit Policy for the Year 2001–2002.' 22 October 2001. https://rbi.org.in/Scripts/BS_PressReleaseDisplay.aspx?prid=5896, accessed on 29 October 2017

405 Ibid.

406 Ministry of Finance. Budget 2002–03 Speech of Shri Yashwant Sinha. 28 February 2002. http://indiabudget.nic.in/ub2002-03/bs/speech_a.htm, accessed on 29 October 2017

407 Yashwant Sinha. *Confessions of a Swadeshi Reformer: My Years as Finance Minister*. Penguin, 2007, p.150

408 Harish Khare. 'Yashwant, Jaswant swap Ministries.' *The Hindu*, 2 July 2002. http://www.thehindu.com/2002/07/02/stories/2002070204560100.htm, accessed on 29 October 2017

409 'The importance of being Bimal Jalan.' *Financial Express*, 30 June 2002. http://www.financialexpress.com/archive/the-importance-of-being-bimal-jalan/50742/, accessed on 29 October 2017

410 Reserve Bank of India. 'Dr. Rakesh Mohan Takes Over as RBI Deputy Governor.' 9 September 2002. https://rbi.org.in/Scripts/BS_PressReleaseDisplay.aspx?prid=7401, accessed on 29 October 2017

411 'Diluted Fiscal Responsibility Bill gets nod.' *Indian Express*, 5 February 2003. http://archive.indianexpress.com/oldStory/17828/, accessed on 29 October 2017

412 'Y. V. Reddy to be new RBI Governor.' *The Tribune*, 19 July 2003. http://www.tribuneindia.com/2003/20030719/biz.htm#6, accessed on 29 October 2017

413 Reserve Bank of India. 'India Should be the Strongest in External Sector: Bimal Jalan.' 5 September 2003. https://rbi.org.in/Scripts/BS_PressReleaseDisplay.aspx?prid=9072, accessed on 29 October 2017

414 C.R.L. Narasimham. 'Bimal Jalan and the art of demystification.' *The Hindu*, 18 September

2003. http://www.thehindu.com/2003/09/18/stories/ 2003091802681800.htm, accessed on 29 October 2017

415   S. Venkitaramanan. 'Dr Jalan on exchange rate, reserves—India's currency model best for Asia'. *The Hindu*, 2 September 2003. http://www.thehindubusinessline.com/2003/09/02/stories/2003090200110900.htm, accessed on 29 October 2017

416   'RBI believes in continuity, says new Governor Y. V. Reddy. *The Hindu*, 7 September 2003. http://www.thehindu.com/2003/09/07/stories/2003090701651300.htm, accessed on 29 October 2017

417   Sanajaya Baru. 'Breakfast With Y.V. Reddy'. *Business Standard*, 23 November 2010. http://www.business-standard.com/article/opinion/breakfast-with-bs-y-v-reddy-110112300037_1.html, accessed on 29 October 2017

418   Y.V. Reddy. 'Autonomy of the Central Bank: Changing Contours in India'. Speech, Reserve Bank of India. 3 October 2001. https://rbi.org.in/scripts/BS_SpeechesView.aspx?Id=88, accessed on 29 October 2017

419   Reserve Bank of India. 'Redemption of Resurgent India Bonds'. 1 October 2003. https://rbi.org.in/Scripts/BS_PressReleaseDisplay.aspx?prid=9208, accessed on 29 October 2017

420   Reserve Bank of India. 'Ceiling on Interest Rate on NRE Deposits'. 18 October 2003. https://rbi.org.in/Scripts/BS_PressReleaseDisplay.aspx?prid=9278, accessed on 29 October 2017

421   Reserve Bank of India. 'RBI Governor Announces Mid-term Review of Monetary and Credit Policy for the Year 2003–04'. 3 November 2003. https://rbi.org.in/Scripts/BS_PressReleaseDisplay.aspx?prid=9341, accessed on 29 October 2017

422   Reserve Bank of India. 'RBI Releases LAF Report and Sterilisation Paper for Public Comment'. 2 December 2003. https://rbi.org.in/Scripts/BS_PressReleaseDisplay.aspx?prid=9448, accessed on 29 October 2017

423   P.A. Seshan. 'Forex reserves and high liquidity in banking system'. *The Hindu*, 15 December 2003. http://www.thehindu.com/2003/12/15/stories/ 2003121500281600.htm, accessed on 29 October 2017

424   'Jaswant Singh rules out full convertibility'. *The Hindu*, 24 December. http://www.thehindu.com/2003/12/24/stories/2003122404601600.htm, accessed on 29 October 2017

425   Reserve Bank of India. 'Prepayment of Foreign Currency Loans'. 2 January 2004. https://rbi.org.in/Scripts/BS_PressReleaseDisplay.aspx?prid=9587, accessed on 29 October 2017

426   Y.V. Reddy. 'Capital flows and Indian policy response'. Speech, Reserve Bank of India, 21 January 2004. https://rbi.org.in/scripts/BS_SpeechesView.aspx?Id=153, accessed on 29 October 2017

427   Reserve Bank of India. 'Report on Currency and Finance, 2002–03'. 28 January 2004. https://rbi.org.in/Scripts/BS_PressReleaseDisplay.aspx?prid=9680, accessed on 29 October 2017

428   Harish Khare. '13th Lok Sabha dissolved'. *The Hindu*, 7 February 2004. http://www.thehindu.com/2004/02/07/stories/2004020704020100.htm, accessed on 29 October 2017

429   'Moody's upgrades India's foreign currency ratings'. *The Hindu Businessline*, 23 January 2004. http://www.thehindubusinessline.com/2004/01/23/stories/ 2004012302520100.htm, accessed on 29 October 2017

430   Reserve Bank of India. 'Revised Guidelines on External Commercial Borrowings'. 31 January 2004. https://rbi.org.in/Scripts/BS_PressReleaseDisplay.aspx?prid=9702, accessed on 29 October 2017

431   Reserve Bank of India. 'External Commercial Borrowings (ECB) for Overseas Direct Investment/Mergers and Acquisitions'. 23 February 2004. https://rbi.org.in/Scripts/BS_PressReleaseDisplay.aspx?prid=9789, accessed on 29 October 2017

432   Reserve Bank of India. 'Launching of Market Stabilisation Scheme'. 23 February 2004. https://rbi.org.in/Scripts/BS_PressReleaseDisplay.aspx?prid=9788, accessed on 29 October 2017

433   S. Balakrishnan. 'Market Stabilisation Funds-induced Jitters in Bonds'. *The Hindu*

Businessline, 25 February 2004. http://www.thehindubusinessline.com/2004/02/25/stories/2004022502021000.htm, accessed on 29 October 2017

434 'Soaking it up.' The *Economist*, 26 February 2004. http://www.economist.com/node/2464338, accessed on 29 October 2017

435 Harish Khare. 'NDA out, Sonia set to become PM.' *The Hindu*, 14 May 2004. http://www.thehindu.com/2004/05/14/stories/2004051409780100.htm, accessed on 29 October 2017

436 'Panic selling reduces Dalal Street to rubble—Erodes ₹2 lakh cr.' *The Hindu Businessline*, 18 May 2004. http://www.thehindubusinessline.com/bline/2004/05/18/stories/2004051802870100.htm, accessed on 29 October 2017

437 V. Anantha Nageswaran. 'What is "reforms with human face"?' *The Hindu Businessline*, 24 May 2004. http://www.thehindubusinessline.com/2004/05/24/stories/2004052400130800.htm, accessed on 29 October 2017

438 Reserve Bank of India. 'RBI Governor Announces Annual Policy Statement for 2004–05.' 18 May 2004. https://rbi.org.in/Scripts/BS_PressReleaseDisplay.aspx?prid=10132, accessed on 29 October 2017

439 Speech of P. Chidambaram presenting 2004–05 budget. 8 July 2004. http://indiabudget.nic.in/ub2004-05/bs/speecha.htm, accessed on 29 October 2017

440 Reserve Bank of India. 'RTGS Services now for Bank Customers: RBI.' 16 August 2004. https://rbi.org.in/Scripts/BS_PressReleaseDisplay.aspx?prid=10516, accessed on 29 October 2017

441 'What's India doing with its vast forex reserves?' Rediff.com, 3 March 2004. http://www.rediff.com/money/2004/mar/03forex.htm, accessed on 29 October 2017

442 Kaushik Basu. 'India's economy: Can the boom last?' BBC.com, 7 January 2004. http://news.bbc.co.uk/2/hi/south_asia/3357957.stm, accessed on 29 October 2017

443 Wanda Tseng and Matthew Fisher. 'India: 2004 Article IV Consultation—Staff Report.' IMF, March 2005. https://www.imf.org/~/media/Websites/IMF/imported-full-text-pdf/external/pubs/ft/scr/2005/_cr0586.ashx, accessed on 29 October 2017

444 Y.V. Reddy. *Advice and Dissent: My Life in Public Service*. Harper Business, 2017, p.282–285

445 Bimal Jalan. 'Exchange Rate Management, An Emerging Consensus?' Speech, Reserve Bank of India, 14 August 2003. https://rbi.org.in/Scripts/BS_SpeechesView.aspx?Id=133, accessed on 29 October 2017

446 'Inflation rate higher than expected, admits RBI.' *The Hindu Businessline*, 8 August 2004 http://www.thehindubusinessline.com/2004/08/09/stories/ 2004080902450100.htm, accessed on 29 October 2017

447 Y.V. Reddy. 'Current Concerns and Some Perspectives on Inflation.' Speech, Reserve Bank of India, 27 August 2004. https://rbi.org.in/Scripts/BS_SpeechesView.aspx?Id=164, accessed on 29 October 2017

448 Reserve Bank of India. 'RBI Increases Cash Reserve Ratio (CRR) for Scheduled Banks.' 11 September 2004. https://rbi.org.in/Scripts/BS_PressReleaseDisplay.aspx?prid=10637, accessed on 29 October 2017

449 'Anti-inflationary steps—4 more commodities under scanner.' *The Hindu Businessline*, 14 September 2004. http://www.thehindubusinessline.com/2004/09/14/stories/2004091402620100.htm, accessed on 29 October 2017

450 Reserve Bank of India. 'RBI Governor Announces Mid-term Review of Annual Policy Statement for the Year 2004–05.' 26 October 2004. https://rbi.org.in/Scripts/BS_PressReleaseDisplay.aspx?prid=10772, accessed on 29 October 2017

451 'Rakesh Mohan's new designation raises eyebrows.' *The Hindu Businessline*, 27 October 2004. http://www.thehindubusinessline.com/2004/10/28/stories/ 2004102802780100.htm, accessed on 29 October 2017

452 Y.V. Reddy. *Advice and Dissent: My Life in Public Service*. Harper Business, 2017, p.338–339

453 'Rakesh Mohan returns to RBI.' *Business Standard*, 5 July 2005. http://www.business-

standard.com/article/finance/rakesh-mohan-returns-to-rbi-105070501048_1.html, accessed on 29 October 2017

454   Reserve Bank of India. 'RBI Activates Relief Measures Through Banks in States Affected by Tsunami.' 27 December 2004. https://rbi.org.in/Scripts/BS_PressReleaseDisplay. aspx?prid=11007, accessed on 29 October 2017

455   Reserve Bank of India. 'Report on Currency and Finance, 2003–04 Theme: Monetary Policy.' 23 December 2004. https://rbi.org.in/Scripts/BS_PressReleaseDisplay.aspx?prid=10994#3, accessed on 29 October 2017

456   Y.V. Reddy. 'Indian Economy: Current Status and Select Issues.' Speech, Reserve Bank of India, 12 January 2005. https://rbi.org.in/Scripts/BS_SpeechesView.aspx?Id=175, accessed on 29 October 2017

457   Speech by P. Chidambaram for budget 2005–06. 28 February 2005. http://indiabudget. nic.in/ub2005-06/bs/speecha.htm, accessed on 29 October 2017

458   Reserve Bank of India. 'RBI Unveils Roadmap for Presence of Foreign Banks in India and Guidelines on Ownership and Governance in Private Banks.' 28 February 2005. https:// rbi.org.in/Scripts/BS_PressReleaseDisplay.aspx?prid=11256, accessed on 29 October 2017

459   Y.V. Reddy. 'Banking Sector Reforms in India: An Overview.' Speech, Reserve Bank of India, 18 May 2005. https://rbi.org.in/Scripts/BS_SpeechesView.aspx?Id=196, accessed on 29 October 2017

460   Y.V. Reddy. 'Globalisation of Monetary Policy and Indian Experience.' Speech, Reserve Bank of India, 7 June 2005. https://rbi.org.in/Scripts/BS_SpeechesView.aspx?Id=202, accessed on 29 October 2017

461   Reserve Bank of India. 'RBI Places Draft Report of the Internal Technical Group on Forex Markets in Public Domain for Comments.' 24 June 2005. https://rbi.org.in/Scripts/ BS_PressReleaseDisplay.aspx?prid=13261, accessed on 29 October 2017

462   Reserve Bank of India. 'RBI's Technical Advisory Committee on Monetary Policy.' 8 July 2005. https://rbi.org.in/Scripts/BS_PressReleaseDisplay.aspx?prid=13316, accessed on 29 October 2017

463   'Macro-economic events under close watch, says RBI chief.' *The Hindu Businessline*, 27 July 2005. http://www.thehindubusinessline.com/todays-paper/tp-money-banking/ macroeconomic-events-under-close-watch-says-rbi-chief/article2184410.ece, accessed on 29 October 2017

464   Reserve Bank of India. 'RBI Governor Announces Mid-term Review of Annual Policy Statement for the Year 2005–06.' 25 October 2005. https://rbi.org.in/Scripts/BS_ PressReleaseDisplay.aspx?prid=13784, accessed on 29 October 2017

465   Rakesh Mohan. 'Some Apparent Puzzles for Contemporary Monetary Policy.' Speech, Reserve Bank of India, 27–28 October 2005. https://rbi.org.in/Scripts/BS_SpeechesView. aspx?Id=217, accessed on 29 October 2017

466   'Industry hails mid-term review of credit policy.' *The Tribune*, 26 October 2005. http:// www.tribuneindia.com/2005/20051026/biz.htm#2, accessed on 29 October 2017

467   Reserve Bank of India. 'NEFT System Goes Live.' 21 November 2005. https://rbi.org.in/ Scripts/BS_PressReleaseDisplay.aspx?prid=13898, accessed on 29 October 2017

468   Statement by Dr Y. Venugopal Reddy, Governor, Reserve Bank of India, on the Third Quarter Review of Annual Monetary Policy for the Year 2005–06. 24 January 2006. https://rbi.org. in/Scripts/BS_PressReleaseDisplay.aspx?prid=14214#1, accessed on 29 October 2017

469   S. Venkitaramanan. 'Third Quarter Review of Monetary Policy Soft Now, But Can Get Tough.' *The Hindu Businessline*, 25 January 2006. http://www.thehindubusinessline.com/ todays-paper/tp-opinion/third-quarter-review-of-monetary-policy-soft-now-but-can-get-tough/article1722775.ece, accessed on 29 October 2017

470   Tamal Bandyopadhyay. 'North Block versus Mint Road.' *Business Standard*, 2 February 2006. http://www.business-standard.com/article/opinion/tamal-bandyopadhyay-north-block-versus-mint-road-106020201046_1.html, accessed on 29 October 2017

471 Y.V. Reddy. *Advice and Dissent: My Life in Public Service*. Harper Business, 2017, p.358–366

472 Reserve Bank of India. 'RBI Governor Announces Annual Policy Statement for the Year 2006–07.' 18 April 2006. https://rbi.org.in/Scripts/BS_PressReleaseDisplay.aspx?prid=14623, accessed on 29 October 2017

473 Reserve Bank of India. 'RBI Increases Repo/Reverse Repo Rates.' 8 June 2006. https://rbi.org.in/Scripts/BS_PressReleaseDisplay.aspx?prid=14891, accessed on 29 October 2017

474 'FM does not see rate hike in July monetary policy review.' *The Tribune*, 13 June 2006. http://www.tribuneindia.com/2006/20060613/biz.htm#5, accessed on 29 October 2017

475 Reserve Bank of India. 'Highlights of First Quarter Review of Annual Policy 2006–2007.' 25 July 2006. https://rbi.org.in/Scripts/BS_PressReleaseDisplay.aspx?prid=15124, accessed on 29 October 2017

476 A.O. Ninan. 'RBI hikes short-term rates.' *The Hindu*, 26 July 2006. http://www.thehindu.com/todays-paper/tp-business/rbi-hikes-short-term-rates/article18464165.ece, accessed on 29 October 2017

477 Y.V. Reddy. *Advice and Dissent: My Life in Public Service*. Harper Business, 2017, p.369–371

478 Ibid., p.366–379

479 Ibid., p.377–379

480 Reserve Bank of India. 'RBI increases Cash Reserve Ratio (CRR).' 8 December 2006. https://rbi.org.in/Scripts/BS_PressReleaseDisplay.aspx?prid=15803, accessed on 29 October 2017

481 'FM sure of bounce-back.' *The Telegraph*, 11 December 2006. https://www.telegraphindia.com/1061212/asp/business/story_7128892.asp, accessed on 29 October 2017

482 'Call rates spurt on tight liquidity.' *The Hindu Businessline*, 23 December 2006. http://www.thehindubusinessline.com/todays-paper/call-rates-spurt-on-tight-liquidity/article1755805.ece, accessed on 29 October 2017

483 Jo Johnson. 'India's sovereign credit rating upgraded.' *Financial Times*, 30 January 2007. https://www.ft.com/content/714d6a02-b0b0-11db-8a62-0000779e2340?mhq5j=e6, accessed on 29 October 2017

484 Reserve Bank of India. 'RBI Governor Announces Third Quarter Review of Annual Statement on Monetary Policy for 2006–07.' 31 January 2007. https://rbi.org.in/Scripts/BS_PressReleaseDisplay.aspx?prid=16039, accessed on 29 October 2017

485 Reserve Bank of India. 'Liquidity Management—Modified Arrangements.' 2 March 2007. https://rbi.org.in/Scripts/BS_PressReleaseDisplay.aspx?prid =16199, accessed on 29 October 2017

486 'Call rates plunge to 10-year low.' *The Hindu Businessline*, 1 June 2007. http://www.thehindubusinessline.com/todays-paper/tp-money-banking/call-rates-plunge-to-10year-low/article1659784.ece, accessed on 29 October 2017

487 Reserve Bank of India. 'First Quarter Review of the Annual Policy Statement on Monetary Policy for the Year 2007–08.' 31 July 2007. https://rbi.org.in/Scripts/BS_PressReleaseDisplay.aspx?prid=16995, accessed on 29 October 2017

488 'RBI looking at ideal inflation rate of 3%: Reddy.' *The Economic Times*, 24 September 2007. http://economictimes.indiatimes.com/news/economy/indicators/rbi-looking-at-ideal-inflation-rate-of-3-reddy/articleshow/2398511.cms, accessed on 29 October 2017

489 'Tarapore against govt taking SBI ownership.' *The Economic Times*, 16 November 2006. http://economictimes.indiatimes.com/news/economy/policy/tarapore-against-govt-taking-sbi-ownership/articleshow/459924.cms, accessed on 29 October 2017

490 Reserve Bank of India. 'RBI Transfers its Share Holding in SBI to Government of India.' 29 June 2007. https://rbi.org.in/Scripts/BS_PressReleaseDisplay.aspx?prid=16837, accessed on 29 October 2017

491 Reserve Bank of India. 'RBI Transfers Surplus Profit to Government of India.' 9 August 2007. https://rbi.org.in/Scripts/BS_PressReleaseDisplay.aspx?prid=17055, accessed on 29 October 2017

492   Reserve Bank of India. 'Third Quarter Review of Annual Policy 2007–08.' 29 January 2008. https://rbi.org.in/scripts/NotificationUser.aspx?Id=4031&Mode =0, accessed on 29 October 2017

493   N.S. Vageesh. 'The Guv does it again!' *The Hindu Businessline*, 30 January 2008. http://www.thehindubusinessline.com/todays-paper/the-guv-does-it-again/article1614612.ece, accessed on 29 October 2017

494   'Chidambaram backs RBI's decision to keep rates unchanged.' *The Hindu Businessline*, 30 January 2008. http://www.thehindubusinessline.com/todays-paper/chidambaram-backs-rbis-decision-to-keep-rates-unchanged/article1614606.ece, accessed on 29 October 2017

495   'Govt announces Rs60,000-crore loan waiver for farmers.' *Livemint*, 29 February 2008. http://www.livemint.com/Politics/XeGU40jlsHGKrfwfJK1ccL/Govt-announces-Rs60000crore-loan-waiver-for-farmers.html, accessed on 29 October 2017

496   Ramesh Golait. 'Current Issues in Agriculture Credit in India: An Assessment.' Research report, Reserve Bank of India, 6 February 2008. https://www.rbi.org.in/SCRIPTs/PublicationsView.aspx?id=10198, accessed on 29 October 2017

497   'RBI supports farm loan waiver scheme.' *The Hindu Businessline*, 6 March 2008. http://www.thehindubusinessline.com/todays-paper/rbi-supports-farm-loan-waiver-scheme/article1618343.ece, accessed on 29 October 2017

498   'Inflation rate crosses 5% as food items turn dearer.' *The Hindu Businessline*, 7 March 2008. http://www.thehindubusinessline.com/todays-paper/inflation-rate-crosses-5-as-food-items-turn-dearer/article1618420.ece, accessed on 29 October 2017

499   Reserve Bank of India. 'RBI Increases CRR.' 17 April 2008. https://rbi.org.in/Scripts/BS_PressReleaseDisplay.aspx?prid=18190, accessed on 29 October 2017

500   Reserve Bank of India. 'RBI Governor Announces Annual Policy Statement for the Year 2008–09.' 29 April 2008. https://rbi.org.in/Scripts/BS_PressReleaseDisplay.aspx?prid=18237, accessed on 29 October 2017

501   'RBI aims at price stability; key rates unchanged.' *The Hindu Businessline*, 30 April 2008. http://www.thehindubusinessline.com/todays-paper/rbi-aims-at-price-stability-key-rates-unchanged/article1622993.ece, accessed on 29 October 2017

502   'Marginal price increase in Petrol, Diesel and Domestic LPG price.' Press Information Bureau, 4 June 2008.

503   Reserve Bank of India. 'RBI Increases Repo Rate.' 11 June 2008. https://rbi.org.in/Scripts/BS_PressReleaseDisplay.aspx?prid=18425, accessed on 29 October 2017

504   Y.V. Reddy. *Advice and Dissent: My Life in Public Service*. Harper Business, 2017, p.386–387

505   Interview with Jehangir Aziz. January 2017

506   Reserve Bank of India. 'Dr D. Subbarao takes over as RBI Governor.' 5 September 2008. https://rbi.org.in/Scripts/BS_PressReleaseDisplay.aspx?prid=19052, accessed on 29 October 2017

507   'Does RBI know that Reddy will continue?' *Livemint*, 28 August 2008. http://www.livemint.com/Politics/H43IYz5PBUeNbRI8QNDosI/Does-RBI-know-that-Reddy-will-continue.html, accessed on 29 October 2017

508   Tamal Bandyopadhyay. 'Who will be the next RBI governor?' *Livemint*, 22 June 2008. http://www.livemint.com/Money/nAz0KVfW7mUmbiHY9mUORP/Who-will-be-the-next-RBI-governor.html, accessed on 29 October 2017

509   Duvvuri Subbarao. *Who Moved My Interest Rate? Leading the Reserve Bank of India Through Five Turbulent Years*. Penguin Books India, 2016, p.4–6

510   Tamal Bandyopadhyay. 'After Raghuram Rajan, who?' *Livemint*, 20 June 2016. http://www.livemint.com/Opinion/uh5VRmQ7c34CMUyPeAANbJ/After-Raghuram-Rajan-who.html, accessed on 29 October 2017

511   'The decoupling debate.' *The Economist*, 6 March 2008. http://www.economist.com/node/10809267, accessed on 29 October 2017

512   'Timeline: Key events in financial crisis.' *USA Today*, 8 September 2013. https://www.usatoday.com/story/money/business/2013/09/08/chronology-2008-financial-crisis-lehman/2779515/, accessed on 29 October 2017

513   Reserve Bank of India. 'Governor Dr D. Subbarao's Press Statement.' 9 September 2008. https://rbi.org.in/Scripts/BS_PressReleaseDisplay.aspx?prid=19067, accessed on 29 October 2017

514   Reserve Bank of India. 'RBI Announces Market Measures.' 16 September 2008. https://rbi.org.in/Scripts/BS_PressReleaseDisplay.aspx?prid=19103, accessed on 29 October 2017

515   P. Vaidyanathan Iyer. 'How They Saved The India Story.' *The Indian Express*, 27 September 2010. http://archive.indianexpress.com/news/how-they-saved-the-india-story/683133/0, accessed on 29 October 2017

516   Megha Bahree. 'Rumors Spark Run On Indian Bank.' *Forbes*, 30 September 2008. https://www.forbes.com/2008/09/30/banking-india-icici-biz-wall-cz_mb_0930icici.html, accessed on 29 October 2017

517   'How Chanda Kochhar saved ICICI Bank from being engulfed by Lehman bankruptcy.' *The Economic Times*, 18 September 2013. http://economictimes.indiatimes.com/industry/banking/finance/banking/how-chanda-kochhar-saved-icici-bank-from-being-engulfed-by-lehman-bankruptcy/articleshow/22678026.cms?intenttarget=no, accessed on 29 October 2017

518   P. Vaidyanathan Iyer. 'How They Saved The India Story.' *The Indian Express*, 27 September 2010. http://archive.indianexpress.com/news/how-they-saved-the-india-story/683133/0, accessed on 29 October 2017

519   Tamal Bandyopadhyay. 'Liquidity crisis: where has all the money gone?' *Livemint*, 13 October 2008. http://www.livemint.com/Politics/DytSTbajYT0pZpZBzQDY5M/Liquidity-crisis-where-has-all-the-money-gone.html, accessed on 29 October 2017

520   Reserve Bank of India. 'RBI Announces Reduction in CRR for Liquidity Management.' 10 October 2008. https://rbi.org.in/Scripts/BS_PressRelease Display.aspx?prid=19233, accessed on 29 October 2017

521   Duvvuri Subbarao. *Who Moved My Interest Rate? Leading the Reserve Bank of India Through Five Turbulent Years.* Penguin Books India, 2016, p.18–19

522   'Sensex recovers from early losses on FM's comments.' *Livemint*, 10 October 2008. http://www.livemint.com/Money/FLj54VtBJOmrSnRXxIhjeK/Sensex-recovers-from-early-losses-on-FM8217s-comments.html, accessed on 29 October 2017

523   Duvvuri Subbarao. *Who Moved My Interest Rate? Leading the Reserve Bank of India Through Five Turbulent Years.* Penguin Books India, 2016, p.25–26

524   P. Vaidyanathan Iyer. 'How They Saved The India Story.' *The Indian Express*, 27 September 2010. http://archive.indianexpress.com/news/how-they-saved-the-india-story/683133/0, accessed on 29 October 2017

525   Reserve Bank of India. 'RBI Announces 14-day Term Repo facility.' 14 October 2008. https://rbi.org.in/Scripts/BS_PressReleaseDisplay.aspx?prid=19249, accessed on 29 October 2017

526   Statement by Finance Minister. Press Information Bureau, 14 October 2008

527   Statement by Finance Minister. Press Information Bureau, 15 October 2008

528   'Centre may overshoot fiscal deficit target.' *The Hindu Businessline*, 23 October 2008. http://www.thehindubusinessline.com/todays-paper/centre-may-overshoot-fiscal-deficit-target/article1639705.ece, accessed on 29 October 2017

529   Reserve Bank of India. 'RBI Announces Further Measures for Monetary and Liquidity Management.' 1 November 2008. https://rbi.org.in/Scripts/BS_PressReleaseDisplay.aspx?prid=19373, accessed on 29 October 2017

530   Duvvuri Subbarao. *Who Moved My Interest Rate? Leading the Reserve Bank of India Through Five Turbulent Years.* Penguin Books India, 2016, p.23–24

531   'India's home minister resigns over Mumbai attacks.' *Financial Times*, 30 November

2008. https://www.ft.com/content/e1ccc782-bd7e-11dd-bba1-0000779fd18c, accessed on 29 October 2017

532   Rakesh Mohan. 'Global Financial Crisis: Causes, Impact, Policy Responses and Lessons.' Speech, Reserve Bank of India, 23 April 2009. https://rbi.org.in/Scripts/BS_SpeechesView.aspx?Id=417, accessed on 29 October 2017

533   Duvvuri Subbarao. *Who Moved My Interest Rate? Leading the Reserve Bank of India Through Five Turbulent Years*. Penguin Books India, 2016, p.30–31

534   Kounteya Sinha and Risha Chitlangia. 'PM has 3 arteries blocked, surgery underway.' *The Times of India*, 24 January 2009. http://timesofindia.indiatimes.com/india/PM-has-3-arteries-blocked-surgery-underway/articleshow/4020769.cms, accessed on 29 October 2017

535   'Sensex skyrockets, trading halted on UPA victory.' Rediff.com, 18 May 2009. http://business.rediff.com/slide-show/2009/may/18/slide-show-1-sensex-rockets-on-upa-victory.htm, accessed on 29 October 2017

536   Speech of Pranab Mukherjee, Interim Budget 2009–2010. 16 February 2009. http://indiabudget.nic.in/ub2009-10(I)/bs/speecha.htm, accessed on 29 October 2017

537   'Highlights of India's fiscal stimulus package.' *DNA*, 7 December 2008. http://www.dnaindia.com/money/report-highlights-of-india-s-fiscal-stimulus-package-1212043, accessed on 29 October 2017

538   Ashok Dasgupta. 'Second stimulus package unveiled.' *The Hindu*, 3 January 2009. http://www.thehindu.com/todays-paper/Second-stimulus-package-unveiled/article16344800.ece, accessed on 29 October 2017

539   Reserve Bank of India. 'Open Market Operations.' 18 February 2009. https://rbi.org.in/Scripts/BS_PressReleaseDisplay.aspx?prid=20118, accessed on 29 October 2017

540   Duvvuri Subbarao. *Who Moved My Interest Rate? Leading the Reserve Bank of India Through Five Turbulent Years*. Penguin Books India, 2016, p.48

541   Reserve Bank of India. 'Dr. Rakesh Mohan Relinquishes Office of Deputy Governor.' 10 June 2009. https://rbi.org.in/Scripts/BS_PressReleaseDisplay.aspx?prid=20829, accessed on 29 October 2017

542   Indian Meteorological Department. 2009 Monsoon Report. http://reliefweb.int/sites/reliefweb.int/files/resources/B1AD548B25ED07C84925764A001F30D6-Full_Report.pdf, accessed on 29 October 2017

543   Ashwin Ramarathinam. 'The monetary policy dilemma.' *Livemint*, 26 October 2009. http://www.livemint.com/Politics/tR0vT8JV8opGDhYfZ7uurJ/The-monetary-policy-dilemma.html, accessed on 29 October 2017

544   Reserve Bank of India. 'Second Quarter Review of Monetary Policy 2009–10: Press Statement by Dr. D. Subbarao, Governor.' 27 October 2009. https://rbi.org.in/Scripts/BS_PressReleaseDisplay.aspx?prid=21577, accessed on 29 October 2017

545   'Govt appoints Gokarn as RBI deputy governor.' Livemint, 18 November 2009. http://www.livemint.com/Politics/JdDZCRjkZdaJna2TTY7bBL/Govt-appoints-Gokarn-as-RBI-deputy-governor.html, accessed on 29 October 2017

546   Subir Gokarn. 'India's Economic Recovery: Drivers and Risks.' Speech, Reserve Bank of India, 30 December 2009. https://rbi.org.in/Scripts/BS_SpeechesView.aspx?Id=454, accessed on 29 October 2017

547   Reserve Bank of India. 'RBI Purchases Gold under IMF's Limited Gold Sales Programme.' 3 November 2009. https://rbi.org.in/Scripts/BS_PressReleaseDisplay.aspx?prid=21598, accessed on 29 October 2017

548   S.Venkitaramanan. 'Return of India's gold.' *The Hindu Businessline*, 16 November 2009. http://www.thehindubusinessline.com/todays-paper/return-of-indias-gold/article1069429.ece, accessed on 29 October 2017

549   Reserve Bank of India. 'Third Quarter Review of Monetary Policy 2009–10.' 29 January 2010. https://rbi.org.in/Scripts/BS_PressReleaseDisplay.aspx?prid=21997, accessed on 29 October 2017

550 'RBI hikes key rates to battle inflation.' *The Hindu Businessline*, 21 April 2010. http://www.thehindubusinessline.com/todays-paper/rbi-hikes-key-rates-to-battle-inflation/article989701.ece, accessed on 29 October 2017

551 Rajan Bharti Mittal. 'How to control inflation.' *The Economic Times*, 29 July 2010. http://economictimes.indiatimes.com/opinion/et-commentary/how-to-control-inflation/articleshow/6230764.cms, accessed on 29 October 2017

552 Duvvuri Subbarao. *Who Moved My Interest Rate? Leading the Reserve Bank of India Through Five Turbulent Years*. Penguin Books India, 2016, p. 61

553 Ibid., p. 175–176

554 M.C. Govardhana Rangan. 'Subbarao learns to call a spade a spade.' *The Economic Times*, 4 July 2010. http://epaper.timesofindia.com/Default/Layout/Includes/ETNEW/ArtWin.asp?From=Archive&Source=Page&Skin=ETNEW&Continuation=1&BaseHref=ETM%2F2010%2F07%2F14&ViewMode=HTML&PageLabel=1&EntityId=Ar00104&AppName=1, accessed on 29 October 2017

555 Bimal Jalan. 'North Block and Mint Road.' *Business Standard*, 28 August 2010. http://www.business-standard.com/article/opinion/bimal-jalan-north-block-and-mint-road-110082800001_1.html, accessed on 29 October 2017

556 Nikhil Pahwa. 'India's Broadband Wireless Auction Ends; Operator & Circlewise Results.' *Medianama*, 11 June 2010. http://www.medianama.com/2010/06/223-indias-broadband-wireless-auction-ends-operator-circlewise-results/, accessed on 29 October 2017

557 Reserve Bank of India. Annual Report 2009–2010. 24 August 2010. https://rbi.org.in/Scripts/AnnualReportMainDisplay.aspx, accessed on 29 October 2017

558 Subir Gokarn. 'The Price of Protein.' Speech, Reserve Bank of India, 26 October 2010. https://rbi.org.in/Scripts/BS_SpeechesView.aspx?Id=531, accessed on 29 October 2017

559 Subodh Varma. 'Does the govt know how to control rising prices?' *The Times of India*, 29 July 2010. http://timesofindia.indiatimes.com/india/Does-the-govt-know-how-to-control-rising-prices/articleshow/6230111.cms, accessed on 29 October 2017

560 Duvvuri Subbarao. *Who Moved My Interest Rate? Leading the Reserve Bank of India Through Five Turbulent Years*. Penguin Books India, 2016, p. 96–97

561 Reserve Bank of India. 'Third Quarter Review of Monetary Policy 2010–11.' 25 January 2011. https://rbi.org.in/Scripts/BS_PressReleaseDisplay.aspx?prid=23812, accessed on 29 October 2017

562 Niranjan Rajyadhaksha. 'The year of living dangerously.' *Livemint*, 3 February 2011. http://www.livemint.com/Politics/eGhSx5V538eza63x6MwsWO/The-year-of-living-dangerously.html, accessed on 29 October 2017

563 Anup Roy. 'Hawkish RBI raises rate 50 bps to fight inflation.' *Livemint*, 4 May 2011. http://www.livemint.com/Home-Page/LCZ5RZGXVav7GueWDMN8UJ/Hawkish-RBI-raises-rate-50-bps-to-fight-inflation.html, accessed on 29 October 2017

564 Reserve Bank of India. 'Monetary Policy Statement for 2011–12.' 4 May 2011. https://rbi.org.in/Scripts/BS_PressReleaseDisplay.aspx?prid=24335, accessed on 29 October 2017

565 Reserve Bank of India. 'First Quarter Review of Monetary Policy 2011–12.' 26 July 2011. https://rbi.org.in/Scripts/BS_PressReleaseDisplay.aspx?prid=24786, accessed on 29 October 2017

566 'Term may not be extended in September.' *The Times of India*, 29 April 2011. http://www.pressreader.com/india/the-times-of-india-new-delhi-edition/20110429/282140697940947, accessed on 29 October 2017

567 Duvvuri Subbarao. *Who Moved My Interest Rate? Leading the Reserve Bank of India Through Five Turbulent Years*. Penguin Books India, 2016, p. 205–207

568 Sugata Ghosh. 'RBI governor Duvvuri Subbarao: Is this man killing India's growth?' The Economic Times, 18 September 2011. http://economictimes.indiatimes.com/news/economy/indicators/RBI-governor-Duvvuri-Subbarao-Is-this-man-killing-Indias-growth/

articleshow/10022057.cms, accessed on 29 October 2017

569   Duvvuri Subbarao. *Who Moved My Interest Rate? Leading the Reserve Bank of India Through Five Turbulent Years.* Penguin Books India, 2016, p. 97–98

570   Sunil Prabhu. 'Cabinet reshuffle.' NDTV, 1 August 2012. http://www.ndtv.com/india-news/cabinet-reshuffle-p-chidambaram-back-as-finance-minister-sushil-kumar-shinde-gets-home-494961, accessed on 29 October 2017

571   'Finance Minister Confident of Bringing Economy Back on Desired Track; Gives an Overview of Map for Recovery.' Press Information Bureau, 6 August 2012

572   'Raghuram Rajan takes over as Chief Economic Advisor.' *The Hindu*, 29 August 2012. http://www.thehindu.com/business/Economy/raghuram-rajan-takes-over-as-chief-economic-advisor/article3836528.ece, accessed on 29 October 2017

573   'CRR cut by 0.25 per cent, repo rate unchanged.' NDTV, 18 September 2012. http://profit.ndtv.com/news/banking-finance/article-crr-cut-by-0-25-per-cent-repo-rate-unchanged-310912, accessed on 29 October 2017

574   'Statement of the Union Finance Minister Shri Chidambaram on Fiscal Roadmap and Consolidation.' Press Information Bureau, 29 October 2012

575   Duvvuri Subbarao. *Who Moved My Interest Rate? Leading the Reserve Bank of India Through Five Turbulent Years.* Penguin Books India, 2016, p.170–174

576   Ashok Dasgupta. 'We will "walk alone" if need be: Chidambaram.' *The Hindu*, 30 October 2012. http://www.thehindu.com/business/Economy/we-will-walk-alone-if-need-be-chidambaram/article4046910.ece, accessed on 29 October 2017

577   Duvvuri Subbarao. *Who Moved My Interest Rate? Leading the Reserve Bank of India Through Five Turbulent Years.* Penguin Books India, 2016, p. 176–179

578   Rajeev Malik. 'Silencing the RBI.' *Business Standard*, 9 January 2013. http://www.business-standard.com/article/opinion/rajeev-malik-silencing-the-rbi-113010900132_1.html, accessed on 29 October 2017

579   Duvvuri Subbarao. 'Volatility in Capital Flows: Some Perspectives.' Speech, Reserve Bank of India, 12 May 2010. https://rbi.org.in/Scripts/BS_SpeechesView.aspx?Id=504, accessed on 29 October 2017

580   Reserve Bank of India. 'Deregulation of Interest Rates on Non-Resident (External) Rupee (NRE) Deposits and Ordinary Non-Resident (NRO) Accounts.' 16 December 2011. https://rbi.org.in/Scripts/NotificationUser.aspx?Id=6875&Mode=0, accessed on 29 October 2017

581   Tamal Bandyopadhyay. 'This is not the way to protect rupee.' *Livemint*, 18 December 2011. http://www.livemint.com/Opinion/lJkI5zT3Xz5At6XaJe2YzN/This-is-not-the-way-to-protect-rupee.html, accessed on 29 October 2017

582   'S&P cuts India's outlook to negative.' *Financial Times*, 25 April 2012. http://blogs.ft.com/beyond-brics/2012/04/25/sp-cuts-indias-outlook-to-negative/?mhq5j=e3, accessed on 29 October 2017

583   Reserve Bank of India. 'Third Quarter Review of Monetary Policy 2012–13.' 29 January 2013. https://rbi.org.in/Scripts/BS_PressReleaseDisplay.aspx?prid= 2803, accessed on 29 October 2017

584   Agustino Fontevecchia. 'Bernanke's QE Dance.' *Forbes*, 22 May 2013. https://www.forbes.com/sites/afontevecchia/2013/05/22/bernankes-qe-dance-fed-could-taper-in-next-two-meetings-tightening-would-collapse-the-market/#78c96e1f7747, accessed on 29 October 2017

585   'The Fragile Five.' Morgan Stanley, 5 August 2013. http://graphics8.nytimes.com/packages/pdf/business/MorganStanleyFragileFive.pdf, accessed on 29 October 2017

586   Anup Roy and Joel Robello. 'Indian rupee hits record low.' *Livemint*, 10 June 2013. http://www.livemint.com/Money/h1vytj4thybwrEUQE8ThSI/Indian-rupee-hits-record-low-RBI-intervention-eyed.html, accessed on 29 October 2017

587   Joel Robello and Ami Shah. 'Rupee tests all-time intra-day low of 59.98.' *Livemint*, 20 June

2013. http://www.livemint.com/Money/z0EjbVjVqJpWvw5ehNV2UO/Indian-rupee-dives-to-a-record-low-of-5974-on-Fed-policy.html, accessed on 29 October 2017

588 Siddhartha Singh and Kartik Goyal. 'Govt plans talks on overseas debt sale after rupee slide.' *Livemint*, 11 July 2013. http://www.livemint.com/Money/9LDKfu3TuJX6qYhR6l3feO/Govt-plan-talks-on-overseas-debt-sale-after-rupee-slide.html, accessed on 29 October 2017

589 Duvvuri Subbarao. *Who Moved My Interest Rate? Leading the Reserve Bank of India Through Five Turbulent Years.* Penguin Books India, 2016, p.116–118

590 Reserve Bank of India. 'RBI announces Measures to address Exchange Rate Volatility.' 15 July 2013. https://rbi.org.in/Scripts/BS_PressReleaseDisplay.aspx?prid=29086, accessed on 29 October 2017

591 'RBI concedes influence of NDF on domestic market.' *Financial Express*, 23 August 2013. http://www.financialexpress.com/archive/rbi-concedes-influence-of-ndf-on-domestic-market/1158931/, accessed on 29 October 2017

592 Duvvuri Subbarao. *Who Moved My Interest Rate? Leading the Reserve Bank of India Through Five Turbulent Years.* Penguin Books India, 2016, p.135–136

593 'Customs Duty on Gold, Platinum & Silver Raised.' Press Information Bureau, 13 August 2013

594 '36.05 % duty on import of high-end TV sets.' *The Hindu*, 19 August 2013. http://www.thehindu.com/business/Economy/3605-duty-on-import-of-highend-tv-sets/article5038815.ece, accessed on 29 October 2017

595 Reserve Bank of India. 'Dr. Raghuram Rajan appointed as the next Governor of RBI.' 8 August 2013. https://rbi.org.in/Scripts/BS_PressReleaseDisplay.aspx?prid=29278, accessed on 29 October 2017

596 Pallavi Pengonda. 'The Joke Is On The Rupee.' *Livemint*, 22 August 2013. http://www.livemint.com/Leisure/LCRbGIjOZ0ZIPQgYtK1U7H/The-joke-is-on-the-rupee.html, accessed on 29 October 2017

597 Reserve Bank of India. 'RBI Introduces Forex Swap Window for Public Sector Oil Marketing Companies.' 28 August 2013. https://rbi.org.in/Scripts/BS_PressReleaseDisplay.aspx?prid=29423, accessed on 29 October 2017

598 Reserve Bank of India. 'Statement by Dr. Raghuram Rajan on taking office on September 4, 2013.' 5 September 2013. https://rbi.org.in/Scripts/BS_PressReleaseDisplay.aspx?prid=29479, accessed on 29 October 2017

599 Duvvuri Subbarao. *Who Moved My Interest Rate? Leading the Reserve Bank of India Through Five Turbulent Years.* Penguin Books India, 2016, p. 139

600 Shobha De. 'Economy with Raghuram Rajan will be sizzling hot.' *The Economic Times*, 13 September 2013. http://economictimes.indiatimes.com/economy-with-raghuram-rajan-will-be-sizzling-hot/articleshow/22533265.cms, accessed on 29 October 2017

601 Raghuram Rajan. 'RBI days.' *I Do What I Do.* Harper Business, 2017

602 Raghuram Rajan. 'Has Financial Development Made the World Riskier?' Presented at Jackson Hole, August 2005

603 Reserve Bank of India. 'Statement by Dr. Raghuram Rajan on taking office on September 4, 2013.' 5 September 2013. https://rbi.org.in/Scripts/BS_PressReleaseDisplay.aspx?prid=29479, accessed on 29 October 2017

604 Reserve Bank of India. 'The Expert Committee to Revise and Strengthen the Monetary Policy Framework Submits its Report.' 21 January 2014. https://rbi.org.in/Scripts/BS_PressReleaseDisplay.aspx?prid=30446, accessed on 29 October 2017

605 Manojit Saha. 'Should RBI target inflation?' *Business Standard*, 28 March 2014. http://www.business-standard.com/article/finance/should-rbi-target-inflation-114032700887_1.html, accessed on 29 October 2017

606 Dinesh Unnikrishnan and Asit Ranjan Mishra. 'Unease in govt over Urjit Patel

panel report. *Livemint*, 23 January 2014. http://www.livemint.com/Politics/VxKNQduzuY9BqdLUDYyPOL/Premature-to-use-CPI-as-anchor-for-inflation-target-Arvind.html, accessed on 29 October 2017

607 'Chidambaram: Government to set up inflation target, RBI to implement. *Deccan Chronicle*, 8 March 2014. http://www.deccanchronicle.com/140308/business-latest/article/chidambaram-government-set-inflation-target-rbi-implement, accessed on 29 October 2017

608 Raghuram Rajan. 'Filtering out the real India. Speech, Reserve Bank of India. 13 October 2013. https://rbi.org.in/Scripts/BS_SpeechesView.aspx?Id=848, accessed on 29 October 2017

609 Manoj Kumar. 'Post-Modi win, RBI governor Raghuram Rajan could be in trouble. *Firstpost*, 4 April 2014. http://www.firstpost.com/entertainment/post-modi-win-rbi-governor-raghuram-rajan-could-be-in-trouble-1465417.html, accessed on 29 October 2017

610 'Differences with BJP a media speculation, says Rajan. Rediff.com, 11 April 2014. http://www.rediff.com/money/report/slide-show-1-differences-with-bjp-a-media-speculation-says-rajan/20140411.htm, accessed on 29 October 2017

611 Raghuram Rajan. 'Hawks, Doves, or Owls.' *I Do What I Do*. Harper Business, 2017

612 Raghuram Rajan. 'Competitive Monetary Easing: Is it yesterday once more?' Speech, Reserve Bank of India, 10 April 2014. https://rbi.org.in/Scripts/BS_SpeechesView.aspx?Id=886, accessed on 29 October 2017

613 'Global Monetary Policy: A View from Emerging Markets. Brookings Institution, 10 April 2014. https://www.youtube.com/watch?v=SZe3issLIb8, accessed on 29 October 2017

614 Reserve Bank of India. 'RBI Decides to Grant "In-principle" Approval for Banking Licences. 2 April 2014. https://rbi.org.in/Scripts/BS_PressReleaseDisplay.aspx?prid=30931, accessed on 29 October 2017

615 Reserve Bank of India. 'RBI Releases Report of the Committee on Comprehensive Financial Services for Small Business and Low Income Households. 7 January 2014. https://rbi.org.in/Scripts/BS_PressReleaseDisplay.aspx?prid=30353, accessed on 29 October 2017

616 Gayatri Nayak. 'Prachi Mishra: An early top level lateral recruit. *The Economic Times*, 19 June 2017. http://economictimes.indiatimes.com/industry/banking/finance/banking/prachi-mishra-an-early-top-level-lateral-recruit-at-rbi-quits-in-less-than-three-years/articleshow/59222081.cms, accessed on 29 October 2017

617 A.B. Manju. 'No outsider to hold RBI COO post, Governor assures staff. *DNA*, 20 August 2014. http://www.dnaindia.com/money/report-no-outsider-to-hold-rbi-coo-post-governor-assures-staff-2012151, accessed on 29 October 2017

618 Latha Venkatesh. 'Raghuram Rajan, Nachiket Mor deserve better. Moneycontrol.com, 23 August 2014. http://www.moneycontrol.com/news/business/cnbc-tv18-comments/raghuram-rajan-nachiket-mor-deserve-better-1358591.html, accessed on 29 October 2017

619 'Take five. *The Hindu Businessline*, 19 August 2014. http://m.thehindubusinessline.com/opinion/editorial/the-rbi-should-initiate-a-dialogue-with-all-stakeholders-on-its-organisational-restructuring-proposal/article6332259.ece, accessed on 29 October 2017

620 Reserve Bank of India. 'RBI's Recent simplified KYC Measures For Public Awareness. 26 August 2014. https://rbi.org.in/Scripts/BS_PressReleaseDisplay.aspx?prid=31935, accessed on 29 October 2017

621 Raghuram Rajan. 'Economic & Financial Outlook. Speech, Reserve Bank of India, 15 September 2014. https://rbidocs.rbi.org.in/rdocs/Speeches/PDFs/REFICSPF150914.pdf, accessed on 29 October 2017

622 'RBI Guv Raghuram Rajan softens stance on Jan Dhan Yojana, says it is a welcome scheme. *Financial Express*, 30 September 2014. http://www.financialexpress.com/archive/rbi-guv-raghuram-rajan-softens-stance-on-jan-dhan-yojana-says-it-is-a-welcome-scheme/1294433/, accessed on 29 October 2017

623   Siddhartha Singh. 'Modi said to give Raghuram Rajan veto power to meet India's CPI goal.' *Livemint*, 10 October 2014. http://www.livemint.com/Politics/PCAb2ws66itgsQbG6rF7NP/Modi-said-to-give-Raghuram-Rajan-veto-power-to-meet-Indias.html, accessed on 29 October 2017

624   Raghuram Rajan. 'Make in India, Largely for India.' Speech, Reserve Bank of India, 12 December 2014. https://rbi.org.in/Scripts/BS_SpeechesView.aspx?Id=930, accessed on 29 October 2017

625   'Arun Jaitley rejects Raghuram Rajan's criticism of "Make in India".' *The Economic Times*, 5 January 2015. http://economictimes.indiatimes.com/news/economy/policy/arun-jaitley-rejects-raghuram-rajans-criticism-of-make-in-india/articleshow/45673933.cms?intenttarget=no, accessed on 29 October 2017

626   Mahim Pratap Singh. 'Diesel prices deregulated.' *The Hindu*, 18 October 2014. http://www.thehindu.com/business/Economy/diesel-prices-deregulated/article6514970.ece, accessed on 29 October 2017

627   Reserve Bank of India. 'Statement by Dr. Raghuram G Rajan, Governor on Monetary Policy.' 15 January 2015. https://rbi.org.in/Scripts/BS_PressReleaseDisplay.aspx?prid=33012, accessed on 29 October 2017

628   Reserve Bank of India. 'Statement by Dr. Raghuram G Rajan, Governor, on Monetary Policy.' 4 March 2015. https://rbi.org.in/Scripts/BS_PressReleaseDisplay.aspx?prid=33372, accessed on 29 October 2017

629   Narendra Modi. 'Prime Minister's remarks at the inaugural session of RBI Conference on Financial Inclusion.' Speech, Reserve Bank of India, 2 April 2015. https://rbidocs.rbi.org.in/rdocs/PressRelease/PDFs/RBI80Y020315.pdf, accessed on 29 October 2017

630   Reserve Bank of India. 'Edited Transcript of Reserve Bank of India's Post Policy Conference Call.' 8 April 2015. https://rbi.org.in/scripts/bs_viewcontent.aspx?Id=2991, accessed on 29 October 2017

631   'Rajan rids banks of "nonsense".' *The Telegraph*, 8 April 2015. https://www.telegraphindia.com/1150408/jsp/frontpage/story_13400.jsp, accessed on 29 October 2017

632   'Government requests RBI Governor Raghuram Rajan to cut interest rates.' India TV, 31 May 2015. http://m.indiatvnews.com/business/india/government-requests-rbi-raghuram-rajan-to-cut-interest-rates-18846.html, accessed on 29 October 2017

633   Reserve Bank of India. 'RBI Grants "In-principle" Approval to 11 Applicants for Payments Banks.' 19 August 2015. https://rbi.org.in/Scripts/BS_PressReleaseDisplay.aspx?prid=34754, accessed on 29 October 2017

634   Raghuram Rajan. 'Introduction.' *I Do What I Do*. Harper Business, 2017

635   Sunil Jain. 'RBI vs GDP.' *Financial Express*, 4 February 2015. http://thesuniljain.com/index.php?view=article&catid=69%3Amiscellaneous&id=2648%3Arbi-versus-gdp&tmpl=component&print=1&page=&option=com_content&Itemid=108, accessed on 29 October 2017

636   Reserve Bank of India. 'RBI Announces Marginal Cost of Funds Methodology for Interest Rate on Advances.' 17 December 2015. https://rbi.org.in/Scripts/BS_PressReleaseDisplay.aspx?prid=35749, accessed on 29 October 2017

637   Reserve Bank of India. 'Financial Stability Report 2015.' 25 June 2015. https://rbidocs.rbi.org.in/rdocs/PublicationReport/Pdfs/0fs15a56030b88bd047b4a7124ba5af1d8cf2.pdf, accessed on 29 October 2017

638   Reserve Bank of India. 'Edited Transcript of Reserve Bank of India's Post Policy Conference Call with Media.' 2 December 2015. https://www.rbi.org.in/Scripts/bs_viewcontent.aspx?Id=3110, accessed on 29 October 2017

639   Aparna Iyer and Vishwanath Nair. 'Weak corporate balance sheets need monitoring: RBI report.' *Livemint*, 24 December 2015. http://www.livemint.com/Industry/Ke9jk1lF1Mk0AlPEtaPbsI/Weak-corporate-balance-sheets-need-monitoring-RBI-report.html, accessed on 29 October 2017

640   'Raghuram Rajan Conferred Central Banker of the Year Award.' NDTV Profit, 7 January 2016. http://profit.ndtv.com/news/banking-finance/article-raghuram-rajan-conferred-central-banker-award-by-ft-group-arm-1263360, accessed on 29 October 2017
641   'Asset quality review by RBI may put public sector banks in red: AIBOC.' The Tribune, 17 January 2017. http://www.tribuneindia.com/news/chandigarh/community/asset-quality-review-by-rbi-may-put-public-sector-banks-in-red-aiboc/184537.html, accessed on 29 October 2017
642   Vishwanath Nair. 'Banks must hike provisions to tackle stressed assets: RBI.' Livemint, 16 January 2016. http://www.livemint.com/Industry/jps9i6ywi3d3aVWprg9IiP/Banks-must-hike-provisions-to-tackle-stressed-assets-RBI.html, accessed on 29 October 2017
643   Shekhar Gupta. 'Walk The Talk With Raghuram Rajan.' NDTV, 22 January 2016. http://www.ndtv.com/video/business/walk-the-talk/walk-the-talk-with-raghuram-rajan-400257, accessed on 29 October 2017
644   Raghuram Rajan. 'The Resolution of Distress.' I Do What I Do. Harper Business, 2017
645   Rahul Oberoi. '20 PSU banks' loss stand at ₹16,272 cr in Q4, should you invest in them?' Financial Express, 23 May 2016. http://www.financialexpress.com/industry/banking-finance/20-psu-banks-loss-stands-at-rs-16272-34-cr-should-you-retain-them-in-you-portfolio/263164/, accessed on 29 October 2017
646   Reserve Bank of India. 'Tolerance and Respect for Economic Progress.' 31 October 2015. https://rbi.org.in/Scripts/BS_SpeechesView.aspx?Id=979, accessed on 29 October 2017
647   'Raghuram Rajan speaks up against culture of bans and intolerance, Subramanian Swamy lashes out.' India Today, 31 October 2015, accessed on 29 October 2017
648   'Rajan defends his speech calling for tolerance, mutual respect.' The Hindu, 4 November 2015. http://www.thehindu.com/news/national/rajan-defends-his-speech-calling-for-tolerance-mutual-respect/article7841863.ece, accessed on 29 October 2017
649   Greg Robb. 'Central banks may do more harm than good, says head of India's central bank.' Marketwatch, 16 April 2016. http://www.marketwatch.com/story/in-interview-indias-rajan-says-monetary-policy-has-run-its-course-2016-04-15, accessed on 29 October 2017
650   Nistula Hebbar. 'Rajan's choice of words could have been better.' The Hindu, 18 April 2016. http://www.thehindu.com/news/national/%E2%80%98Rajan%E2%80%99s-choice-of-words-could-have-been-better%E2%80%99/article14246048.ece, accessed on 29 October 2017
651   Raghuram Rajan. 'Introduction.' I Do What I Do. Harper Business, 2017
652   P.G. Gurus. 'Swamy's letter to PM Modi.' May 18 2016. https://www.pgurus.com/wp-content/uploads/2016/05/Subramanian-Swamy%20s-letter-to-RBI-Governor-Raghuram-Rajan-on-hushing-up-ED-case-on-Karti-page-001.jpg, accessed on 29 October 2017
653   'Subramanian Swamy embarrasses government, says Raghuram Rajan not fit as RBI Governor.' The Economic Times, 12 May 2016. http://economictimes.indiatimes.com/news/politics-and-nation/subramanian-swamy-embarrasses-government-says-raghuram-rajan-not-fit-as-rbi-governor/articleshow/52237381.cms, accessed on 29 October 2017
654   Janmejaya Sinha. 'All the bank's men.' Indian Express, 2 May 2016. http://indianexpress.com/article/opinion/columns/all-the-banks-men/, accessed on 29 October 2017
655   'Raghuram Rajan's reappointment should not be of media's interest.' The Times of India, 27 May 2016. http://timesofindia.indiatimes.com/india/PM-Narendra-Modi-Raghuram-Rajans-reappointment-should-not-be-of-medias-interest/articleshow/52464518.cms, accessed on 29 October 2017
656   'With Modi's patronage, govt most likely to reappoint Raghuram Rajan.' The Hindu Businessline, 1 June 2016. http://www.thehindubusinessline.com/money-and-banking/with-modis-support-raghuram-rajan-most-likely-to-be-offered-a-second-term-as-rbi-governor/article8676876.ece, accessed on 29 October 2017

657   Reserve Bank of India. 'RBI releases Governor's message to staff for wider dissemination.' 18 June 2016. https://rbi.org.in/Scripts/BS_PressReleaseDisplay.aspx?prid=37259, accessed on 29 October 2017

658   'Raghuram Rajan is no less patriotic: Modi.' *The Hindu*, 27 June 2016. http://www.thehindu.com/news/national/Raghuram-Rajan-is-no-less-patriotic-Modi/article14404916.ece, accessed on 29 October 2017

659   'After Raghuram Rajan, Who? 4 Shortlisted For RBI Chief.' *NDTV Profit*, 27 June 2016. http://profit.ndtv.com/news/economy/article-after-rajan-who-these-4-candidates-shortlisted-report-1423799, accessed on 29 October 2017

660   'New panel likely to set rate in next monetary policy.' *Indian Express*, 28 June 2016. http://indianexpress.com/article/business/economy/new-panel-likely-to-set-rate-in-next-monetary-policy-2880058/, accessed on 29 October 2017

661   Reserve Bank of India. 'Governor's Opening Statement to the Post-Policy Press Conference.' 9 August 2016. https://rbi.org.in/Scripts/BS_PressReleaseDisplay.aspx?prid=37735, accessed on 29 October 2017

662   Reserve Bank of India. 'RBI Governor argues for Independent Central Bank for Macroeconomic Stability of the Country.' 3 September 2016. https://rbi.org.in/Scripts/BS_PressReleaseDisplay.aspx?prid=37966, accessed on 29 October 2017

663   Reserve Bank of India. 'Urjit Patel appointed RBI Governor.' 20 August 2016, http://www.thehindu.com/business/Economy/Urjit-Patel-appointed-RBI-Governor/article14580496.ece, accessed on 29 October 2017

664   Tamal Bandyopadhyay. 'An open letter to Urjit Patel.' *Livemint*, 12 September 2016. http://www.livemint.com/Opinion/3bMKJPHOMCUvaiEC57K44L/An-open-letter-to-Urjit-Patel.html, accessed on 29 October 2017

665   'Modi warns of crackdown on tax evaders.' *The Hindu*, 27 June 2016. http://www.thehindu.com/news/national/Modi-warns-of-crackdown-on-tax-evaders/article14403543.ece, accessed on 29 October 2017

666   'Declare black money by 30 Sept or face action: PM Modi passes ultimatum.' *Firstpost*, 24 July 2016. http://www.firstpost.com/business/declare-black-money-by-30-sept-or-face-action-pm-modi-passes-ultimatum-2912140.html, accessed on 29 October 2017

667   Narendra Modia. 'Full Text of Indian Prime Minister Narendra Modi's Speech on Replacing Largest Rupee Notes.' *The Wall Street Journal*, 8 November 2016. https://blogs.wsj.com/indiarealtime/2016/11/08/full-text-of-indian-prime-minister-narendra-modis-speech-on-replacing-largest-rupee-notes/, accessed on 29 October 2017

668   'Over 600 jewellers asked to give details of gold sales.' *The Indian Express*, 11 November 2016. http://indianexpress.com/article/india/india-news-india/over-600-jewellers-500-1000-rupee-notes-demonetisation-currency-exchange-asked-to-give-details-of-gold-sales-4370413/, accessed on 29 October 2017

669   'Demonetisation move a standard prescription: Former RBI governor Rangarajan.' *The New Indian Express*, 11 November 2016. http://www.newindianexpress.com/business/2016/nov/11/demonetisation-move-a-standard-prescription-former-rbi-governor-rangarajan-1537458.html, accessed on 29 October 2017

670   Kaushik Basu. 'In India, Black Money Makes for Bad Policy.' *The New York Times*, 27 November 2016. https://www.nytimes.com/2016/11/27/opinion/in-india-black-money-makes-for-bad-policy.html, accessed on 29 October 2017

671   Kenneth Rogoff. 'Kenneth Rogoff: India's Currency Exchange and The Curse of Cash.' Princeton blogs, 17 November 2016. http://blog.press.princeton.edu/2016/11/17/kenneth-rogoff-indias-currency-exchange-and-the-curse-of-cash/, accessed on 29 October 2017

672   'IAF will carry your cash to banks.' *Financial Express*, 14 November 2016. http://www.financialexpress.com/india-news/demonetisation-effects-now-iaf-will-carry-your-cash-to-banks/445403/, accessed on 29 October 2017

673 Vrishti Beniwal and Nag Anirban Nag. 'RBI Governor Urjit Patel missing in action as PM Narendra Modi escalates war on cash.' *The Economic Times*, 24 November 2016. http://economictimes.indiatimes.com/news/economy/policy/rbi-governor-urjit-patel-missing-in-action-as-pm-narendra-modi-escalates-war-on-cash/articleshow/55592017.cms, accessed on 29 October 2017

674 Kritika Banerjee. 'RBI taking steps to ease people's pain.' *India Today*, 27 November 2016. http://indiatoday.intoday.in/story/rbi-governor-urjit-patel-breaks-silence-demonetisation/1/821005.html, accessed on 29 October 2017

675 Reserve Bank of India. 'RBI Announces Measures to Manage Liquidity Conditions.' 26 November 2016. https://rbi.org.in/Scripts/BS_PressReleaseDisplay.aspx?prid=38714, accessed on 29 October 2017

676 Reserve Bank of India. 'Fifth Bi-monthly Monetary Policy Statement, 2016–17 Resolution of the Monetary Policy Committee (MPC).' 7 December 2017. https://rbi.org.in/Scripts/BS_PressReleaseDisplay.aspx?prid=38818, accessed on 29 October 2017

677 'RBI cites inflation risk, holds rate; markets stunned.' *The Hindu Businessline*, 7 December 2017. http://www.thehindubusinessline.com/money-and-banking/rbi-keeps-repo-rate-unchanged-at-625/article9415400.ece, accessed on 29 October 2017

678 Arihant Pawariya. 'How Much Of The "Demonetised" Currency Is Actually Coming Back?' *Swarajya*, 8 December 2016. https://swarajyamag.com/economy/how-much-of-the-demonetised-currency-is-actually-coming-back, accessed on 29 October 2017

679 'Demonetisation: Manmohan Singh's full speech in Rajya Sabha.' 24 November 2016. http://indianexpress.com/article/india/india-news-india/demonetisation-manmohan-singhs-full-speech-in-rajya-sabha-4392829/, accessed on 29 October 2017

680 'I would have resigned if overruled on demonetisation: Reddy.' *Business Standard*, 14 January 2017. http://www.business-standard.com/article/economy-policy/reddy-i-would-have-resigned-if-overruled-on-demonetisation-117011400026_1.html, accessed on 29 October 2017

681 Rahul Shrivatsava. 'Don't Answer That Question, Dr Manmohan Singh Said To RBI Governor.' NDTV, 18 January 2017. http://www.ndtv.com/india-news/dont-answer-that-question-dr-manmohan-singh-said-to-rbi-governor-1650217, accessed on 29 October 2017

682 Arun Janardhanan. 'RBI head must quit for havoc.' *The Indian Express*, 21 November 2016. http://indianexpress.com/article/business/banking-and-finance/demonetisation-rbi-urjit-patel-resignation-all-india-bank-officers-confederation-narendra-modi-4386431/, accessed on 29 October 2017

683 '"Feeling humiliated" by post-note ban events, RBI employees write to Urjit Patel.' *The Times of India*, 13 January 2017. http://timesofindia.indiatimes.com/business/india-business/feeling-humiliated-by-post-note-ban-events-rbi-employees-write-to-urjit-patel/articleshow/56527140.cms, accessed on 29 October 2017

684 Dianne Nongrum. 'RBI Governor Urjit Patel manhandled by Congress workers at Kolkata airport.' *India Today*, 15 December 2016. http://indiatoday.intoday.in/story/rbi-governor-urjit-patel-kolkata-airport-congress-workers/1/835511.html, accessed on 29 October 2017

685 'RBI Governor runs away from reporters.' *Business Standard*, 11 January 2017. http://www.business-standard.com/article/news-ians/rbi-governor-runs-away-from-reporters-117011101286_1.html, accessed on 29 October 2017

686 'RBI's own figures indicate return of 15 lakh cr of banned notes.' *Business Standard*, 14 January 2017. http://www.business-standard.com/article/economy-policy/rbi-s-own-figures-indicate-return-of-15-lakh-cr-of-banned-notes-117011400304_1.html, accessed on 29 October 2017

687 Shilpy Sinha. 'Cash withdrawal limits to go from March 13: RBI.' *The Economic Times*, 8 February 2017. http://economictimes.indiatimes.com/news/economy/policy/cash-withdrawal-limits-to-go-from-march-13-rbi/articleshow/57038629.cms, accessed on 29 October 2017

688 Reserve Bank of India. 'Macroeconomic impact of demonetisation—a preliminary assessment.' 10 March 2017. https://rbidocs.rbi.org.in/rdocs/Publications/PDFs/ MID10031760E85BDAFEFD497193995BB1B6DBE602.PDF, accessed on 29 October 2017

689 C.L. Manoj. 'Still counting returned demonetised currency: RBI Governor tells parliamentary committee.' *The Economic Times*, 13 July 2017. http://economictimes. indiatimes.com/news/economy/policy/rbi-has-cut-staff-holidays-to-count-junked-notes-urjit-patel/articleshow/59566529.cms, accessed on 29 October 2017

690 George Mathew and Aanchal Magazine. 'RBI's dividend to Government falls by almost half to ₹30,659 crore.' *The Indian Express*, 11 August 2017. http://indianexpress.com/ article/business/banking-and-finance/rbis-dividend-to-government-falls-by-almost-half-to-rs-30659-crore-4791420/, accessed on 29 October 2017

691 'P. Chidambaram says add another ₹50,000 cr as cost of demonetization.' *The Economic Times*, 11 August 2017. http://m.economictimes.com/news/economy/policy/p-chidambaram-says-add-another-rs-50000-cr-as-cost-of-demonetisation/articleshow/60017367. cms?from=desktop, accessed on 29 October 2017

692 Reserve Bank of India. 'Annual Report for FY2016–17.' 30 August 2017. https://rbi.org. in/Scripts/AnnualReportPublications.aspx?year=2017, accessed on 29 October 2017

693 Raghuram Rajan. 'Introduction.' *I Do What I Do*. Harper Business, 2017